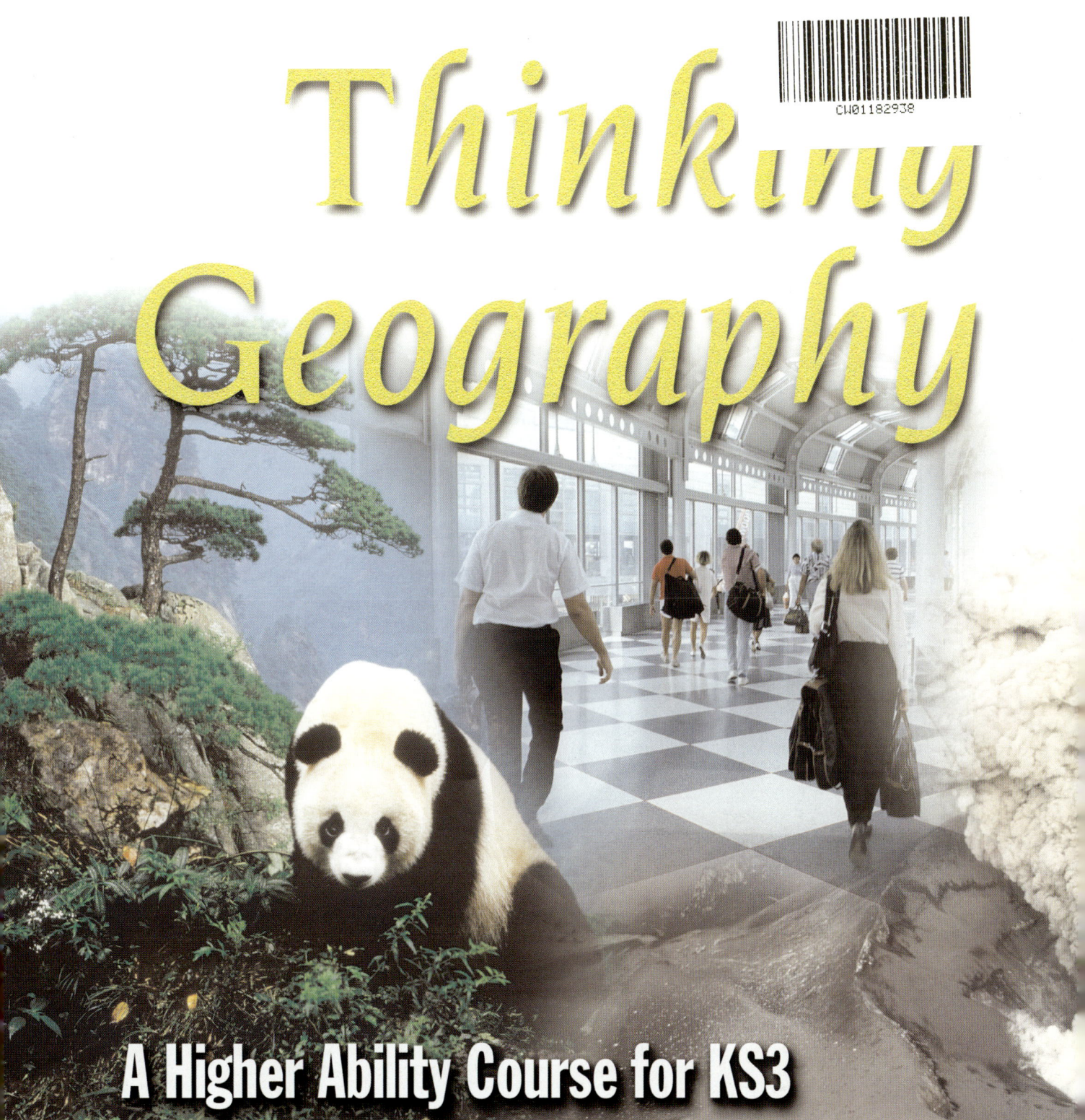

Dedication

To Angela, Rosie, Patrick and Bethany

Acknowledgements

The publishers would like to thank the following individuals, institutions and companies for permission to reproduce copyright illustrations in this book:
Figure 1.19, AP Photo/Brian Cassey; Figure 1.21, AP Photo/Mohamad Sayyad; Figure 1.22, AP Photo/Domenico Stinellis; Figure 1.23, AP Photo/courtesy TG5; Figures 2.4, 2.5, Garrett Nagle; Figure 2.8, PA Photos; Figure 2.10, AP Photo/Philippe Desmazes; Figures 2.15, 2.17, 2.19, 2.20, 2.25, 2.27, 2.28, 2.29, 2.31, 2.32, 2.44, 2.48, 2.49, 2.62, 2.63, 2.64, Garrett Nagle; Figure 3.14, University of Dundee; Figure 3.15, Garrett Nagle; Figure 3.17, University of Dundee; Figure 3.18, Corbis; Garrett Nagle; Figures 4.2, 4.6, 4.9, 4.10, 4.11, 4.13, 4.14, 4.15, Garrett Nagle; Figure 4.17, Dr Nigel Smith/The Hutchison Library; Figures 4.20, 4.21, 4.23, Garrett Nagle; Figure 5.14, The Hutchison Library; Figure 5.16, John Hatt c/o The Hutchison Library; Figures 6.6, 6.7, 6.11, 6.12, Garrett Nagle; Figure 6.13, Liba Taylor/Panos Pictures; Figure 7.4, Garrett Nagle; Figure 7.8 Hulton Getty; Figure 7.9, PA Photos; Figure 7.11 Hulton Getty; Figure 7,12, The Hutchison Library; Figures 7.21, 7.22, 7.23, 8.1, 8.2, 8.8, 8.11, Garrett Nagle; Figure 8.14, © AFP/Corbis; Figure 8.16, Garrett Nagle; Figure 8.17, The Hutchison Library; Figure 8.22, NASA/Goddard Space Flight Center/Science Photo Library; Figure 8.23, AP Photo/Luis Elvir; Figure 9.2, Garrett Nagle; Figure 9.3, Science Photo Library; Figure 9.13 AP Photo/David Gray, Pool; Figure 9.14, AP Photo; Figures 9.17, 9.20, 9.21, 9.23, 9.24, 9.25 Garrett Nagle; Figure 10.3, © Patrick Ward/Corbis;
Figure 10.4, Jim Winkley//Ecoscene/Corbis; Figure 10.8, Garrett Nagle; Figure 11.3, AP Photo/Xinhua, Du huaju; Figure 11.4 Sarah Errington/The Hutchison Library; Figure 11.16, Corbis; Figure 11.17, AP Photo/Xinhua, Liu Yanwu.

The publishers would also like to thank the following for permission to reproduce material in this book:
Maps reproduced from Ordnance Survey mapping with the permission of the Controller of Her Majesty's Stationery Office, © Crown copyright.

Every effort has been made to trace and acknowledge ownership of copyright. The publishers will be glad to make suitable arrangements with any copyright holders whom it has not been possible to contact.

Orders: please contact Bookpoint Ltd, 78 Milton Park, Abingdon, Oxon OX14 4TD. Telephone: (44) 01235 827720, Fax: (44) 01235 400454. Lines are open from 9.00 – 6.00, Monday to Saturday, with a 24 hour message answering service. Email address: orders@bookpoint.co.uk

British Library Cataloguing in Publication Data
A catalogue record for this title is available from The British Library

ISBN 0 340 74283 6

First published 2000
Impression number   10 9 8 7 6 5 4 3 2 1
Year   2005 2004 2003 2002 2001 2000

Copyright © 2000 Garrett Nagle

All rights reserved. No part of this publication may be reproduced or transmitted in any form or by any means, electronic or mechanical, including photocopy, recording, or any information storage and retrieval system, without permission in writing from the publisher or under licence from the Copyright Licensing Agency Limited. Further details of such licences (for reprographic reproduction) may be obtained from the Copyright Licensing Agency Limited, of 90 Tottenham Court Road, London W1P 9HE.

Cover photo from Liz Rowe Design, Rotherfield
Typeset by Clare Brodmann Book Designs, Burton-on-Trent
Printed in Italy for Hodder & Stoughton Educational, a division of Hodder Headline Plc, 338 Euston Road, London NW1 3BH by Printer Trento

Contents

Chapter 1 Natural Hazards	1
Chapter 2 Geomorphology	13
Chapter 3 Weather and climate	41
Chapter 4 Ecosystems	52
Chapter 5 Population	64
Chapter 6 Settlement	73
Chapter 7 Economic activities	82
Chapter 8 Development	92
Chapter 9 Resources and Environmental issues	105
Chapter 10 The UK – an MEDC	120
Chapter 11 China – an LEDC	128
Index	141

Natural Hazards

Plate Tectonics

Plate tectonics is a set of theories which describes and explains the distribution of earthquakes, volcanoes, fold mountains and continental drift. It states that the earth's core consists of semi-molten magma (Figure 1.1) and that the earth's surface or crust moves around on this magma. The cause of the movement is radioactive decay in the core.

This creates huge **convection currents** which rise towards the earth's surface, drag plates apart, and cause them to collide.

The earth is made up of a number of 'plates', solid rock, which float on the mantle. There are seven large plates, such as the African plate and the Eurasian plate, and a large number of small plates, such as the Caribbean plate and the Turkish plate (Figure 1.2). Some plates are formed of continental crust – these are the land masses, whereas others are formed of oceanic crust – these are the ocean floors.

Plates move relative to one another. In some places, such as in Iceland, plates

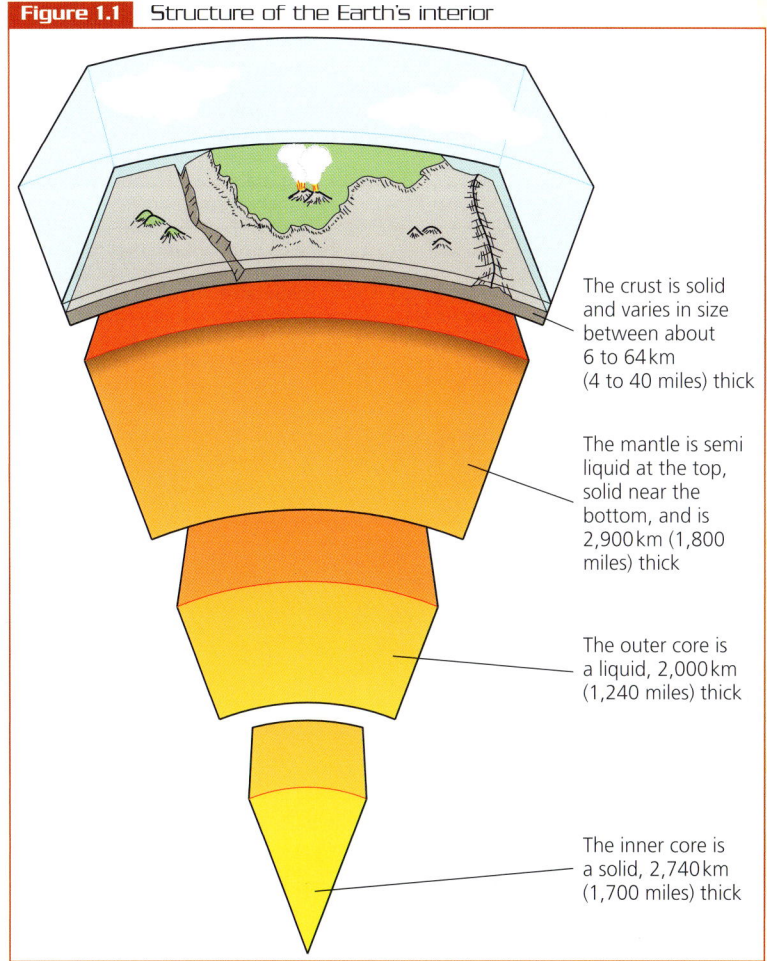

Figure 1.1 Structure of the Earth's interior

The crust is solid and varies in size between about 6 to 64 km (4 to 40 miles) thick

The mantle is semi liquid at the top, solid near the bottom, and is 2,900 km (1,800 miles) thick

The outer core is a liquid, 2,000 km (1,240 miles) thick

The inner core is a solid, 2,740 km (1,700 miles) thick

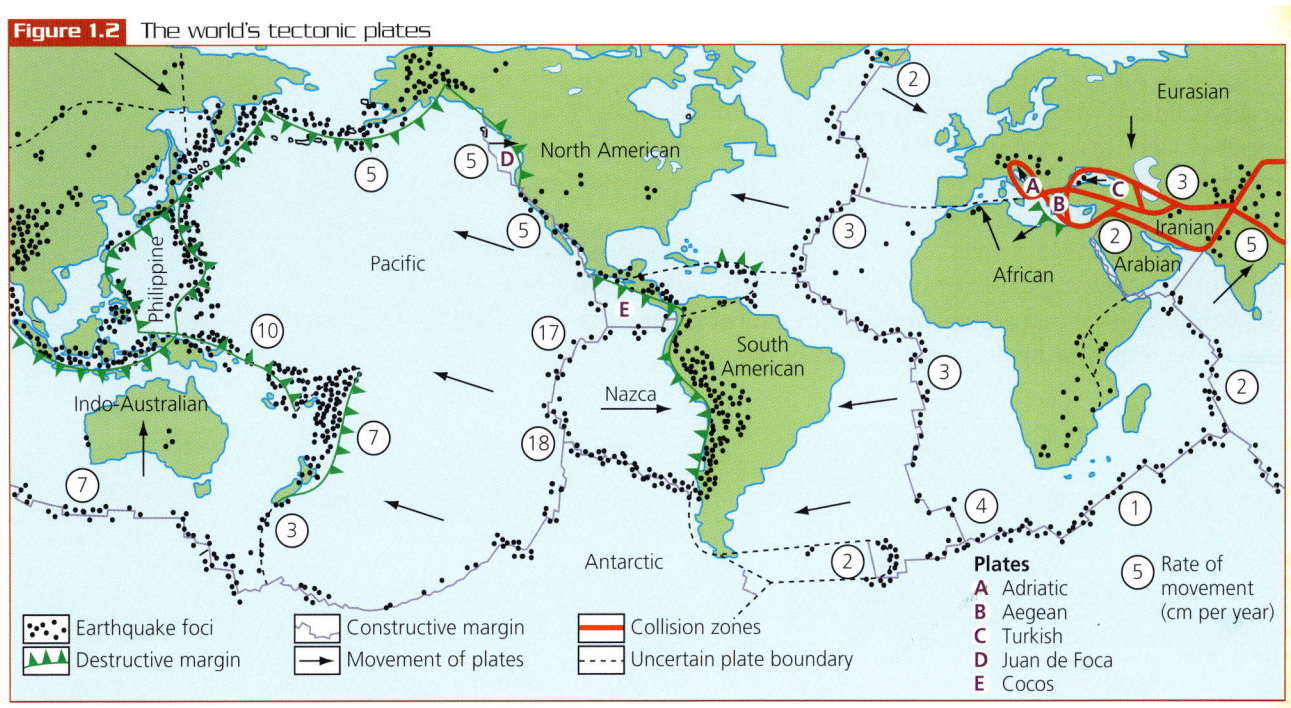

Figure 1.2 The world's tectonic plates

Plates
A Adriatic
B Aegean
C Turkish
D Juan de Foca
E Cocos

5 Rate of movement (cm per year)

Earthquake foci
Destructive margin
Constructive margin
Movement of plates
Collision zones
Uncertain plate boundary

TYPE OF BOUNDARY	PROCESSES	EXAMPLE
Constructive margins (spreading or divergent plates)	Two plates move apart from each other; new oceanic crust is formed, creating mid-ocean ridges; volcanic activity is common.	Mid Atlantic Ridge (Europe is moving away from North America).
Destructive margins (subduction zone)	The oceanic crust moves towards the continental crust and sinks beneath it due to its greater density; deep sea trenches and island arcs are formed; volcanic activity is common.	Nazca plate sinks under the South American plate.
Collision zones	Two continental crusts collide: as neither can sink they are folded up into fold mountains.	The Indian plate collided with the Eurasian plate to form the Himalayas.
Conservative margins (passive margins or transform plates)	Two plates move sideways past each other but land is neither destroyed nor created.	San Andreas fault in California.

Figure 1.3 Types of plate boundary

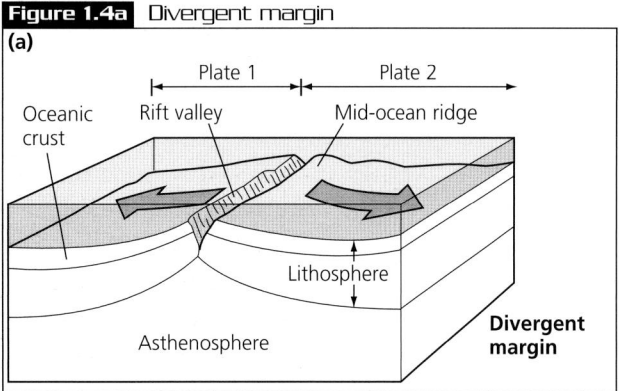

Figure 1.4a Divergent margin

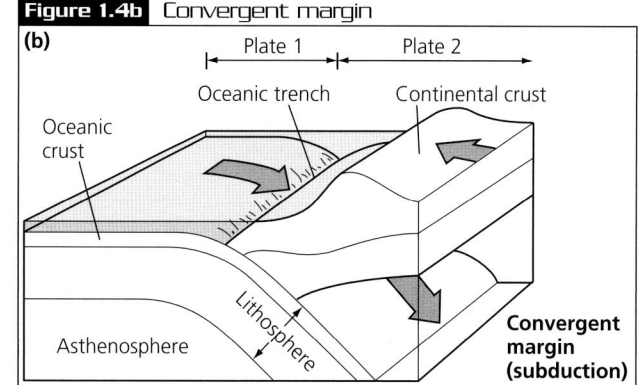

Figure 1.4b Convergent margin

are pulling apart **(Figure 1.4a)**. In other places, such as the west coast of South America, plates are moving together and colliding. When oceanic crust collides with continental crust, the dense oceanic crust plunges underneath (*subducts*) the less dense continental crust. The sinking plate is forced down into the mantle and melts due to the high temperatures and pressure. Some of this molten rock may form volcanoes. The continental crust is crumpled (folded) to form fold mountains. By contrast, at a transform or conservative boundary two similar plates slide past one another **(Figure 1.4b)**.

Although Figure 1.2 suggests that movement occurs every year, plate movement is not constant but occurs at irregular intervals. The greater the length of time that a plate has not moved, the greater the likelihood that when it moves it will have a large impact.

THE EVIDENCE FOR PLATE TECTONICS

1. The shape of the continents – if the shapes of South America and Africa were placed together they would fit closely rather like a jigsaw (Figure 1.5).
2. The fossils of a reptile called mesosaurus found in South America are similar to ones found in Africa suggesting that at one time all these continents were linked together.
3. Glacial deposits in South America have been traced to Africa – there is not enough water on earth for glaciers to have moved from Africa to South America so at some time the continents must have been linked.
4. The geological sequence (the layering of rocks) in South America, Africa, India, Australia and Antarctica are similar, suggesting that when these rocks were formed these continents were all linked together.
5. Rocks on the ocean floor are younger close to the mid ocean ridge and get older with distance away from the mid ocean ridges – this fits it with new materials being formed at ocean ridges and then being moved away.
6. The distribution of volcanoes and earthquakes is mostly along plate boundaries which are regions of crustal instability and tectonic activity.

Volcanoes

A volcano is a weakness in the earth's crust through which magma, molten rock and ash are erupted onto the land during volcanic eruptions. Volcanoes are mostly conical in shape although there are a variety of forms depending upon:

- the type of eruption;
- the nature of the material erupted;
- the amount of change since the eruption.

Active volcanoes that have erupted in recent times include Mount Pinatubo in 1991 and Montserrat in 1997, both of which could erupt again. There are about 1300 active volcanoes, three-quarters of which are in the Pacific Ring of Fire.

Dormant volcanoes are volcanoes that have not erupted for many centuries but may erupt again. An example would be Mount Rainier in the USA.

Extinct volcanoes are not expected to erupt again. Castle Rock in Edinburgh last erupted 340 million years ago.

In a volcanic eruption hot molten magma (lava), ash, gas, and steam are ejected into the atmosphere. Some eruptions let out so much material that the world's climate is affected for a number of years.

Figure 1.5 The evidence for plate tectonics

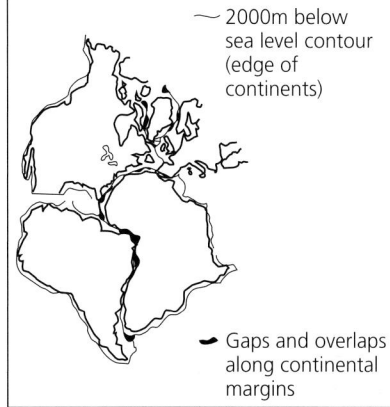

— 2000m below sea level contour (edge of continents)

← Gaps and overlaps along continental margins

Questions

1. What type of plate boundary is found
   a off the coast of Alaska
   b in northern Italy
   c in the East Pacific Ocean?
2. Where is plate movement fastest? By how much do plates move every century?
3. In your own words write a definition for each of the following terms
   a subduction zone
   b destructive plate boundary
   c constructive plate boundary
   d conservative plate boundary.
4. Briefly explain **two** pieces of evidence which support the theory of plate tectonics.
5. What is plate tectonics?

Figure 1.6 The biggest volcanic eruptions

Eruption	Date	Volume of material ejected
Mt St Helens, USA	1980	1 km^{-3}
Mt Vesuvius, Italy	AD79	3 km^{-3}
Mt Katmai, USA	1912	12 km^{-3}
Mt Krakatoa, Indonesia	1883	18 km^{-3}
Mt Tambora, Indonesia	1815	80 km^{-3}

Figure 1.7 The largest number of deaths caused by volcanoes

	Date	Number killed
Tambora	1815	92 000
Mt Pelee	1902	40 000
Krakatoa	1883	36 000
Nevado del Ruiz	1985	23 000

Most volcanoes occur at plate boundaries, especially constructive and destructive ones. At constructive boundaries magma is forced to the surface to form new rock. By contrast, at destructive boundaries rock is melted to form new magma. Some of this escapes, under great pressure, in volcanic eruptions. Other volcanoes, such as those in Hawaii and the East African Rift Valley, are found at **hot spots**, in the middle of plates. In these places, rising magma has burnt a hole through the earth's crust to allow volcanic activity to take place.

The shape of a volcano depends on the type of lava it contains. Runny lava produces gently sloping shield volcanoes.

TYPES OF VOLCANO

Shield volcanoes are formed of runny basaltic lava which travels down the sides of the volcano in lava flows. The volcano therefore has a gentle slope **(Figure 1.8)**. By contrast, thick sticky lava produces steep *cone-shaped volcanoes*. These may be the result of many volcanic eruptions over a long period of time. Part of the volcano may be blasted away during eruption.

THE PACIFIC RING OF FIRE

Three-quarters of the earth's 550 historically active volcanoes lie along the Pacific Ring of Fire **(Figure 1.9)**. This includes most of the world's recent volcanoes, including Mount Pinatubo in the Philippines which erupted in 1991. However, without volcanic activity the Philippines would not exist: they comprise the remains of previous eruptions.

PREDICTING VOLCANOES

The main ways of prediction include:

- *seismometers* to record swarms of tiny earthquakes that occur as the magma rises;
- *chemical sensors* to measure increased sulphur levels;
- *lasers* to detect the physical swelling of the volcano;
- *ultra sound* to monitor low frequency waves in the magma, resulting from the surge of gas and molten rock, as happened at Pinatubo, El Chichon and Mt St Helens.

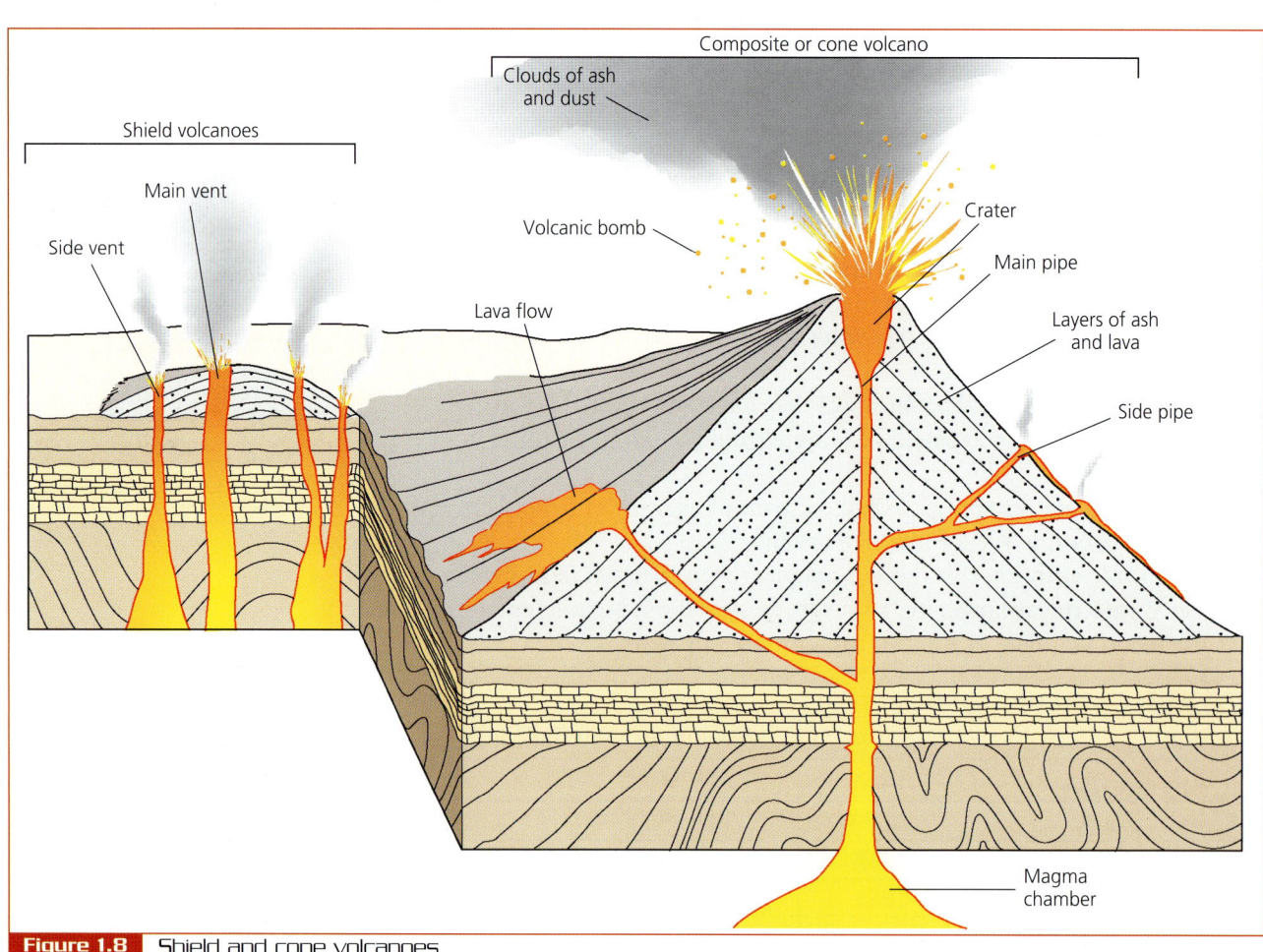

Figure 1.8 Shield and cone volcanoes

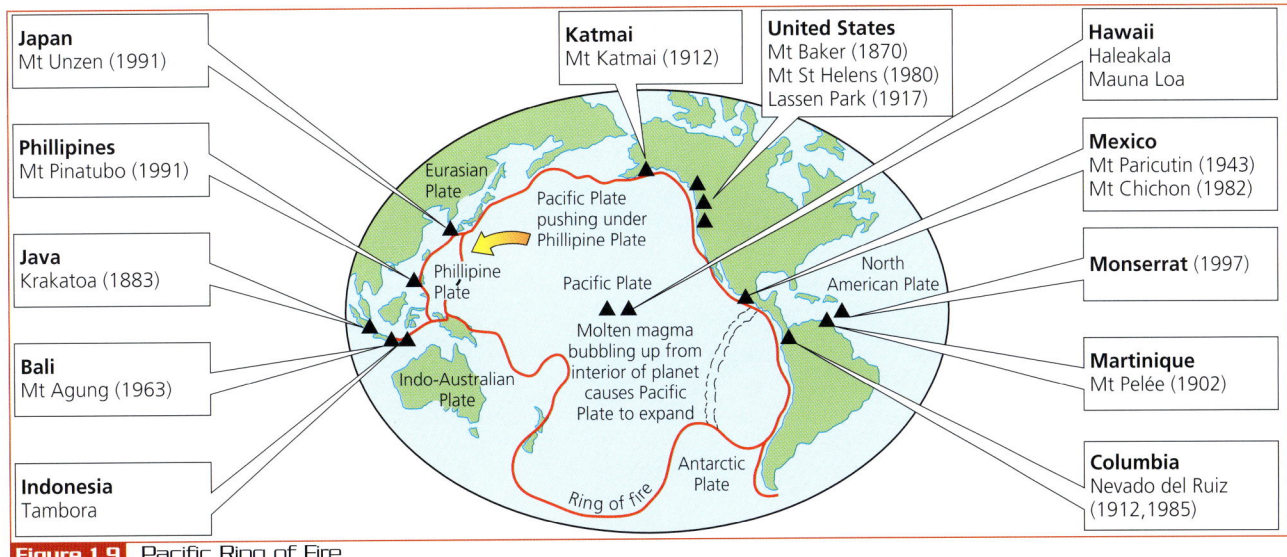

Figure 1.9 Pacific Ring of Fire

MONTSERRAT

Montserrat is a small island in the Caribbean, which has been affected by a number of recent hazards, including, in the mid-1990s, a volcano. The cause of the volcano is a **subduction zone** caused by the South American and North American plates plunging under the Caribbean plate **(Figure 1.10)**. Rocks at the edge of the plate melt and the rising magma forms volcanic islands.

In July 1995 the Soufriere Hills erupted after being dormant for nearly 400 years. At first the Soufriere Hills gave off clouds of ash and steam. Then in 1996 the volcano finally erupted. It caused mudflows and finally it emitted lava flows. Part of the dome collapsed, boiling rocks and ash were thrown out and a new dome was created. Ash, steam and rocks were hurled out, forcing all the inhabitants out of the south, the main agricultural part of the island. The largest settlement, Plymouth, with a population of just 4,000 has been abandoned. This has had a severe impact on Montserrat as it contained all the government offices, most of the shops and services, such as the market, post office, and cinema.

The hazard posed by the volcano was just one side of the risk experienced on Montserrat. For the refugees there were other hazards. For example, up to 50 people had to share a toilet. Sewage tanks in the temporary shelters were often not emptied for weeks on end. The risk of contamination in water and the spread of diseases, such as cholera, was greatly increased by large numbers of people living in overcrowded, unhygienic conditions.

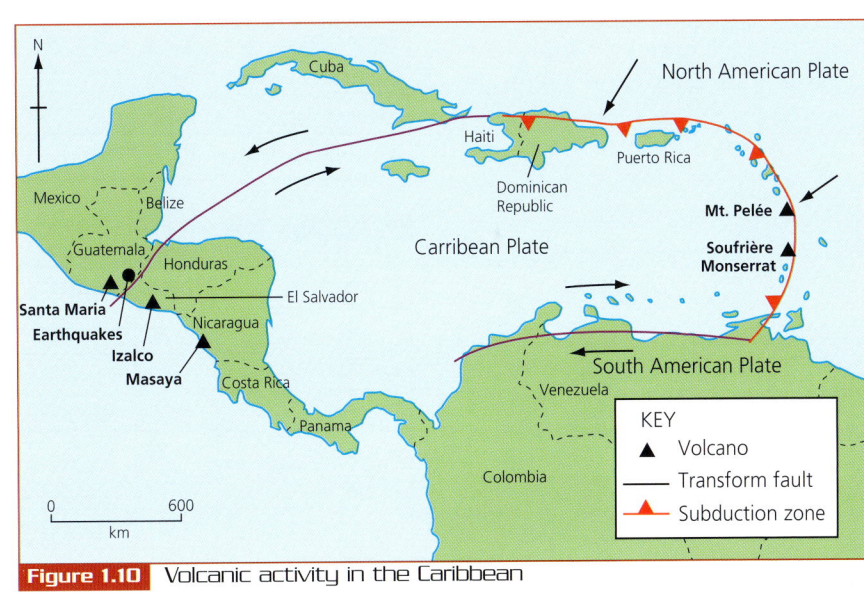

Figure 1.10 Volcanic activity in the Caribbean

Questions

6 What is the Pacific Ring of Fire? How many of the world's active volcanoes are located there?

7 Suggest **three** ways that volcanoes may be predicted.

8 Suggest **two** reasons why people live near volcanoes.

9 Explain why Montserrat is affected by volcanoes.

10 Why was the south part of Montserrat the main agricultural region of the island?

Earthquakes

Figure 1.11 World distribution of earthquakes

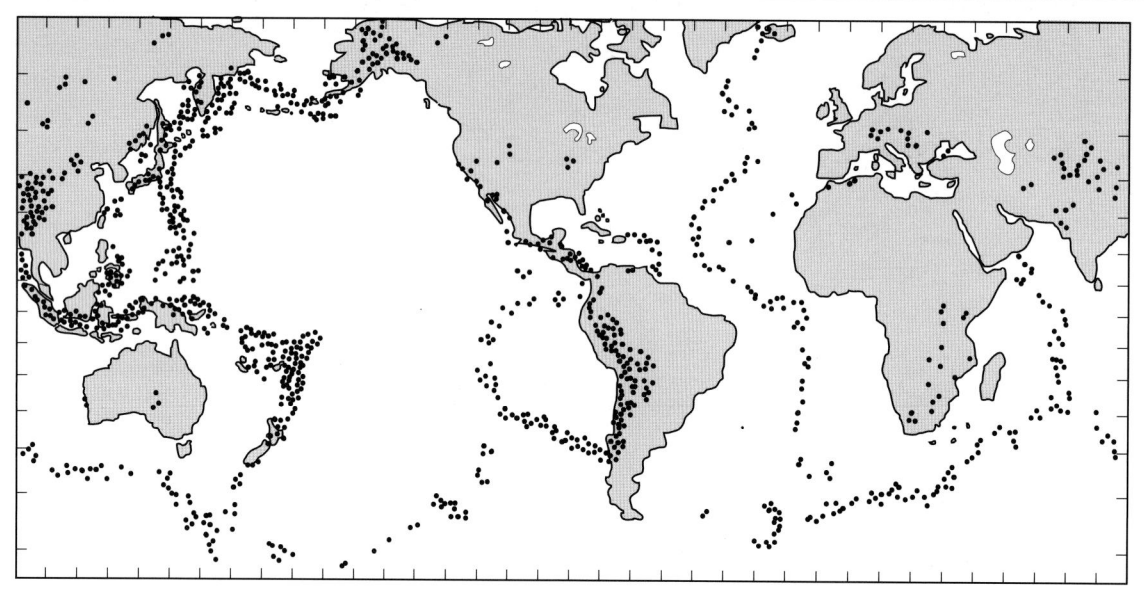

Earthquakes are sudden, violent movements of the earth. They occur after a build up of pressure causes rocks to give way. Most earthquakes occur at plate boundaries **(Figure 1.11)** but others are caused by:

- the weight of large dams;
- drilling for oil;
- nuclear testing;
- coal mining.

Earthquakes occur when two plates are moving apart (*tension*), pushing against each other (*compression*), sliding alongside each other (*tearing*), or when one plate is plunging underneath another (*subduction*). Up to 90% of the world's earthquakes occur around the Pacific Ring of Fire.

The **Richter Scale** measures the amount of energy released by an earthquake. It is a logarithmic scale, which means that every increase of 1.0 on the scale represents 10 times more energy. Thus an earthquake of 5.0 is 100 times more powerful that an earthquake registering 3.0 on the Richter Scale.

EARTHQUAKE DAMAGE

The factors affecting earthquake damage include:

- population density;
- the nature and type of buildings;
- the time of day;
- the distance from the centre (**focus**) of the earthquake; the **epicentre** is the point on the earth's surface directly above the focus (centre) of the earthquake;
- the type of rocks and sediments;
- the strength of the earthquake;
- secondary hazards such as mudslides and tsunami.

Figure 1.12 The world's largest earthquakes

Place	Date	Strength
Kansu	1920	8.6
Tokyo	1923	8.3
Tangshen	1976	8.0
Erzincan (Turkey)	1939	7.9
Mexico City	1985	7.8
North Peru	1970	7.7

Figure 1.13 Loss of life in major earthquakes

Place	Date	Deaths
Tangshen	1976	695 000
Kansu	1920	100 000
Tokyo	1923	99 000
Messina	1908	80 000
Armenia	1988	55 000
North-west Iran	1990	40 000
Erzincan (Turkey)	1939	30 000

EARTHQUAKE PREDICTION

There are a number of ways of predicting and monitoring earthquakes. These include:

- crustal movement;
- historic evidence;
- changes in electrical conductivity;
- strange and unusual animal behaviour.

KOBE

The Kobe earthquake on the 17th January 1995 killed over 5000 people, injured over 30 000, and made almost 750 000 people homeless. It was caused by the subduction of the Pacific Plate underneath the Eurasian Plate **[Figure 1.14]**. Kobe is situated near the northern end of the Philippine Plate.

Conditions were made worse by the rain and strong winds. These increased the risk of landslides. Damp, unhygienic conditions encouraged disease. Fires, broken glass, broken water pipes, and a lack of insurance meant that many people lost their livelihoods.

REDUCING THE EFFECTS OF EARTHQUAKES

There are a number of ways of limiting the damage caused by earthquakes. These include:

- buildings with shock absorbers;
- pyramidal-shaped buildings which withstand stress better;
- remaining indoors during an earthquake and staying underneath a table;
- not using a lift during an earthquake.

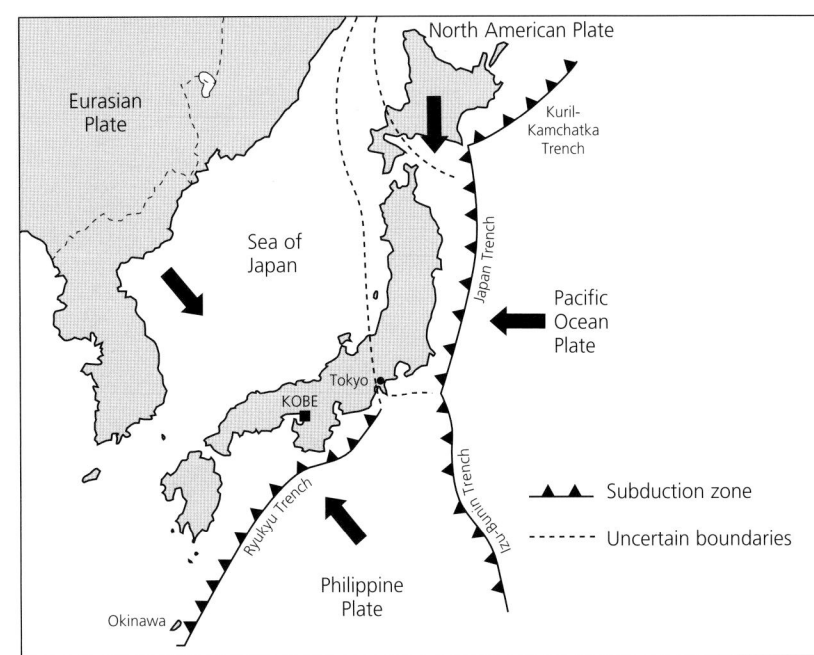

Figure 1.14 Location of Kobe

Questions

11 What is an earthquake?
12 What are the human causes of earthquakes?
13 Explain why there are many earthquakes in California and Japan but few earthquakes in the UK.
14 Using an atlas, locate the earthquakes mentioned in Figures 1.12 and 1.13. How do they support the theory of a tectonic origin of earthquakes?

Hazards

A **hazard** is a natural event which threatens both life and property – a **disaster** occurs when the hazard takes place and human life and property are destroyed.

Environmental hazards are caused by people's use of **dangerous environments**, such as floodplains and volcanic soils. Hazards also occur because **vulnerable populations** (the poor) are forced to live in hazardous environments, such as steep slopes and floodplains. Moreover, the same river that causes floods is also a **resource** – it brings fertile alluvial material and water.

Hazards are very varied. They include:

- natural and man-made,
- local and global,
- subtle *(invisible)*, such as drought,
- intense *(highly visible)*, such as volcanic eruptions and earthquakes.

Environmental hazards have a number of common characteristics:

- the **cause** of the hazard is clear and produces distinct effects, such as flooding causing death by drowning;
- the **warning time** is short (drought is an exception);
- most losses to life and property occur shortly after the environmental hazard – these are often related to **secondary hazards** such as fire and contaminated water;

- in some areas, especially ELDCs, people are forced to live in hazardous areas; by contrast in most EMDCs people occupy hazard areas as much through choice as through ignorance or necessity;
- the disaster occurs with a **scale** and **intensity** that requires emergency response.

It is possible to characterise hazards and disasters in a number of ways.

1. **Magnitude** – the size of the event e.g. the size of an earthquake on the Richter Scale.
2. **Frequency** – how often an event of a certain size occurs.
3. **Duration** – the length of time that particular environmental hazard exists.
4. **Extent** – the size of the area covered by the hazard.
5. **Speed of onset** – varies from rapid events, such as the Kobe earthquake, to slow time-scale events such as the drought in the Sahel of Africa.
6. **Regularity** – some hazards are regular (such as cyclones) whereas others are much more random (such as earthquakes and volcanoes).

Some of these can be shown on a hazard event profile (Figure 1.16).

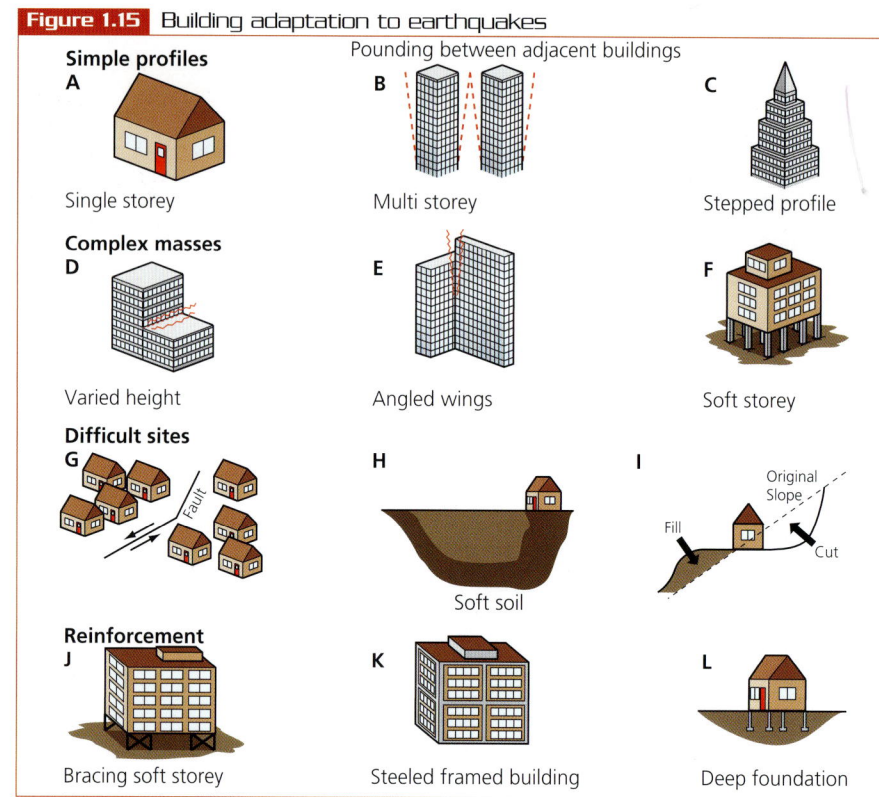

Figure 1.15 Building adaptation to earthquakes

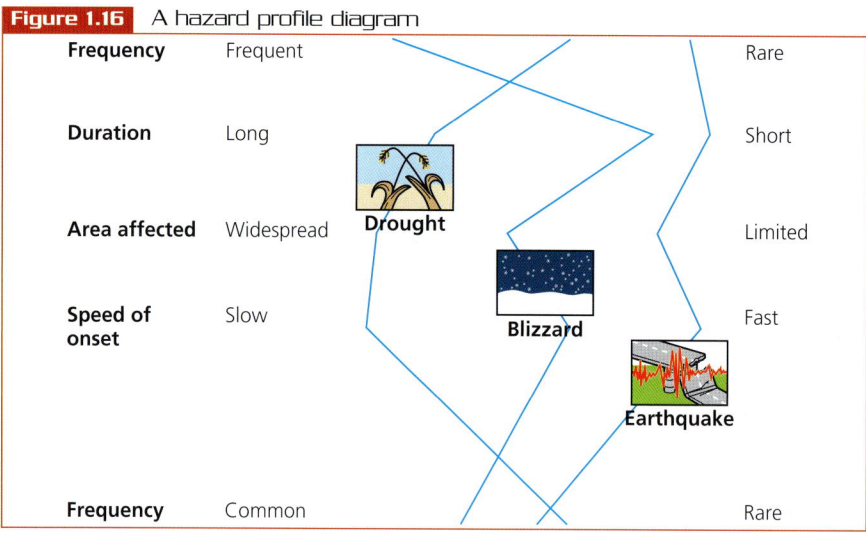

Figure 1.16 A hazard profile diagram

Figure 1.17 Classification of natural hazards by main causal agents

Geophysical		Biological	
Climatic and meteorological	**Geological and geomorphological**	**Floral**	**Faunal**
Snow and ice Floods Hail Heatwaves Tropical cyclones Lightning and fires	Avalanches Earthquakes Erosion, e.g. soil erosion and coastal erosion Tsunami	Fungal diseases, e.g. athlete's foot, Dutch elm disease Infestations, e.g. weeds, water hyacinth	Bacterial and viral diseases, e.g. influenza, smallpox, rabies Infestations, e.g. locusts

TSUNAMIS

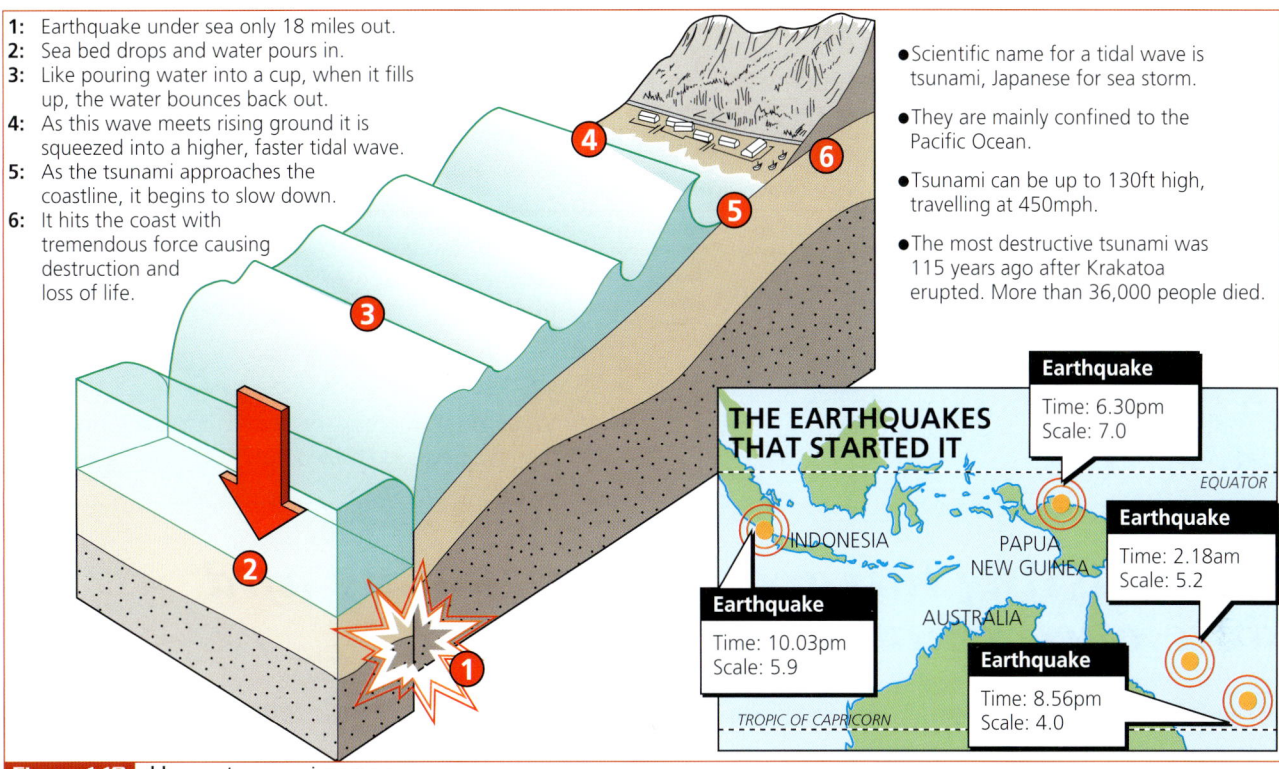

1: Earthquake under sea only 18 miles out.
2: Sea bed drops and water pours in.
3: Like pouring water into a cup, when it fills up, the water bounces back out.
4: As this wave meets rising ground it is squeezed into a higher, faster tidal wave.
5: As the tsunami approaches the coastline, it begins to slow down.
6: It hits the coast with tremendous force causing destruction and loss of life.

- Scientific name for a tidal wave is tsunami, Japanese for sea storm.
- They are mainly confined to the Pacific Ocean.
- Tsunami can be up to 130ft high, travelling at 450mph.
- The most destructive tsunami was 115 years ago after Krakatoa erupted. More than 36,000 people died.

THE EARTHQUAKES THAT STARTED IT

Earthquake Time: 6.30pm Scale: 7.0
Earthquake Time: 2.18am Scale: 5.2
Earthquake Time: 10.03pm Scale: 5.9
Earthquake Time: 8.56pm Scale: 4.0

Figure 1.18 How a tsunami occurs

Tsunami are waves caused by earthquakes, volcanic activity, or by the shocks of massive undersea landslide. The danger from tsunamis rests in their sheer size and energy **[Figure 1.18]**. They have very long wavelengths. Up to 90% of tsunami occur in the Pacific Ocean. Tsunamis travel fast in open oceans reaching speeds of up to 500 km/hour.

One of the strongest tsunamis was the one triggered by the 1883 eruption of Krakatoa killing 36 000 people. In July 1998 tsunamis struck villages along the Sissano Lagoon on the West Sepik Coast of Papua New Guinea **[Figure 1.19]** leaving up to 6000 people dead, half of the area's population. Villagers had little warning of the tsunami, whose approach sounded like the roar of a jet plane. Many of the dead were the young and the old of seven villages on the north coast of Papua New Guinea. The children had gathered at Sissano Lagoon for the school holidays. Most of the young were just swept away by the tsunami. Another 6000 people were made homeless by the tsunami, which was caused by two submarine earthquakes 24 km off the coast and measuring 7.0 on the Richter Scale. As the earthquakes were so close to the shore there was little time to issue any warning. Many of the dead bodies were washed

Figure 1.19 The Papua New Guinea tsunami

up in the lagoon. A few days after the disaster the problem changed. Owing to the contamination of water by the dead bodies the risk of disease escalated. Stray dogs and pigs were scavenging the bodies. Due to the high temperatures and high humidity of the area decomposition of the corpses started quickly. In addition the threat of pneumonia also increased as many of the survivors were hiding in the bush in fear of further tsunami. In the absence of medical equipment disease is a major risk and even minor wounds became dirty and life threatening infections. For those who survived their livelihoods were wiped out. The Sissano Lagoon was declared a prohibited area, and no one was allowed to return there for at least two years.

Questions

15 Make a copy of Figure 1.17. Add the following hazards to the correct column: animal bites; drought; frost; hay fever; landslides; malaria; poisonous plants; rabbits; tornadoes; volcanic eruptions.

16 Draw a hazard profile (similar to Figure 1.16) for a volcano.

17 Why are most tsunami located in the Pacific Ocean?

18 Give **three** reasons why tsunami cause so much damage.

19 What are the secondary hazards associated with tsunami? Why do they occur?

Contrasting hazards in developing and developed countries

We have seen how the effects of earthquakes vary with the strength and intensity of the shock, its depth beneath the earth's surface, the nature of the bedrock (hard or unconsolidated), the nature of the terrain (steep or flat), and the type of country involved (developed or less developed). Much also depends upon chance factors such as the time. However, there are many precautions that can be taken to reduce the impact of earthquakes, although some of these can only be afforded by developed countries. Hazards, it would seem, affect the poor disproportionately. The two examples in the final section of this chapter compare the effects of two earthquakes that occurred in 1997.

THE IRANIAN EARTHQUAKE, MAY 1997

In May 1997 over 2400 people were killed and over 6000 were injured in an earthquake which affected a mountainous area in the northeast of Iran **(Figure 1.20)**. Thousands were made homeless by the earthquake which measured 7.1 on the Richter Scale. It was followed by more than 130 aftershocks. Most of the damage was in a 90 km stretch between Birjand and Qaen, a region characterised by poor villages and mud huts **(Figure 1.21)**. In the village of Ardakul, about 90 km east of Qaen, more than 500 of the 1600 inhabitants were killed during the earthquake and the aftershocks.

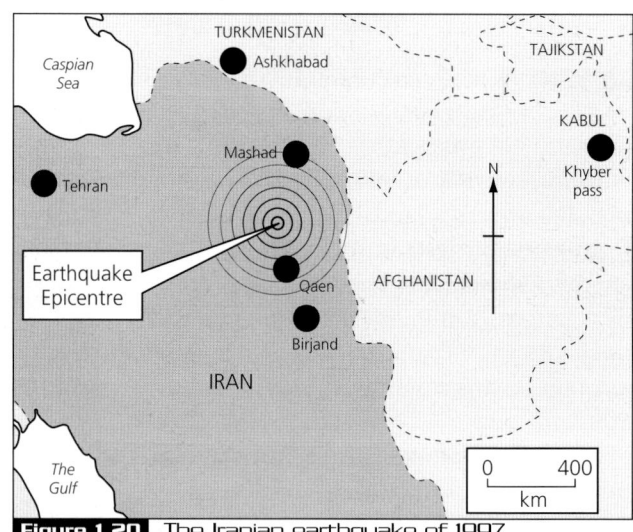

Figure 1.20 The Iranian earthquake of 1997

Figure 1.21 The area between Birjand and Qaen

Iranian officials appealed for aid to help the 50 000 people made homeless. However, much of the aid donated from the West took three or four days to reach the area. However, the critical period is the first twenty four hours, often when there is limited water and power availability.

Attempts to rescue people were made more difficult because the area is very sensitive politically, with a number of ethnic minorities and Afghan refugees. In addition to the political sensitivities, language and cultural differences discouraged foreign rescue teams. The cost of repairing the damage was estimated at over $100 million (£66 million) but the amount of aid offered by other countries amounted to only $10 million. Iran's ability to repair the damage was weakened because the price of oil, Iran's main export, fell by over 12%, and their output was reduced by 25%.

The earthquake was Iran's worst since 1990 when about 35 000 people died. Considerable damage is also believed to have occurred in neighbouring Afghanistan although there are few details available.

THE ITALIAN EARTHQUAKE

During September 1997 more than 400 earth tremors were recorded in the central Italian region around Assisi (Figure 1.22). Two powerful earthquakes, measuring 5.6 and 4.8 on the Richter Scale, struck central Italy on September 26, 1997 killing eleven people, injuring over 125 people and forcing 100 000 people to leave their homes. Up to 70% of Assisi's buildings were evacuated due to safety fears.

Figure 1.22 The Italian earthquake of 1997

Figure 1.23 The Basilica of St Francis of Assisi

However, the earthquake was newsworthy for other reasons – it badly damaged 13th and 14th century paintings in the Basilica of St Francis of Assissi **(Figure 1.23)**.

Since 1900 there have been 19 severe earthquakes in Italy, killing over 120 000 people. This earthquake, therefore, is only minor in its impact on the loss of human life but one of the very few to affect Italian heritage. Although media attention focused upon the Basilica of St Francis, all across the region mediaeval churches and towers have been reduced to rubble. Since 1945 they have cost Italy over L150 000 billion. For example, the 1976 earthquake which shook the north-east of the country killed over 1000 people and in the Naples area in 1980 an earthquake killed nearly 3000 people.

Some local villagers complained that rescue operations were slow and inadequate and that priority was given to Assisi because of its paintings.

Web sites worth browsing
World earthquakes at http://gldfs.cr.usgs.gov/
World quakes at http://www.civeng.carleton.ca/cgi-bin/quakes/
Kobe earthquake information at http://www.msen.com/–emv/kobe.html
Southern California earthquake center at http://scec.gps.caltech.edu/terrascope/terrainfo.html
Northern California earthquake data at http://quake.geo.berkeley.edu

Questions

20 Give reasons why language and cultural differences may discourage rescue teams.
21 Why is Iran subject to earthquakes?
22 a Compare the effects of the Iranian earthquake with that of the Italian earthquake.
b Why did the Italian earthquake receive more media attention than the Iranian one? Give at least **two** contrasting reasons.

Chapter review questions

How might earthquake damage vary with:
a the strength of the earthquake
b time of day
c population density
d level of economic development.
Use examples to support your answer.
Why are earthquakes becoming increasingly hazardous?

Geomorphology

2

Geomorphology is the study of the earth – and includes the **nature of the rock**, the **processes** that shape and change rocks and the **features** on it. Geographers usually separate these three aspects in order to understand the earth more clearly.

The nature of the rock includes whether it is:

- igneous, sedimentary or metamorphic;
- permeable or impermeable;
- hard or soft;
- jointed (fractured) or solid.

The processes include:

- **weathering** (the breakdown of material on the spot such as by acid rain);
- **erosion** (the breakdown of materials by a moving force such as a river);
- **mass movement** (the movement of materials due to gravity and another force such as moisture or temperature changes);
- **transport** (the movement of materials from one place to another);
- **deposition** (the creation of new landforms – features – by the dumping of material).

Rocks and Relief

Rocks vary in strength and permeability [Figure 2.1]. The **strength** determines whether they produce highlands or lowlands whereas the **permeability** (the ability to transmit water) determines whether the landscape is wet at the surface or dry. **Permeable** rocks allow water to pass through whereas **impermeable** rocks do not allow much water to pass through. Hence, strong permeable limestone gives dry upland areas whereas soft, impermeable clay produces wet lowland areas [Figure 2.2].

THE ROCK CYCLE

Sedimentary rocks are formed of fragments of older rocks and/or the remains of organic material. They are forced together to form solid rock, such as sandstone and limestone [Figure 2.3].

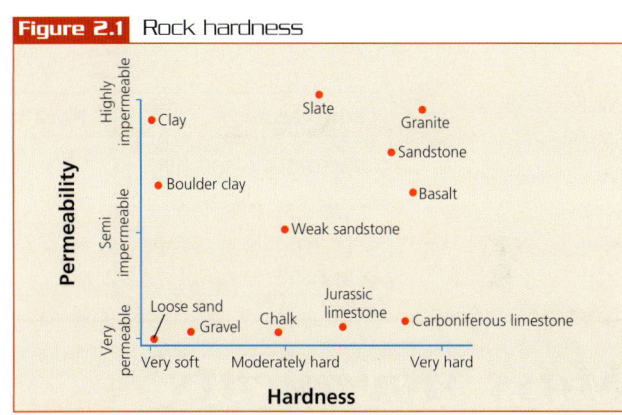

Figure 2.1 Rock hardness

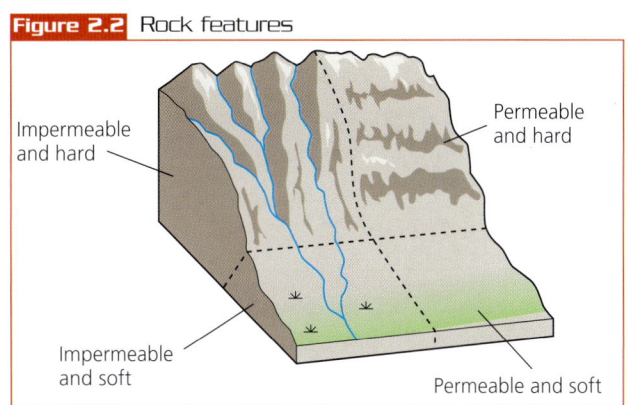

Figure 2.2 Rock features

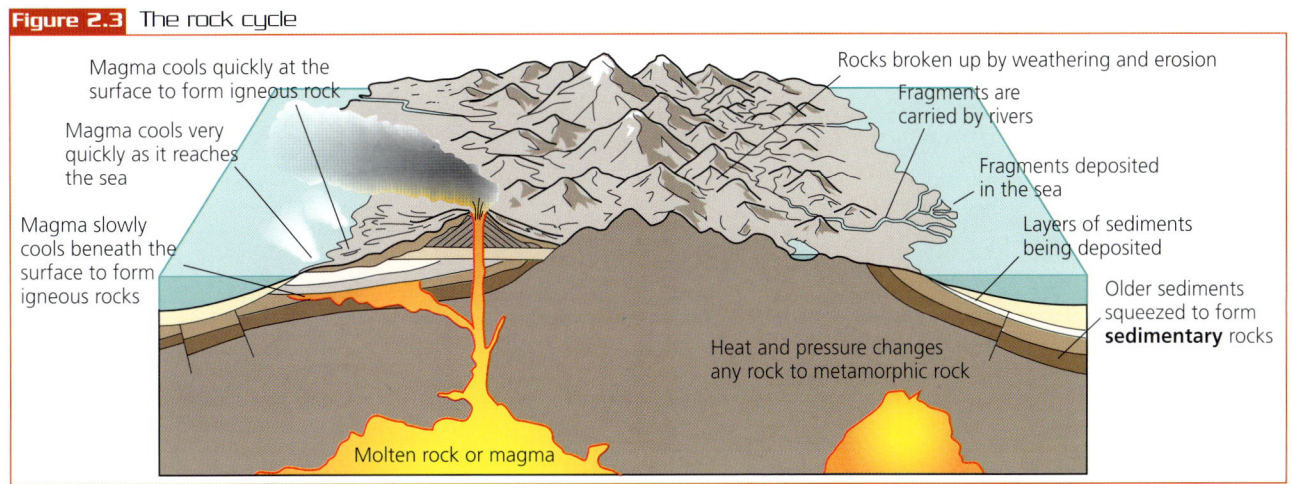

Figure 2.3 The rock cycle

13

Metamorphic rocks are formed when intense heat and pressure changes existing rocks. Limestone is changed by heat and pressure into marble.

Igneous rocks are formed when molten magma cools, forming granite and basalt.

Questions

1 Define the terms permeable and impermeable. Classify the following rock types as either permeable or impermeable: granite; clay; gravel; chalk; limestone.

2 Make a copy of Figure 2.2. Study Figure 2.1 and then decide which of the following four rock types give you each of the four landscapes in Figure 2.3 – limestone, granite, clay, gravel.

Landscape	Rock type
Impermeable and hard	....
Permeable and hard	....
Impermeable and soft	....
Permeable and soft	....

Figure 2.4 The effects of soil creep

Mass Movements

Mass movements involve any large scale movements of the earth's surface that are not accompanied by a moving force such as a river, glacier or ocean wave. They include very small movements, such as soil creep **(Figure 2.4)**, and fast movements, such as avalanches. They vary from dry movement, such as rock falls, to very fluid movements like mud flows **(Figure 2.5)**.

LANDSLIDES

The sliding rocks keep their shape and cohesion until they hit something at the bottom of the slope **(Figure 2.6)**. They range from small-scale slides close to roads, to large-scale movements killing thousands of people such as the Vaiont Dam, Italy where over 2000 people died on the 9th October 1963.

Figure 2.5 A mudflow

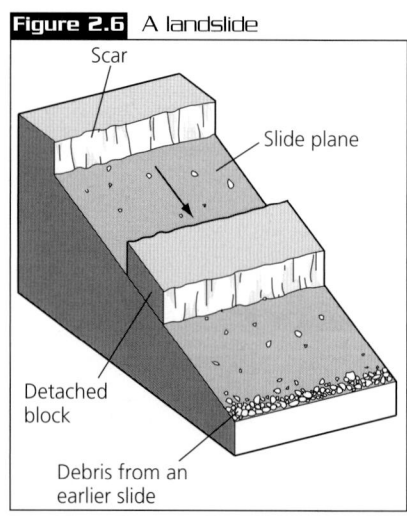

Figure 2.6 A landslide
- Scar
- Slide plane
- Detached block
- Debris from an earlier slide

FALLS

Falls occur on steep slopes. The initial cause of the fall may be weathering which prises open lines of weakness. Once the rocks are detached they fall under the influence of gravity **(Figure 2.7)**. An excellent example of rockfalls forming scree (collections of broken rock which settle at an angle of between 32° and 38°) is Wastwater in the Lake District.

SLUMPS

Slumps occur on weaker rocks, especially clay, and have a curved movement. Clay absorbs water, becomes saturated, and slumps. It then flows along a slip plane. Human activity can intensify the condition by increasing pressure on the rocks such as the Holbeck Hall Hotel, Scarborough **(Figure 2.8)**.

Figure 2.7 Rock falls

Figure 2.8 The Holbeck Hall slump

Avalanches

Avalanches are rapid movements of snow, ice, rock or earth down a slope **(Figure 2.9)**. They are common in mountainous areas: newly fallen snow may fall off older snow, especially in winter (a dry avalanche) while in spring partially melted snow moves (a wet avalanche), often triggered by skiing. Avalanches frequently occur on steep slopes over 22°, especially on North facing slopes where the lack of sun makes the snow unstable (unsafe).

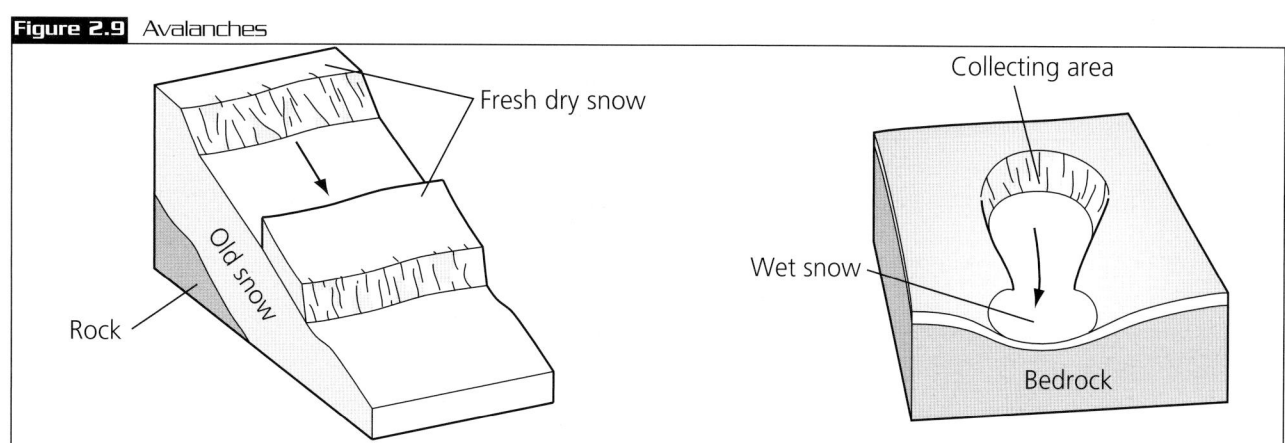

Figure 2.9 Avalanches

Figure 2.10 The avalanches of Europe 1999

Questions

3. What are the factors that increase the risk of an avalanche?
4. What were the conditions in Europe in February 1999 that led to widespread avalanches?
5. How and why may the threat of avalanches change in the next decades?
6. Imagine you are a journalist. Write a 200-word report describing the causes and consequences of the avalanche, and the effects it has had on a school ski trip caught up in the area.

THE EUROPEAN AVALANCHES OF 1999

The avalanches in the Alps in February 1999 were the worst in the area for nearly a century (Figure 2.10). Moreover, they occurred in an area which was thought to be fairly safe. The avalanche that swept through the Chamonix Valley killed 11 people and destroyed 18 chalets. Rescue work was hampered by the low temperatures (−7°C) which caused the snow to compact, and made digging almost impossible. The avalanche was about 150m wide, 6m high and travelled at a speed of up to 90 kmph. It crossed a stream and even travelled uphill for some 40m. Residents were shocked since they had not experienced an avalanche so powerful, so low in the mountains, and certainly not one capable of moving uphill.

The area received over 2m of snow in just three days. However, buildings in Montroc were not considered to be at risk. In fact, they were classified as being in the 'white zone' almost completely free of danger. By contrast, in the avalanche danger zones no new buildings have been developed for many decades. Avalanche monitoring is so old and elaborate that it had caused villagers and tourists in the 'safe' zone to think that they were safe. In Montroc the avalanche that occurred was the equivalent of an extinct volcano – the last time the snow above Montroc had caused an avalanche was in 1908.

Meteorologists have suggested that the disruption of weather patterns resulting from global warming will lead to increased snow falls in the Alps, which are increasingly heavier and later in the season.

Italian Mudslides 1998

In May 1998 mudslides swept through towns and villages in Campania, killing nearly 300 people. Hardest hit was Sarno, a town of 35 000 people (Figure 2.11). Up to a year's rainfall fell in the two weeks previous. Geologically the area is unstable – it has active volcanoes, such as Etna and Vesuvius, many mountains and scores of fast-flowing rivers. A state of emergency was declared in the Campania region and up to £18 million was earmarked for curing the damage done by the landslides. Campania is Italy's most vulnerable corner, and since 1892 scientists have recorded at least 1000 serious landslides in Campania and Calabria. Since 1945, landslides and floods have caused an average of seven deaths every month (Figure 2.12).

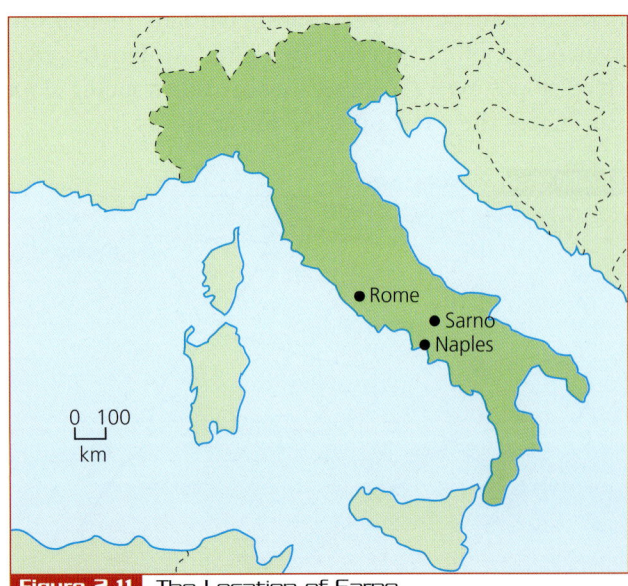

Figure 2.11 The Location of Sarno

Figure 2.12 Natural disasters in Italy since 1950

Date	Location	Disaster	Deaths
1951	Calabria	Floods	100
1951	Polesine, Veneto	Floods	89
1954	Salerno, Campania	Floods	297
1963	Longarone, Veneto	Landslide, floods	1,800
1966	Florence, Tuscany	Floods	35
1985	Val di Stava, Trentino	Landslide, floods	269
1987	Valtelina, Lombardy	Floods, landslide	53
1994	Alessandria, Piedmont	Floods	68
1996	Versilia, Tuscany	Floods, landslide	14
1998	Sarno and Siano,	Mudslide, floods	285

However, the disaster was only partially natural, much of it being down to human error. The River Sarno's riverbed had been cemented over. The clay soils of the surrounding mountains had become dangerously loose due to forest fires and deforestation. Houses had been built up hillsides identified as landslide zones. Italy's sudden entry into the industrial age in the 1960s led to the uncontrolled building of houses and roads, and deforestation. Nowhere was this more evident than in Campania. Over 20% of the houses in Sarno were built without permission. Most are shoddily built over a two-metre thick layer of lava formed by the eruption of Vesuvius in 79 AD. Heavy rain can make it liquid and up to 900 million tonnes of land are washed down in this way every year. Hence, much of the region's fragility is due to mass construction, poor infrastructure and poor planning. The strategy that occurred in Sarno was only partially a natural disaster.

In Italy 217 000 houses have been built without permission. Like many of the hundreds and thousands of other houses thrown up since Italy's economic miracle they are without proper drainage or foundations. Many stand close to river beds that seem empty and remain empty until storms occur. One of the worst examples is a Campanian town of 15 000 people called Villaggio Coppola Di Castelvolturno which was created entirely without permission.

Questions

7 Design a poster illustrating the causes, consequences and possible solutions to mudslides in Italy. Include a map of the area and an information box to define the terms mass movement and mudslide.

Weathering

Weathering is the **decomposition** and **disintegration** of rocks **in situ**, that is without any movement involved. Decomposition refers to chemical weathering and creates altered rock substances. By contrast disintegration or mechanical weathering produces smaller, angular fragments of the same rock. Weathering is important for landscape evolution as it breaks down rock and facilitates erosion and transport.

MECHANICAL (PHYSICAL) WEATHERING

There are three main types of mechanical weathering:

1 **freeze thaw** occurs when water in joints and cracks freezes at 0°C and expands by 10% **(Figure 2.13)**. This is enough to crack and split most rocks. It is most effective in environments where there is lots of moisture and there are frequent fluctuations above and below freezing point. Hence it is very common in arctic and mountainous regions;

2 **disintegration** is found in hot desert areas where there is a large **diurnal** (day and night) temperature range. Rocks heat up by day and cool down by night. As rock is a poor conductor of heat, stresses occur only in the outer layers and cause peeling or **exfoliation** to occur **(Figure 2.14)**. A little moisture is essential for this to happen;

Figure 2.13 Freeze-thaw weathering

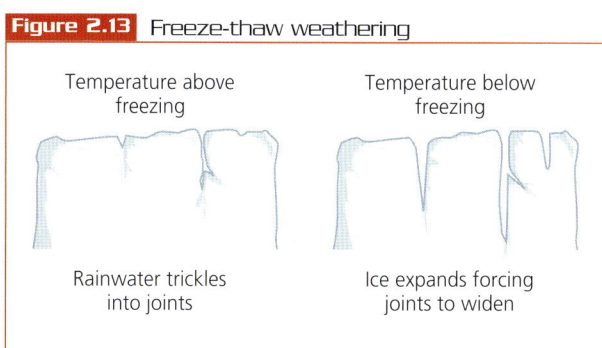

3 pressure release is the process whereby overlying rocks are removed by erosion thereby causing underlying ones to expand and fracture. The removal of a great weight, such as a glacier, has the same effect.

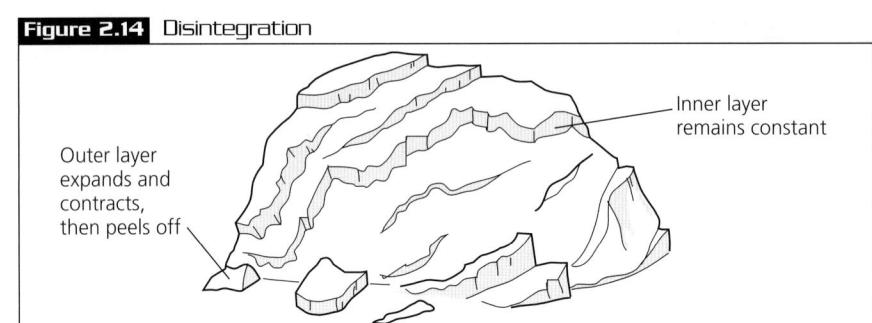

Figure 2.14 Disintegration
- Outer layer expands and contracts, then peels off
- Inner layer remains constant

CHEMICAL WEATHERING

There are three main types of chemical weathering:

1 **carbonation-solution** occurs on rocks with calcium carbonate e.g. **chalk** and **limestone**. Rainfall and dissolved carbon dioxide forms a weak carbonic acid. Calcium carbonate reacts with an acid water and forms calcium bicarbonate which is soluble and removed by percolating water. Buildings and statues are often disfigured (Figure 2.15];

2 **hydrolysis** occurs on rocks with feldspar such as **granite**. Feldspar reacts with acid water and forms kaolin (or china clay). Other minerals in the granite, such as quartz and mica, remain with the kaolin;

3 **hydration** is the process whereby certain minerals absorb water, expand and change.

Figure 2.15 Weathering of limestone

Limestone scenery

Limestone scenery is unique on account of its permeability and solubility in rain and ground-water.

The two main types of contrasting limestone scenery in the UK are:

1 carboniferous **limestone** (220-280 million years old) such as the Mendips and the Pennines;

2 cretaceous limestone or **chalk** (70-100 million years old) such as the North and South Downs.

Limestone consists mostly of CaCO3 (Calcium Carbonate) and is formed from the remains of organic material such as plants and shells.

Carboniferous limestone has many vertical cracks called *joints* and horizontal cracks called *bedding planes*. These act as lines of weakness allowing water to percolate into the rock and dissolve it. One of the main processes to affect limestone is carbonation-solution.

Questions

8 Define the term weathering.
9 What forms of weathering would you expect to find around your school?
10 Suggest how the following factors would influence the rate of weathering on, for example, a granite gravestone:
   a the age of the rock;
   b whether it faces east or west (west facing rocks are usually warmer and wetter) under a tree or not.

Figure 2.16 Block diagram of limestone

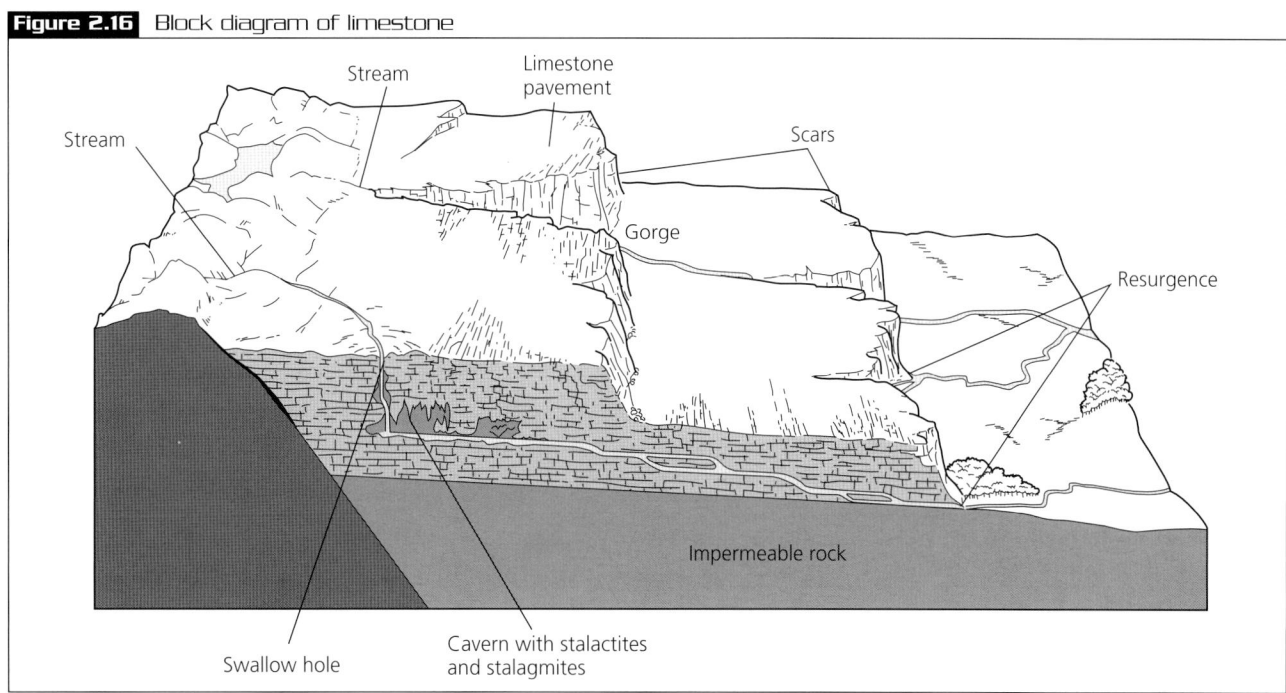

SURFACE FEATURES

As the joints and cracks are weathered and eroded over thousands of years, its permeability increases. **Clints** and **grikes** develop on the limestone surface (Figure 2.16). Large areas of bare exposed limestone containing many clints and grikes are known as **limestone pavements** (Figure 2.17). A good example is at Malham in Yorkshire. The processes involved in the formation of a limestone pavement include carbonation-solution, freeze thaw and ice action. The latter strips away horizontal bedding planes and the overlying soil.

Figure 2.17 A limestone pavement

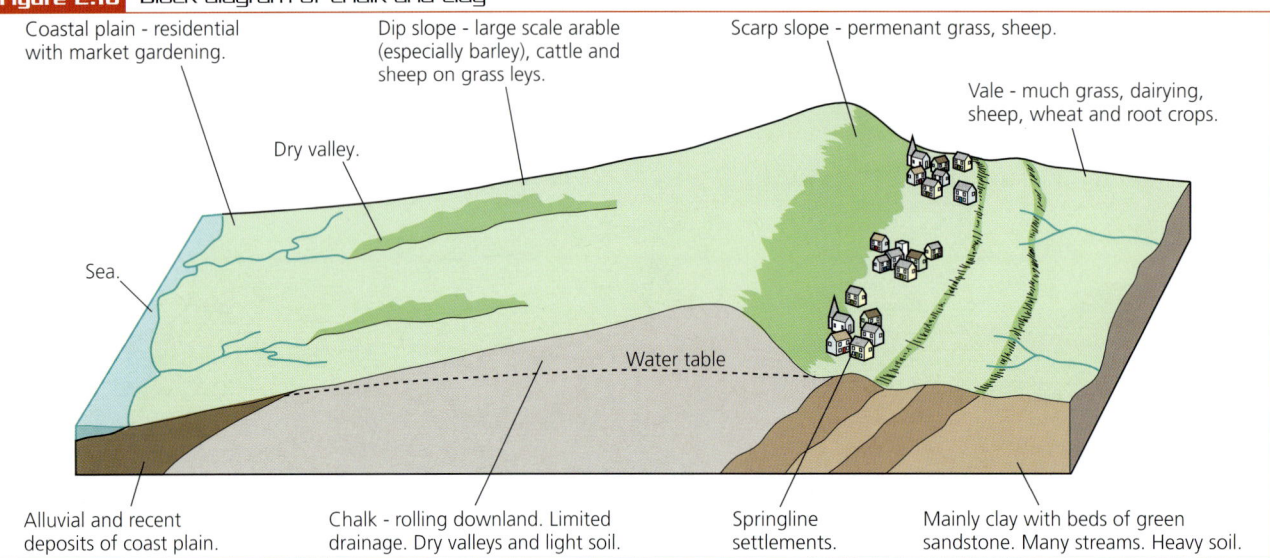

Figure 2.18 Block diagram of chalk and clay

Swallow holes (or **sinks**) are small depressions caused by the solution of limestone. They can also be formed by the enlargement of grikes, by solution or river erosion, or by the collapse of a cavern such as Gaping Ghyll near Malham. Often a river disappears down the hole, hence the term 'sink'.
Resurgent streams are streams which emerge at the base of limestone. They occur when the limestone is underlain by an impermeable rock, such as clay. A good example is the River Axe at Wookey Hole.

The term **karst** refers to well developed features on dry limestone, that is limestone without surface drainage. Underground features include caves formed by carbonation and erosion by rivers.
Stalactites (deposits of calcium) form from the top of the cave whereas **stalagmites** are formed on the base of the cave. Rates of deposition are slow, about 1 mm/100 yrs (thickness of a coat of paint). When water drips slowly from the ceiling of a cave, stalactites are formed; when it drips fast, stalagmites are formed.

Chalk

Unlike carboniferous limestone, which is very hard, grey, angular and jointed, chalk is moderately hard, white, rounded and porous. The most famous outcrops of chalk in England are the North and South Downs. Other areas of chalk include the Hog's Back near Guildford, and the flat Salisbury Plain. Other famous chalk landforms include the Folkestone Warren, the Seven Sisters and the Needles.

Escarpments are not unique to chalk, but they are generally most easily identified on chalk (Figure 2.18). They have a steep **scarp** slope and a gentle **dip** slope. The steepness of the scarp slope depends upon weathering, erosion and mass movement on the slope. Sometimes escarpments are called **cuestas**.

Dry valleys, such as Scratchy Bottom near Lulworth Cove and the Devil's Dyke near Brighton, are common especially on dip slopes (Figure 2.19). In some cases, such as in the Vale of the White Horse, Uffington, *periglacial* avalanches led to the formation of steep 'valleys' on the chalk.

Caves do not generally develop because chalk is not strong enough to support such features.

Figure 2.19 A dry valley

Clay

Clay is a fine grained, soft rock that is easily eroded. It is the end result of chemical weathering and river erosion. Clay is porous (like a sponge) but it is impermeable. It is impermeable because when it is wet the individual particles expand (hydrate) and pack very tightly. This seals off the surface and makes it impermeable. Because of its softness clay forms undulating lowlands with lots of surface drainage, such as rivers, marshes and moors. When drained, clay provides fertile soils, such as those in East Anglia. Settlements are usually found on the higher ground to avoid the risk of flooding.

Granite

Granite is an igneous rock. It has great physical strength and is very resistant to erosion. There are many types of granite and all contain quartz, mica and felspar. These are very resistant minerals. The processes that occur on granite today include weathering such as freeze-thaw and hydrolysis and erosion, especially by rivers.

Characteristic granite landscapes include large-scale **batholiths**, which form mountains. Good examples include the Wicklow Mountains and the Mountains of Mourne in Ireland. **Tors** are isolated masses of bare rock. They can be up to 20m high, such as Hay Tor and Yes Tor in Dartmoor **(Figure 2.20)**. Due to its great resistance, granite forms upland areas.

Due to granite's resistance, weathering results in a thin, gritty soil cover. Such soils are generally infertile, so rough grazing is the dominant land use. Granite is an impermeable rock and many marshy hollows at the heads of the valleys are due to the impermeable nature of granite.

Questions

11 Compare chalk and clay in terms of
  a strength
  b permeability.
12 Which of the two rocks (chalk and clay) is likely to form high ground?
13 What is a dry valley? How is it formed?
14 Why is flooding such a big problem in clay areas?

Figure 2.20 Tors

Figure 2.21 Uses of granite

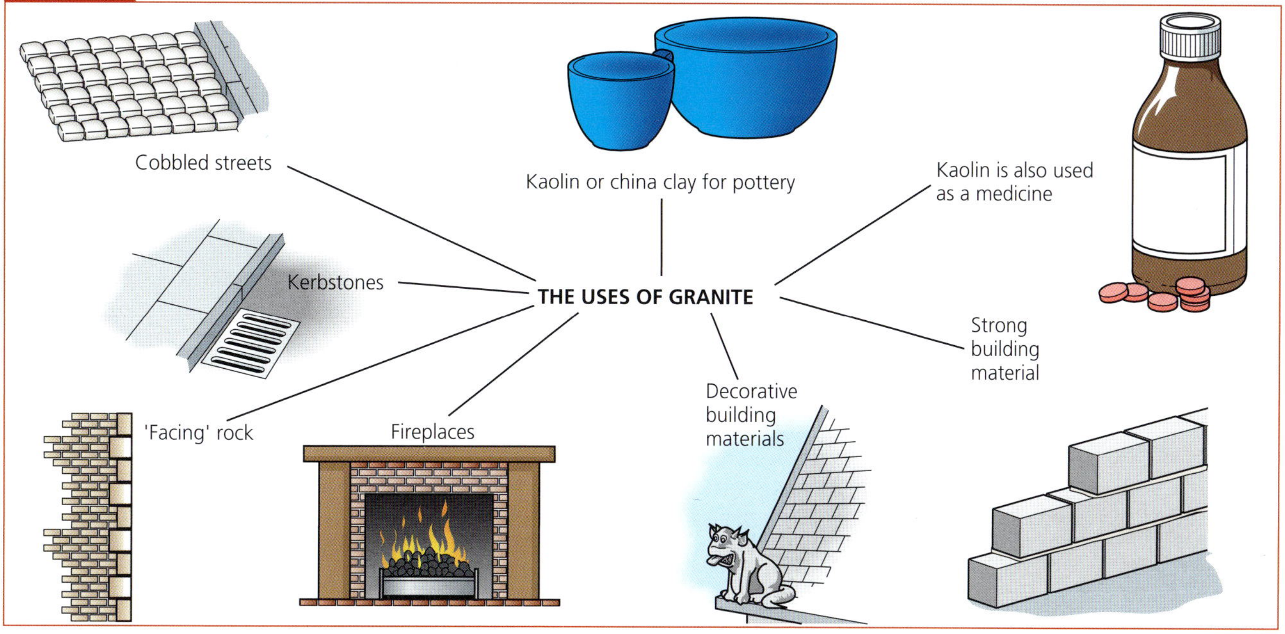

- Cobbled streets
- Kerbstones
- 'Facing' rock
- Fireplaces
- Kaolin or china clay for pottery
- Decorative building materials
- Kaolin is also used as a medicine
- Strong building material

THE USES OF GRANITE

Mining – the debate

Limestone has a wide range of industrial uses compared to other rocks that are heavily quarried, such as granite, gritstone and basalt. It is cheaper to quarry limestone than other rocks, and limestone is a vital ingredient for the chemical industry. In Britain, production of hard limestone for chemical uses is over 21 million tonnes, and for construction is over 65 million tonnes.

Large scale quarrying of the Mendip limestones in Somerset began in 1870 with the arrival of the railways. About 40 large quarries have opened, and 16 are still working or are only temporarily inactive. About 6 per cent of the limestone outcrop has been quarried and 250 million tonnes of limestone removed. The greatest impact has been on Mendip scenery. A small limestone hill at Vobster has disappeared, and larger hills at Sandford, Milton and Dulcote have shrunk by between one-quarter and two-thirds of their volume.

Between 1756 and 1966 60 million tonnes of limestone were blasted out of the Mendips. By 1988, only 22 years later, 190 million tonnes more had gone! The value of the 250 million tonnes of limestone was about £900 million. On the same basis, sales of limestone from Mendip quarries are worth about £43 million a year.

In the Mendips, annual production of hard limestone 'aggregate' (crushed rock) rose from three million tonnes in 1965 to 10 million tonnes in 1980. Since the mid-1980s, the Mendip quarries produced more than 12 million tonnes of limestone annually, and production from East Mendip will rise to 15.3 million tonnes in 2005.

Quarrying has shrunk or polluted five of the once large and clear Mendip springs. About 600 000 people in Somerset and Avon get their water supply from springs in the Mendips, which, thanks to their high rainfall of 1000-1200 millimetres a year, produce at least 40 per cent more water per unit of area than any other aquifer (water bearing rock) in southern England. Some researchers argue that deep quarries, when abandoned, will fill with water to become vast reservoirs but waste disposal companies in Somerset and Avon are keen to use old quarries more profitably as rubbish tips.

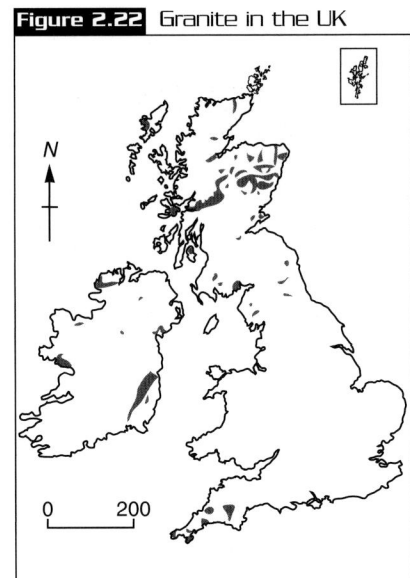

Figure 2.22 Granite in the UK

Questions

15 Make a copy of Figure 2.22. On it label the following areas: Dartmoor, the Scottish Uplands, the Mountains of Mourne; the Wicklow Mountains.

16 Using Figure 2.21 identify the ways in which granite is used in:
  a your home
  b your school.

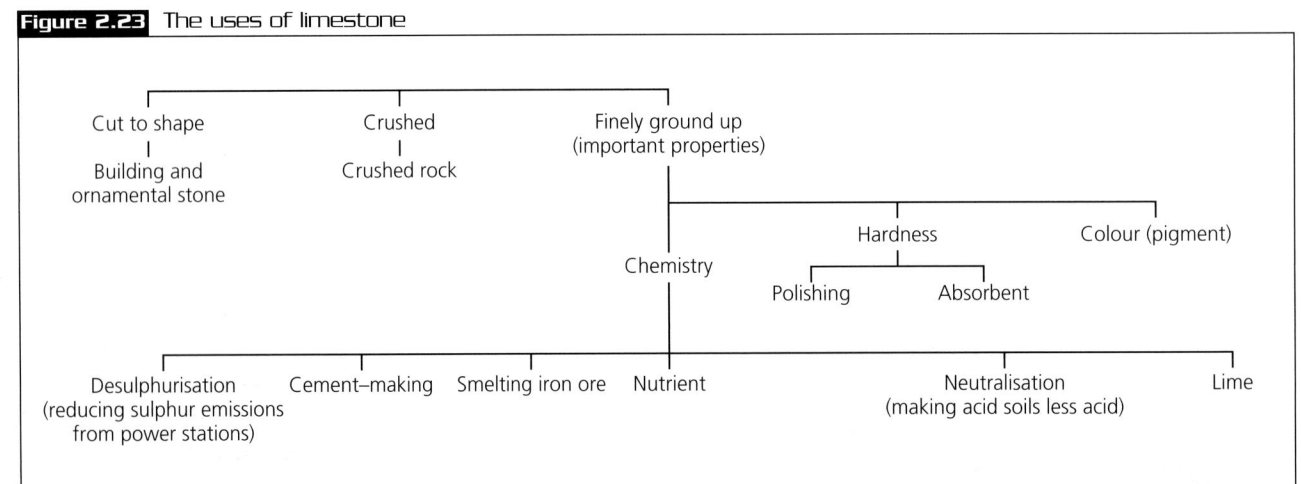

Figure 2.23 The uses of limestone

"Already, the road infrastructure cannot support the scale of quarrying. The increase in lorry traffic is intolerable: on one day there were more than 3000 outward journeys from East Mendip quarries."

"Now that quarrying is largely automated fewer jobs depend on it. For many people, tourism generates jobs and the sites such as Cheddar Gorge [Figure 2.25], the hills around Wells and Wookey Hole need protection."

"Britain needs to keep going forward. There is demand for new housing, for more industries, and these create demand for more materials. We are providing the resources that are needed. Otherwise we would have to import limestone from overseas."

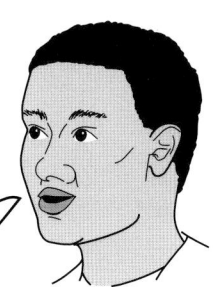

"Visitors to attractions created by Mendip limestone bring about £23 million into the area a year. Destruction of the karst landscape would dry up this revenue. Further damage to the Mendips' limestone aquifer would mean finding a replacement: water suppliers consider that a new source on this scale could only be the River Severn, which would cost about £12 million a year."

Figure 2.24 Mining – the debate

Figure 2.25 Cheddar Gorge

Questions

17 Study Figure 2.23. What are the uses of limestone in modern society?

18 Study the views of the individuals shown in Figure 2.24. What are the conflicts of interest over how best to use the resources of the Cheddar region?

2 Rivers

- The River Nile, in north east Africa, is the world's longest river.
- The Amazon in South America has the biggest discharge (amount) of water.
- The Yangtze in China carries 1.6 million tonnes of silt each year.
- Antarctica has no rivers; it is all ice.
- The largest lake is the Caspian Sea (in the former USSR) – it is much bigger than the British Isles.
- The Ganges delta in south east Asia is the largest in the world. It is about 75 000 km^2.
- The widest waterfall is the Khone Falls in Laos. It is over 10 km wide.

River	Length (km)
Nile	6695
Amazon	6437
Yangtze	6379
Mississippi	6264
Ob-Irtysh	5411
Hwange He	4672
Zaire (Congo)	4662
Amur	4416
Lena	4400
Mackenzie	4241

KEY TERMS AND DEFINITIONS

The **water cycle** is the movement of water between air, land and sea. It varies from place to place and over time.

A **river regime** is the annual variation in the flow of a river.

A **storm hydrograph** shows us how a river changes over a short period, such as a day or a couple of days.

A **drainage basin** is the area drained by a river, for example the Thames drainage basin or the Severn drainage basin.

A **watershed** is the dividing line between one drainage basin and another.

An **estuary** is the mouth of a large river which is affected by tides.

A **tributary** is a smaller river which joins up with a larger one.

The **discharge** of a river is the amount of water (volume) passing a given point over a certain time and is measured in cubic metres per second (cusecs).

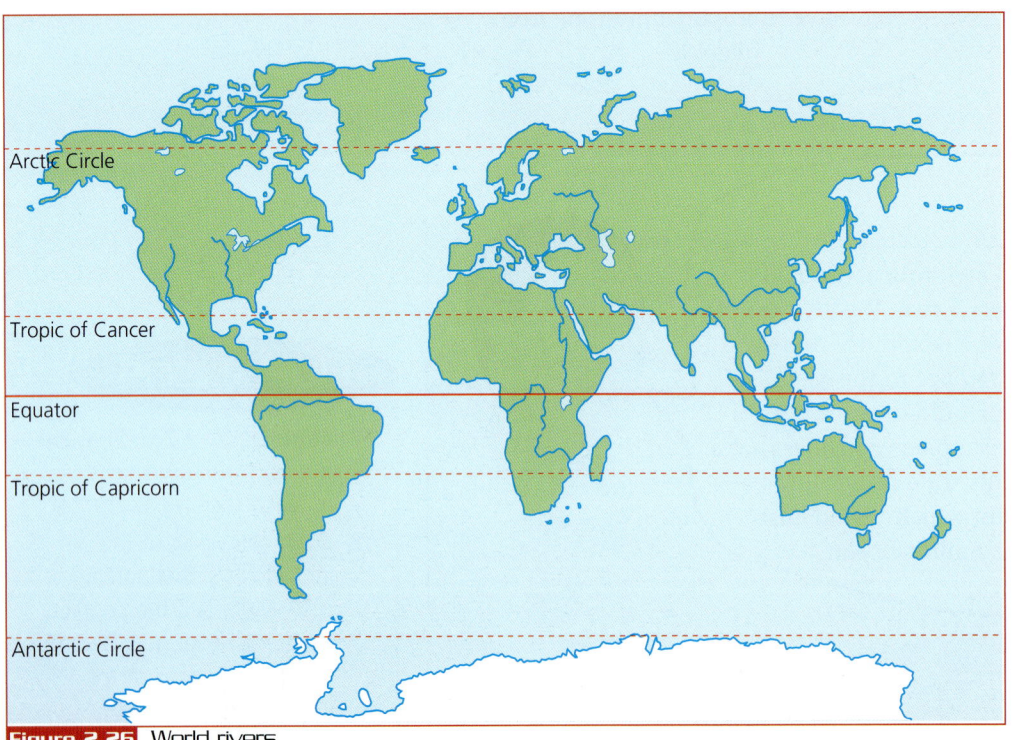

Figure 2.26 World rivers

Questions

19 In which continents are the rivers listed in Figure 2.26?
20 Which continents do not have any of the world's longest rivers?
21 Which rivers are located near these towns:
New York
Paris
Tombouctou (Timbuktu)?
22 The photographs **(Figures 2.27–2.29)** show rivers from South Africa, the Dolomites and the United Kingdom. Match each photo with one of these countries. Give reasons for your choice.
23 Using an atlas (a) find out the approximate length of the River Thames and the River Severn; how do they compare with the rivers listed in Figure 2.26?
(b) find out the approximate areas of the UK and the Aral Sea.

Figure 2.27

Figure 2.28

Figure 2.29

Figure 2.30 The hydrological cycle

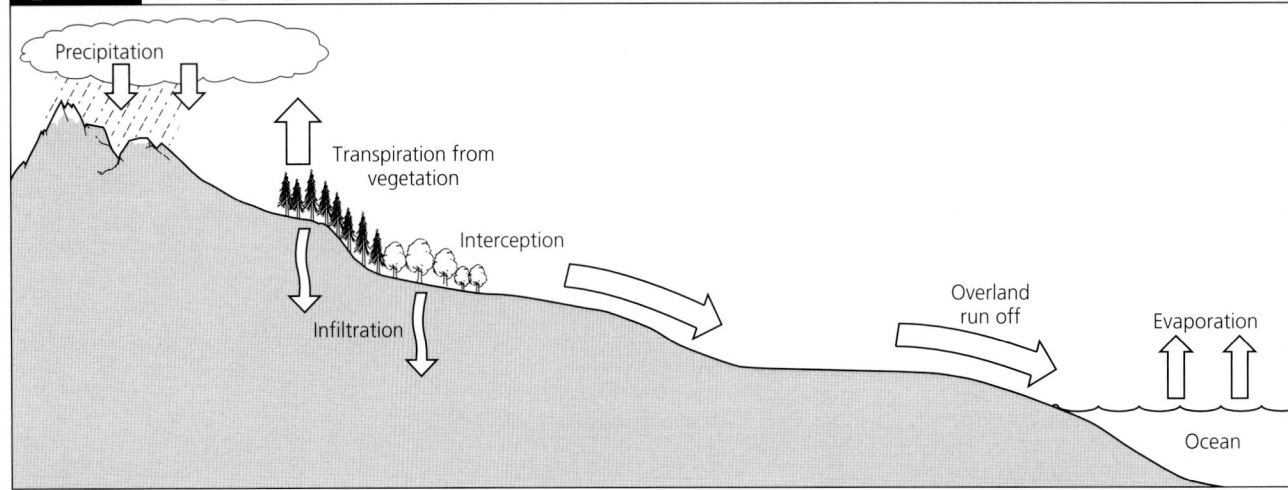

KEY TERMS AND DEFINITIONS

Hydrology is the study of water.

Precipitation includes all types of rainfall, snow, frost, hail and dew.

Interception is the precipitation that is collected and stored by vegetation.

Overland runoff is water that flows over the ground.

Infiltration is water that seeps into the ground.

Evaporation refers to the process by which water from the ground or a lake that changes into a gas.

Transpiration is water loss from vegetation to the atmosphere.

Evapotranspiration is the combined losses of transpiration and evaporation.

Questions

24 Figure 2.30 shows a model of the hydrological cycle. Suggest how the hydrological cycle might change if the underlying bedrock was (a) granite and (b) limestone.

25 **Figures 2.31 and 2.32** show the same river in summer and in winter. How and why does the hydrological cycle vary between winter and summer. In your answer make use of the following terms: *temperature, rainfall, interception, overland runoff, vegetation cover.*

Figure 2.31 The Thames in summer

Figure 2.32 The Thames in winter

River regimes

A **river regime** is the annual variation in the flow of a river **(Figure 2.33)**. In Britain river flows are higher in winter for a number of reasons:

- higher rainfall;
- lower temperatures and hence lower evapotranspiration;
- less interception by deciduous vegetation – such as oak trees, which are in leaf in summer, and so intercept rainfall, whereas in winter when they lose their leaves they do not intercept any rainfall.

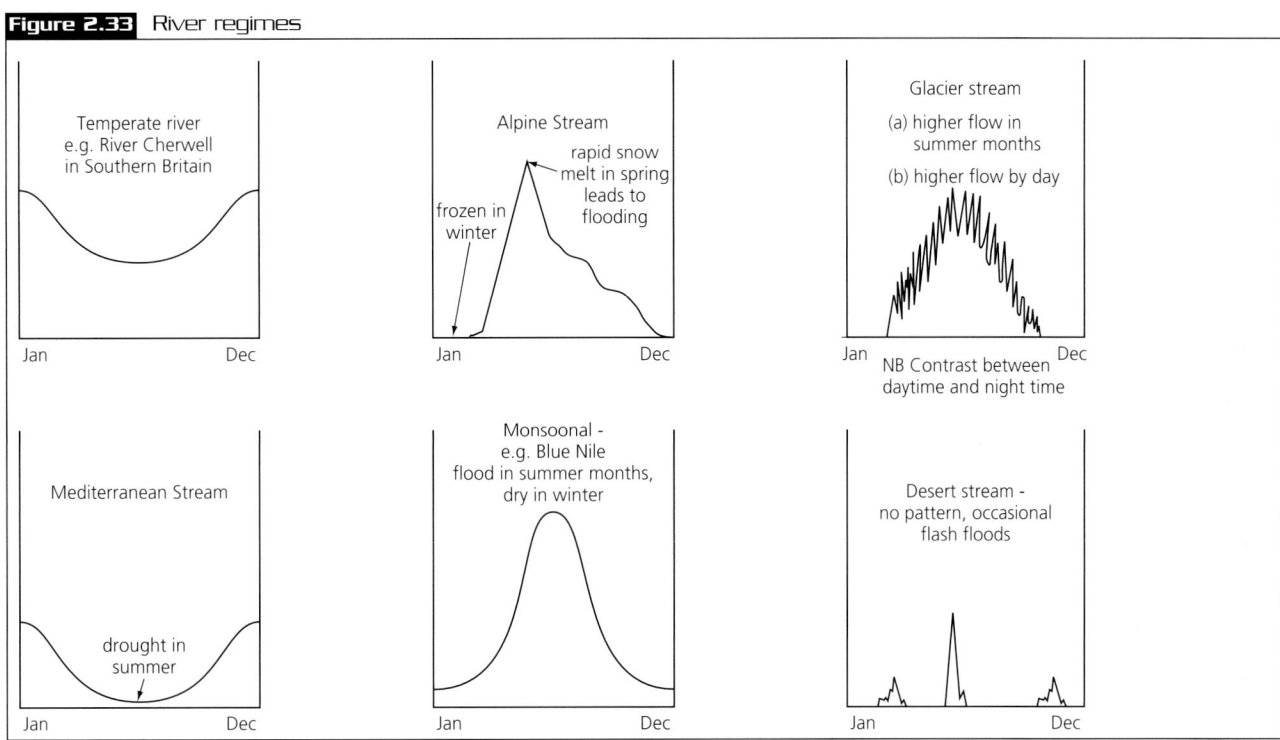

Figure 2.33 River regimes

By contrast, in summer there is:

- less rainfall;
- higher temperatures and more evapotranspiration;
- greater interception by deciduous vegetation.

In general, river regimes reflect climate. It is possible to have complex regimes. For example, some rivers flow through a variety of climate types, and others have tributaries from different climates. The River Nile has three main tributaries (feeder streams): the White Nile, the Blue Nile and the Atbara **(Figure 2.34)**. The White Nile is an equatorial river, and produces a fairly constant flow over the year, whereas the Atbara and the Blue Nile are monsoonal and produce a peak flow in the summer.

The building of the High Dam at Aswan in the 1960s has controlled the flow of the Nile below the dam. Excess water from the summer months is stored in Lake Nasser and released during the winter months.

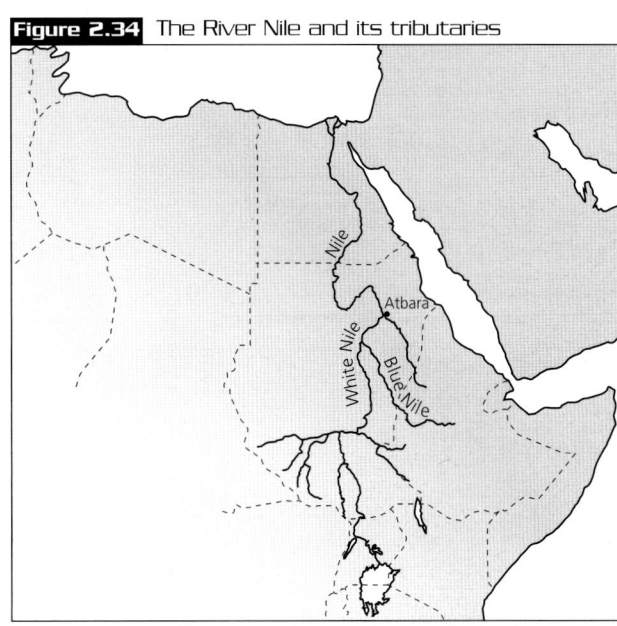

Figure 2.34 The River Nile and its tributaries

Questions

26 When is the biggest flow in British (temperate) rivers?

27 How does the annual flow of an alpine stream differ from that of a monsoonal stream?

28 Plot the data for the equatorial stream **(Figure 2.35)**. The first three points have already been done for you. Join up the points with a free hand curve. Describe the graph that you have drawn. How is this related to climate?

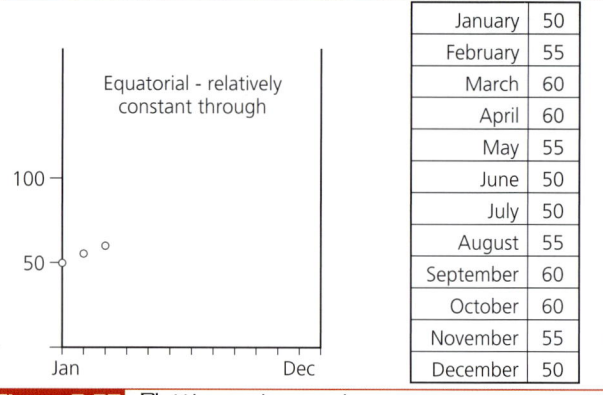

January	50
February	55
March	60
April	60
May	55
June	50
July	50
August	55
September	60
October	60
November	55
December	50

Figure 2.35 Plotting a river regime

Storm hydrographs

A **storm hydrograph (Figure 2.36)** shows us how a river changes over a short period, such as a day or a couple of days. Usually it is drawn to show how a river reacts to an individual storm. Each storm hydrograph has a series of parts (see key terms and definitions).

Flood hydrographs are affected by a number of factors:
- climate (intense rain causes more flooding);
- soils (impermeable clay soils create more flooding);
- vegetation (vegetation intercepts rainfall and so flooding is less likely);
- infiltration capacity (soils with a low infiltration capacity cause much overland runoff);
- rock type (permeable rocks will allow water to infiltrate, thereby reducing the flood peak);

KEY TERMS AND DEFINITIONS

The **rising limb** shows us how quickly the flood waters begin to rise.

The **peak flow** is the maximum discharge of the river as a result of the storm.

The **time lag** is the time between the height of the storm (not the start or the end) and the maximum flow in the river.

The **falling limb** is the speed with which the water level in the river declines after the peak.

Baseflow is the normal level of the river, which is fed by groundwater.

Quickflow or **stormflow** is the water which gets into the river as a result of overland runoff.

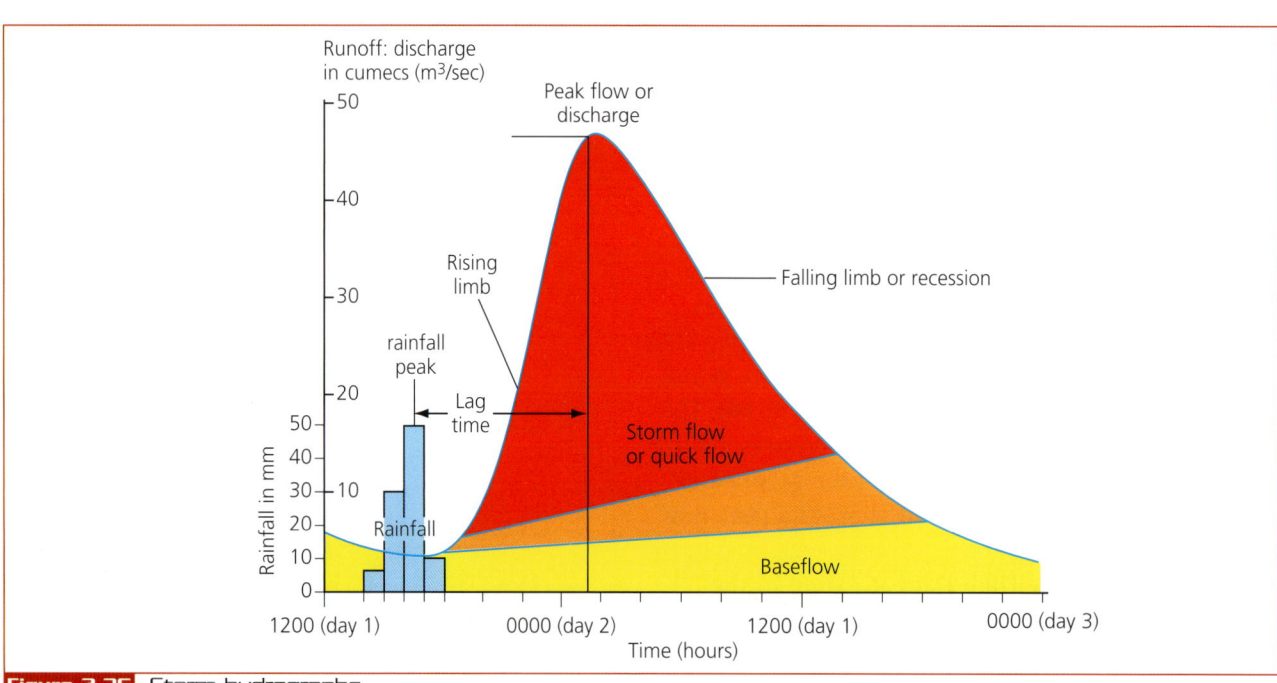

Figure 2.36 Storm hydrographs

- slope angle (on steeper slopes there is greater runoff);
- human impact (creating impermeable surfaces and additional drainage channels increases the risk of flooding).

Urban hydrographs are different to rural ones. They have:

- a shorter time lag;
- a steeper rising limb;
- a higher peak flow;
- a steeper falling limb.

This is because there are more impermeable surfaces in urban areas (roofs, pavements, roads, buildings) as well as more drainage channels (gutters, drains, sewers).

Questions

29 Plot the following figures which were collected from a rural stream and a nearby urban stream during the same storm.

Figure 2.37 Table for hydrographs

Time (mins.)	Discharge (litres per second)	
	Rural stream	Urban stream
0	2.1	2.1
30	2.5	4.0
60	3.0	9.0
90	5.0	16.0
120	7.0	21.0
150	9.0	16.0
180	11.0	10.0
210	13.0	7.0
240	12.0	6.0
270	10.0	5.0
300	8.0	4.0
330	6.0	3.0
360	4.0	2.0
390	3.0	2.0
420	2.0	2.0

30 What is the peak flow and time lag in:
  a the rural hydrograph
  b the urban hydrograph?

31 How do the rising limb and recessional limbs in the urban hydrograph compare with the rural hydrograph?

32 Explain these differences with reference to:
  a the increase in impermeable surfaces (pavements, roads, buildings etc.)
  b number of drainage channels (sewers, gutters, drains, ditches, streams).

River erosion

KEY TERMS AND DEFINITIONS

Abrasion is the wearing away of the bed and bank by the load carried by a river.

Attrition is the wearing away of the load carried by a river. It creates smaller, rounder particles.

Hydraulic action is the force of air and water on the sides of rivers and in cracks.

Solution is the chemical erosion in a river especially of calcium (found in chalk and limestone).

FACTORS AFFECTING EROSION

- load – the heavier and sharper the load the greater the potential for erosion;
- velocity – the greater the velocity the greater the potential for erosion;
- gradient – increased gradient increases the rate of erosion;
- geology – soft, unconsolidated rocks such as sand and gravel are easily eroded;
- pH – rates of solution are increased when the water is more acidic;
- human impact – deforestation, dams and bridges interfere with the natural flow of a river and frequently end up increasing the rate of erosion.

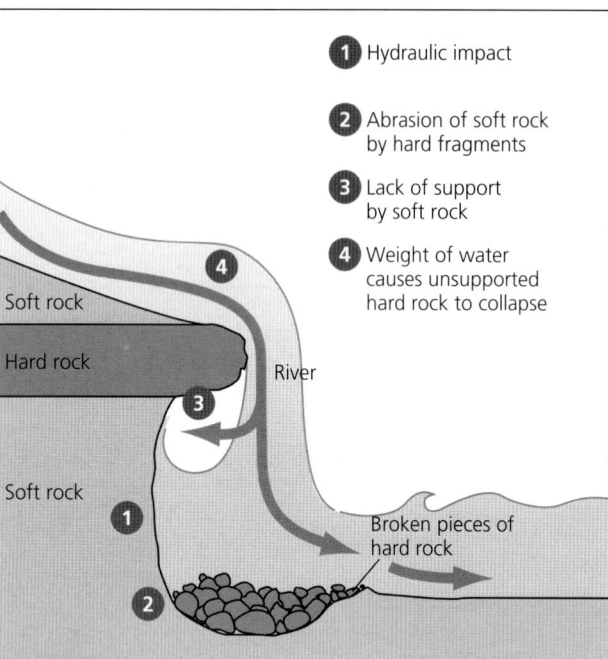

Figure 2.38 The formation of a waterfall

Features of erosion

Waterfalls frequently occur on horizontally bedded rocks **(Figure 2.38)**. The soft rock is undercut by hydraulic action and abrasion. The weight of the water and the lack of support cause the waterfall to collapse and retreat. Over thousands of years the waterfall may retreat enough to form a gorge, a narrow, steep sided valley **(Figure 2.39)**.

Other features of erosion include pot holes **(Figure 2.40)**, river cliffs and V-shaped valleys.

Figure 2.40 The formation of potholes

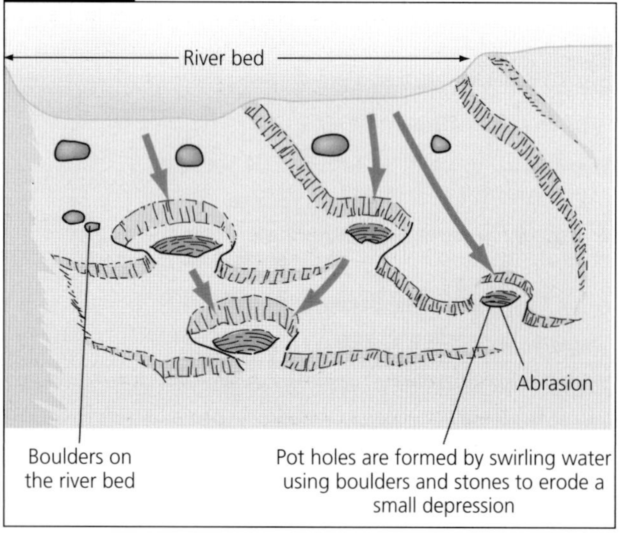

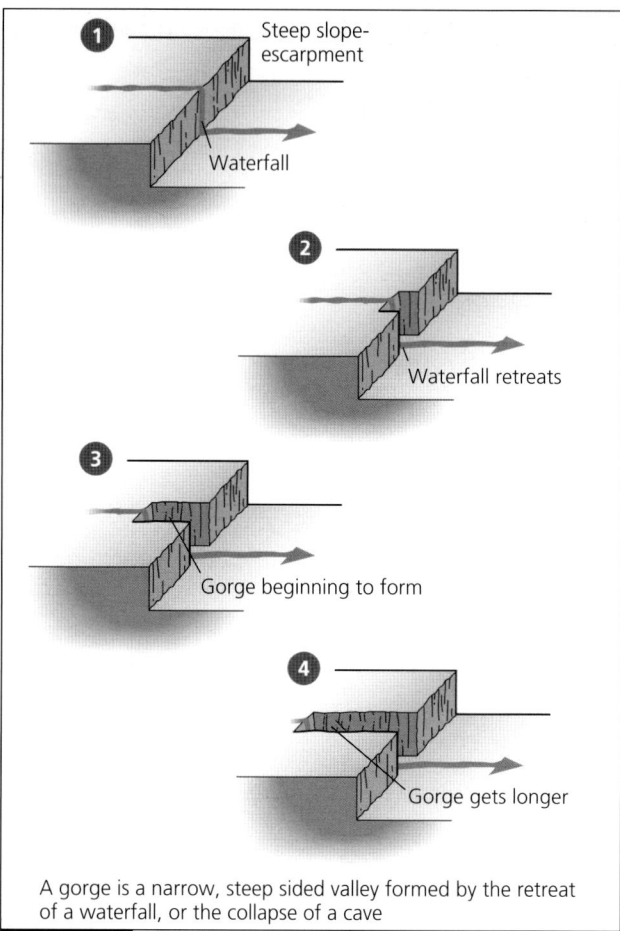

A gorge is a narrow, steep sided valley formed by the retreat of a waterfall, or the collapse of a cave

Figure 2.39 The formation of a gorge

Transport

KEY TERMS AND DEFINITIONS

Suspension – small particles are held up by the turbulent flow in the river.

Saltation – heavier particles are bounced or bumped along the bed of the river.

Solution – the chemical load is carried dissolved in the water.

Traction – the heaviest material is dragged or rolled along the bed of the river.

Floatation – leaves and twigs are carried on the surface of the river.

Questions

33 Under what conditions does river erosion increase?

34 What is a gorge? How can it be formed?

Deposition

Deposition occurs as a river slows down and loses its energy. This occurs as a river floods across a flood plain, or when it enters the sea or a dam. Features include deltas, levees, flood plains and ox-bow lakes.

DELTAS

A delta is a flat, low lying area formed by river deposits. The Nile, Mississippi and Ganges are excellent examples of deltas. For deltas to be formed a river needs to (a) carry a large volume of sediment, and (b) enter a still body of water **(Figure 2.41)**. Deposition is increased if the water is salty, as this causes salt particles to stick together, become heavier and be deposited. Vegetation also increases the rate of deposition by slowing down the water. The heavier material is deposited first, and the finest material last, and furthest away.

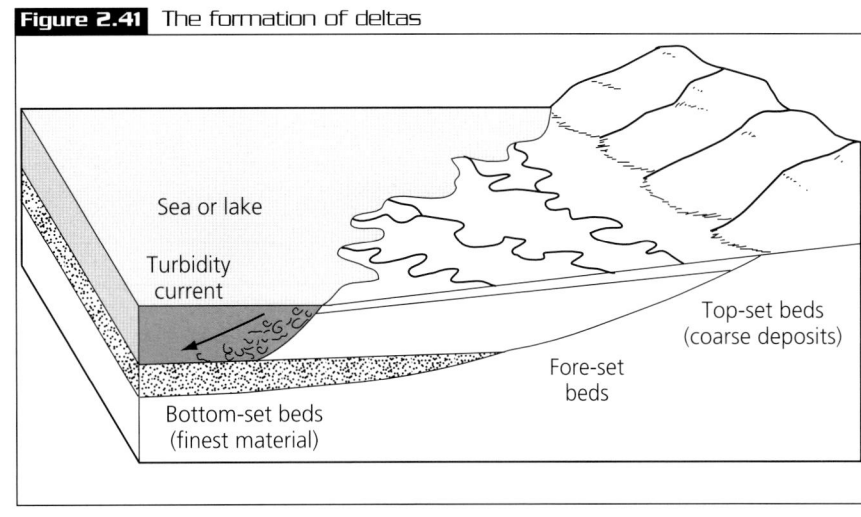

Figure 2.41 The formation of deltas

LEVEES

Levees are raised banks at the edge of a river. They are formed by repeated flooding of the river **(Figure 2.42)**. When the river floods its speed is reduced. This is because it is slowed down by the vegetation on the floodplain. As its speed is reduced it has to deposit some of its load. It drops the coarser, heavier material first and the finer, lighter material last. This means that over time, the levees are built up of coarse material, such as sand and gravel, while the flood plain consists of fine silt and clay.

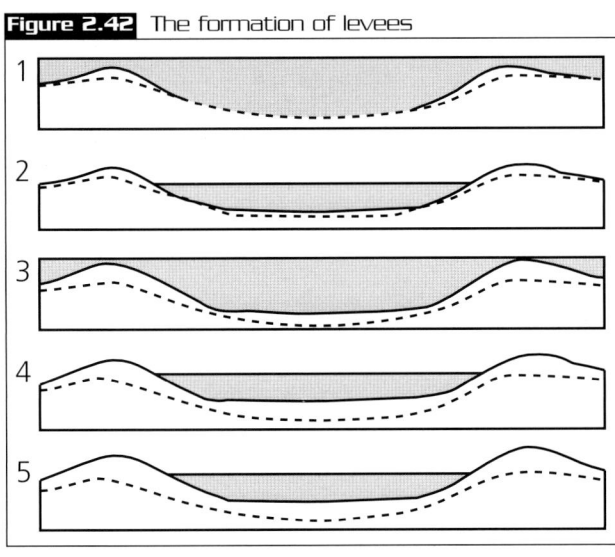

Figure 2.42 The formation of levees

1. When the river floods it bursts its banks. It deposits it coarsest load (grade sand) close to the bank and the finer load - clay and sand further away.

2,3,4 } This continues over a long period of time.

5. The river has built up raised banks called levees - consisting of coarser material and a flood plain consisting of fine material.

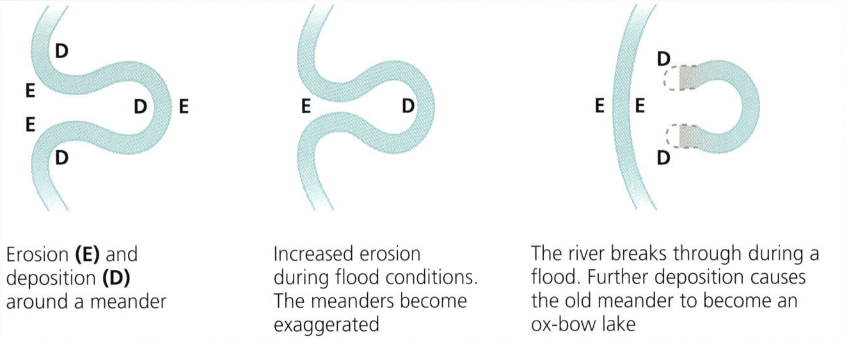

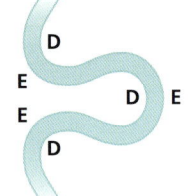
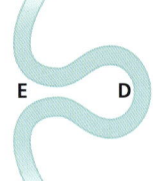

Erosion (E) and deposition (D) around a meander

Increased erosion during flood conditions. The meanders become exaggerated

The river breaks through during a flood. Further deposition causes the old meander to become an ox-bow lake

Figure 2.43 The formation of ox-bow lakes

OX-BOW LAKES

Ox-bow lakes are the result of erosion and deposition. Erosion is concentrated on the outer, deeper bank of a meander (Figure 2.43). During times of flooding, erosion increases. The river breaks through and creates a new, steeper channel. In time, the old meander is closed off by deposition to form an ox-bow lake.

Rivers and human activity

Rivers are very attractive to people for a variety of reasons. But rivers can also cause problems. The flood hazard is extremely dangerous for people's lives and their possessions. Many settlements are built in order to reduce the risk of flooding. Oxford is an excellent example (Figure 2.44). Much of the flood plain of the Thames and the Cherwell has not been built upon. It has been left for farming and for recreational grounds. Housing and industry have tended to locate on the higher ground free from flooding.

Moreover, people have tried to reduce the effect of flooding by reinforcing river banks with steel, concrete and wood, diverting streams and creating new flood relief channels and raising the banks of the river.

Figure 2.44 River meanders

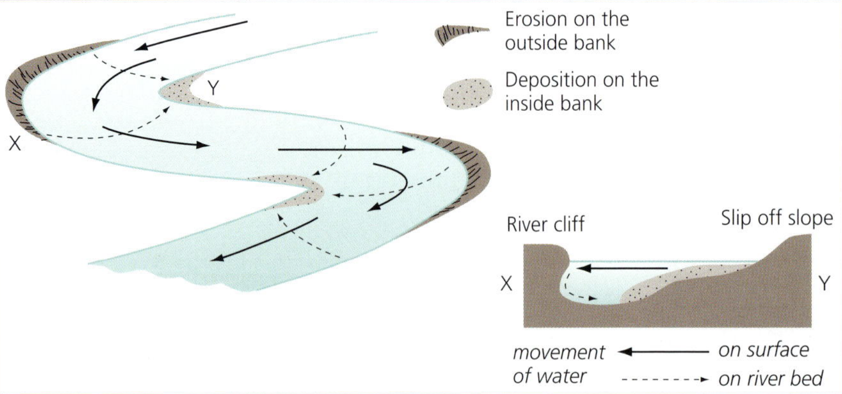

Figure 2.45 Meanders

Questions

35 Make a copy of the photo (Figure 2.44), which shows a meander. On your diagram label the following: *river cliff, slip-off slope, flood plain, area of erosion, area of deposition.*

36 Explain why erosion takes place on one side of the meander and deposition on the other side.

Questions

37 In small groups discuss how the effects of flooding may be reduced. Which do you think is most effective, and why?

38 For a river near you, list:
   a the advantages it provides
   b the problems it causes.

39 Why are so many settlements near rivers? Use examples to support your answer.

RIVERS AND MAPWORK

KEY TERMS AND DEFINITIONS

The **long profile** is the shape or gradient of a river from its start (source) to where it meets the sea **(Figure 2.47a)**.

The **cross profile** is a cross section across a river valley at any point along the river **(Figure 2.47b)**.

Maps tell us a great deal about rivers. We can see if they are in their upper course or lower course, whether they are eroding or depositing, and whether they are having any effect on human activity. There are a number of key things to look for:

- Is the river in its upper course or lower course? If it is in the upper course the land will be higher and the contours close together. If it is in the lower course, the land will be lower and flatter. The contour lines will be further apart.
- Is the river straight of winding (meandering)?
- Are there any features such as ox-bow lakes or waterfalls?
- What evidence is there for human activity – are there any locks, weirs, embankments, drainage channels (these are straight, unlike rivers which are normally winding), are there any canals or dams?

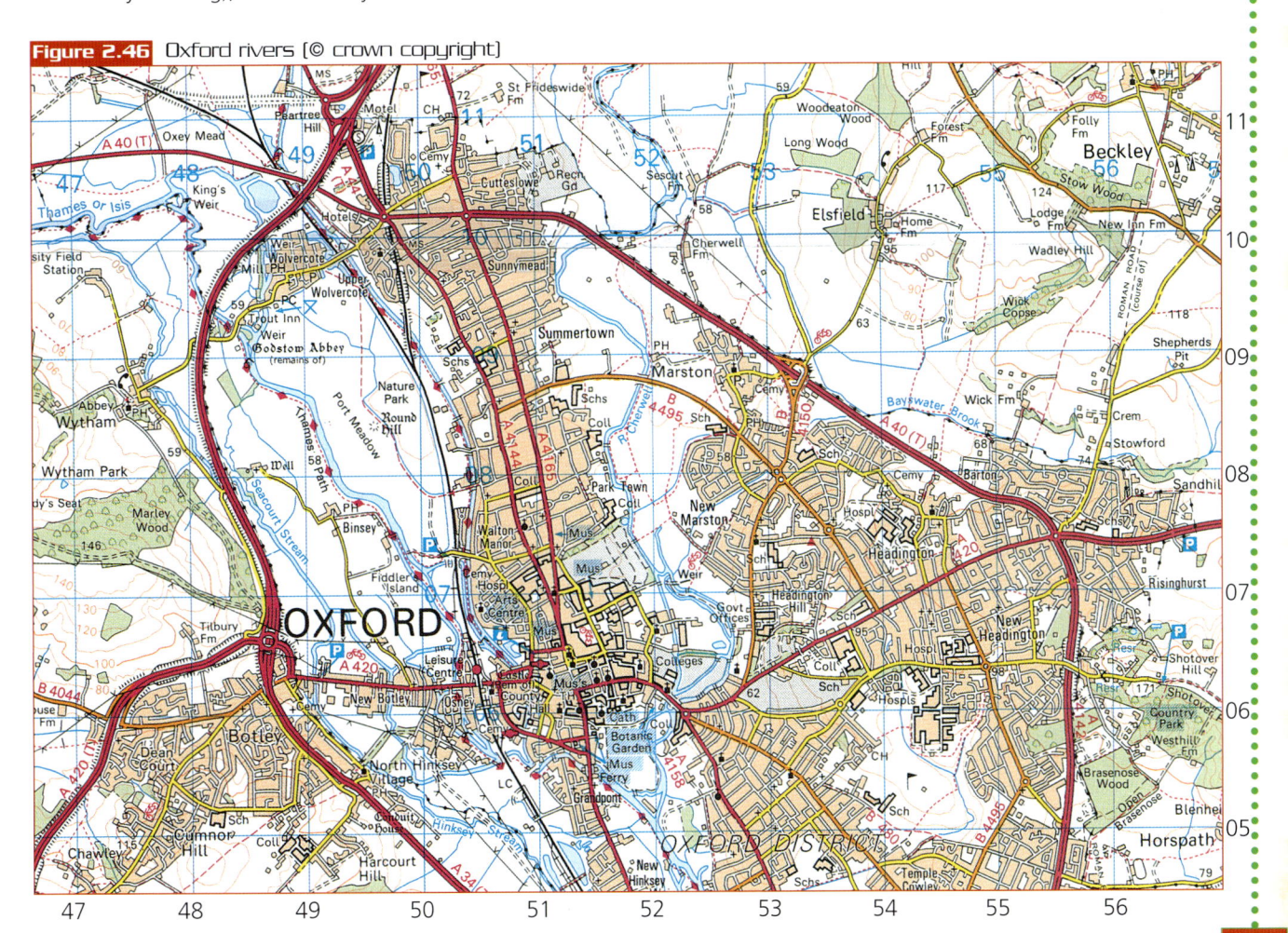

Figure 2.46 Oxford rivers (© crown copyright)

(a) Long profile

Mountain region

A

B

Tributary

Low ground

Flat, low land area

Delta

C

(b) Cross profile

Hard rock
Soft rock
River

Figure 2.47 Long and cross profiles of a river

Questions

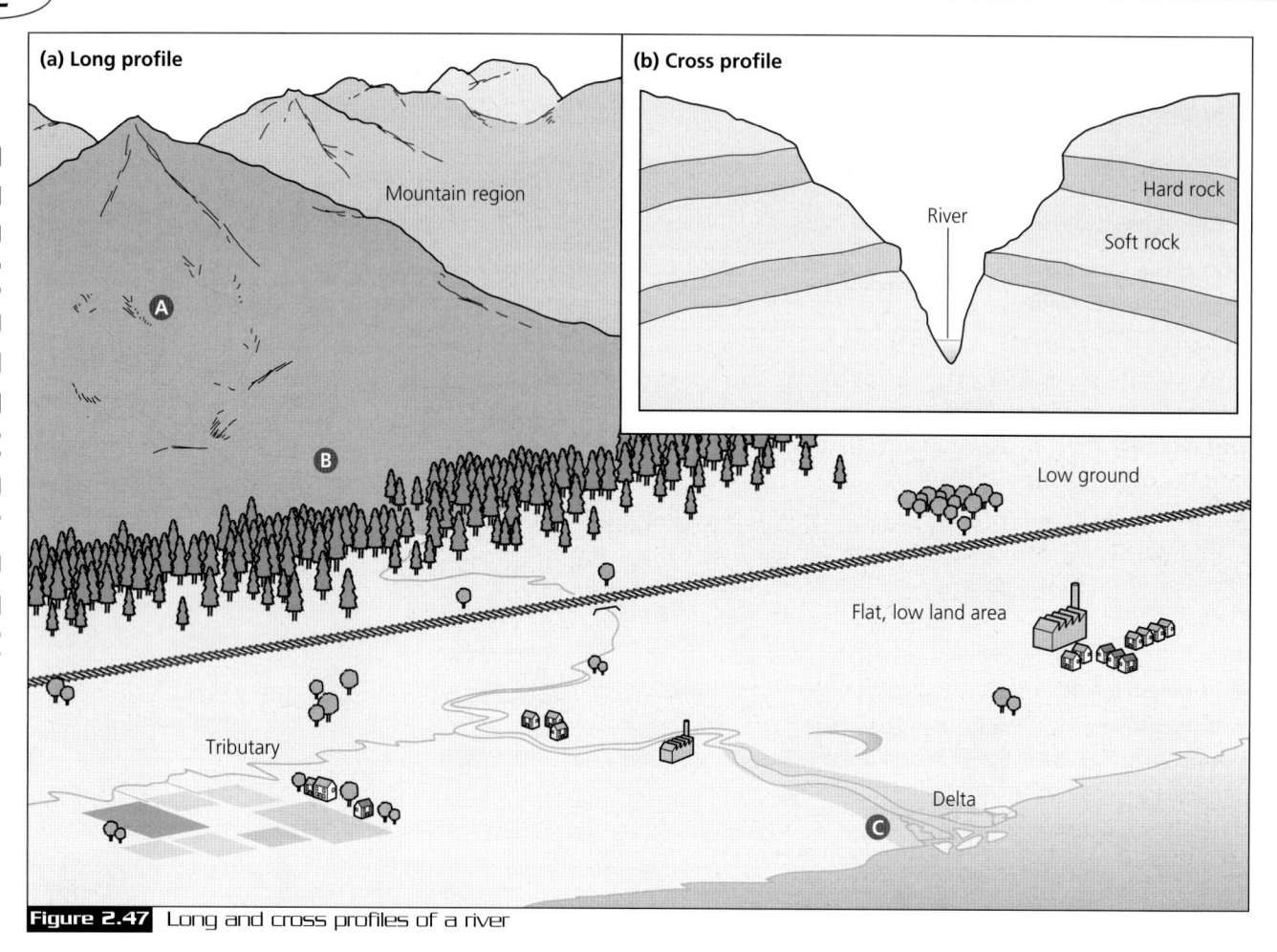

Study the Ordnance Survey extract, **Figure 2.46**, and answer the following questions.

40 Give the four-figure square reference for Port Meadow.
41 Give the six-figure grid reference for the King's Weir.
42 Study the two aerial photos. **Figure 2.48** was taken from 482099. What direction was the camera pointing? What is the river on the left of the photo?
43 **Figure 2.49** was taken from 485091. What does it tell us about the effect of rivers and flooding on the growth of Oxford?
44 Draw a cross-section from the 146m spot height at 472074 (part of Marley Wood) to the 117m spot height at 546105 (near Elsfield). Make a copy of **Figure 2.50**, the grid provided for you. On your cross section mark the following: Marley Wood, the A34, the River Thames, Port Meadow, the built up area (Summertown), the River Cherwell, the A40 and Elsfield.
45 What map evidence is there to suggest that flooding is a problem in Oxford?
46 How have planners reduced the risk of flooding on the A34?
47 Using map evidence show how the the rivers around Oxford have been controlled.

Figure 2.48 Oxford rivers

Figure 2.49 Oxford rivers

Figure 2.50 Grid for cross section

m
200
150
100
50

m
200
150
100
50

472074

546105

Coastal processes

IMPORTANT DEFINITIONS

Wavelength is the distance between two successive crests or troughs.
Wave frequency is the number of waves per minute.
Wave height is the distance between the trough and the crest.
The **fetch** is the amount of open water over which a wave has passed.
Velocity is the speed a wave travels at, and is influenced by wind, fetch and depth of water.
Swash is the movement of water up the beach.
Backwash is the movement of water down the beach.

DESTRUCTIVE WAVES

- Erosional waves.
- Short wavelength, high height **(Figure 2.51)**.
- High frequency (10–12/minute).
- The backwash is stronger than the swash.

CONSTRUCTIVE WAVES

- Depositional waves.
- Long wavelength, low height **(Figure 2.52)**.
- Low frequency (6–8/minute).
- The swash is stronger than the backwash.

FETCH

The fetch is the distance of open water that a wave travels across **(Figure 2.53)**. As fetch increases the potential for erosion also increases.

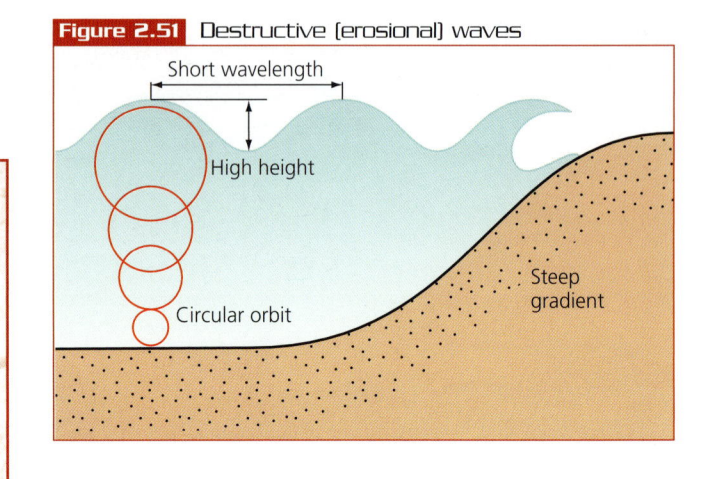

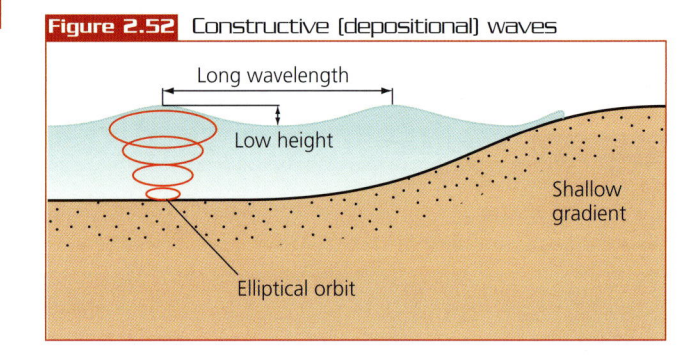

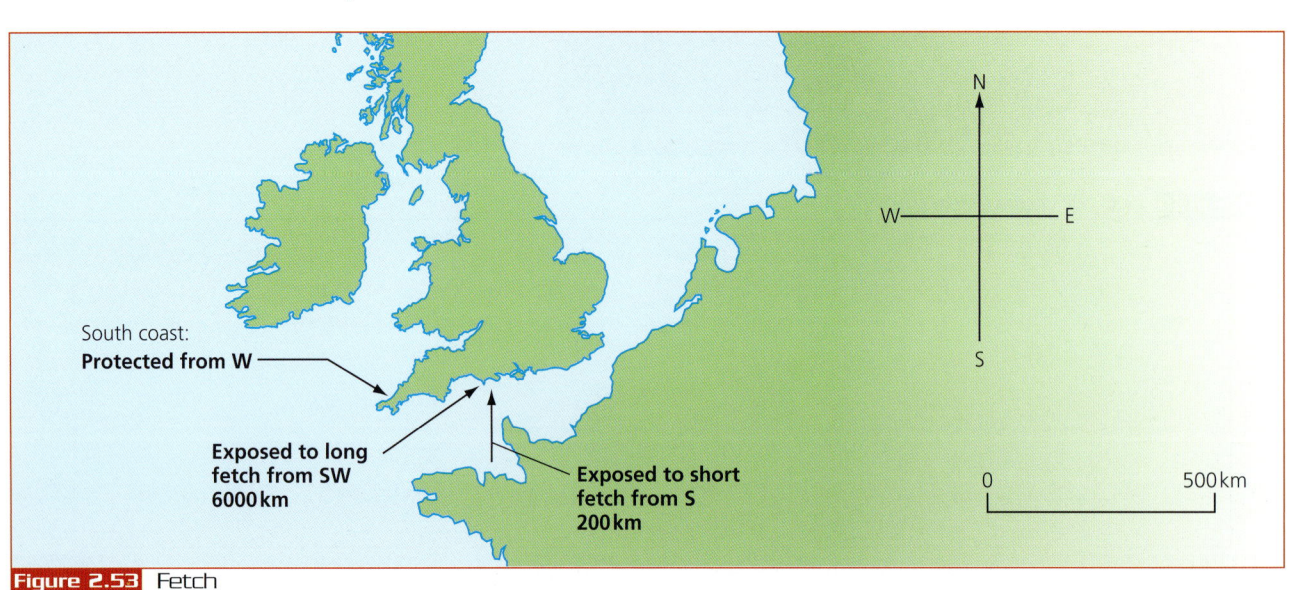

Figure 2.51 Destructive (erosional) waves

Figure 2.52 Constructive (depositional) waves

Figure 2.53 Fetch

South coast: Protected from W
Exposed to long fetch from SW 6000 km
Exposed to short fetch from S 200 km

Figure 2.54 Wave refraction

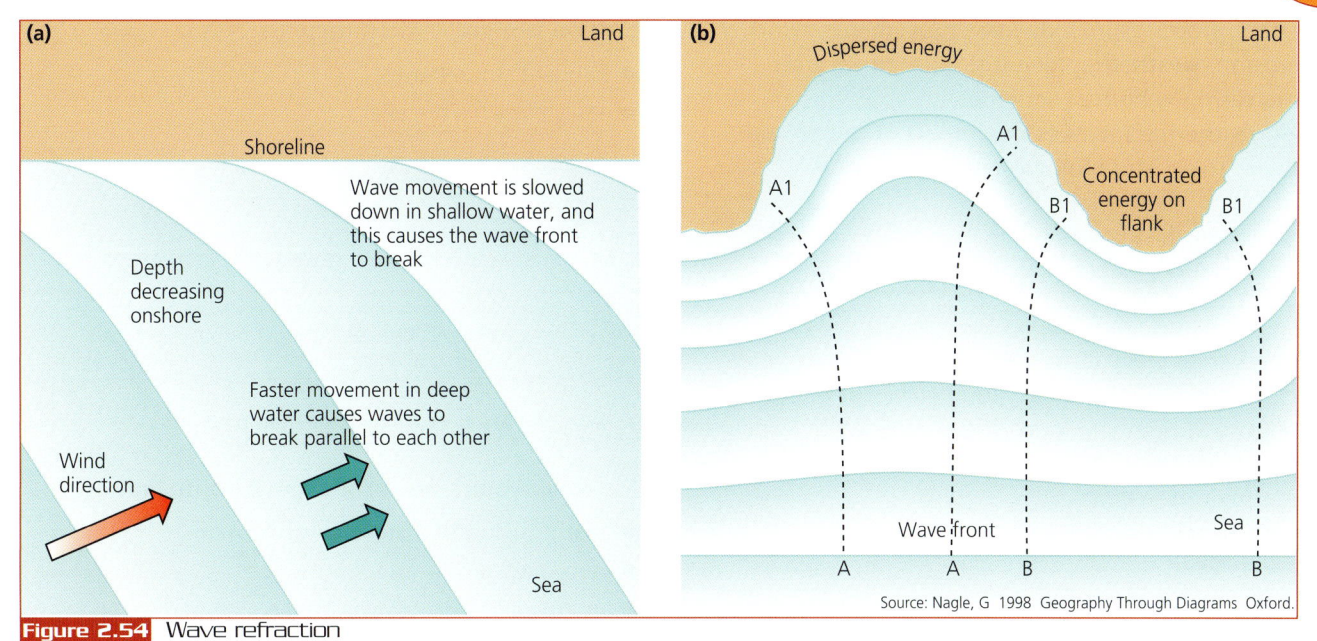

WAVE REFRACTION AND LONG SHORE DRIFT

Wave refraction occurs when waves approach an irregular coastline or when they come at an angle to the shore. As they come in contact with the seabed they are slowed down. Waves in deep water travel faster than those in shallow water. Hence, the wave front begins to change shape. If refraction is complete, the waves break parallel to the shore **(Figure 2.54)**. Wave refraction concentrates energy on the flanks of headlands and weakens energy in bays. However, refraction is rarely complete, therefore long shore drift occurs.

LONG SHORE DRIFT

Long Shore Drift (LSD) is the gradual movement of sediment along the beach **(Figure 2.55)**. On the south coast of Britain LSD occurs from west to east. Drift occurs because the swash travels up the beach in the direction of the prevailing (most common) wind. By contrast, the backwash comes down the beach along the shortest route, that is the steepest slope. The results of LSD include spits, bars, tombolos and the build up of sand and pebbles against groynes.

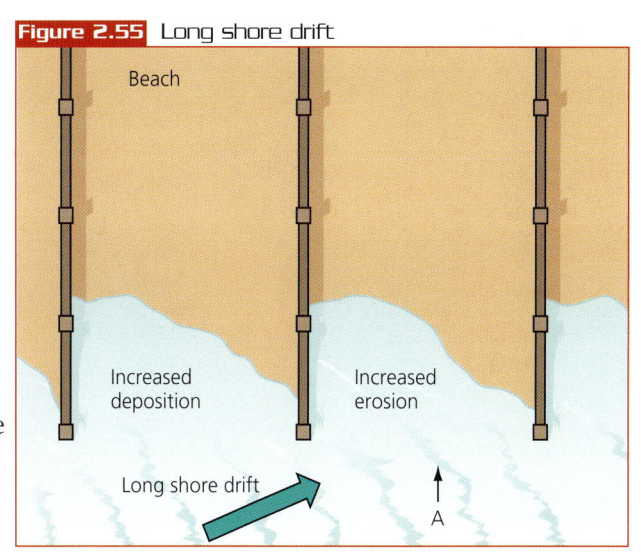

Figure 2.55 Long shore drift

Coastal erosion

MAIN PROCESSES

Abrasion The wearing away of the shoreline by material carried by the waves.
Hydraulic impact The force of water and air on rocks (up to 30 000 kg/m2 in severe storms).
Solution The wearing away of chalk and limestones by an acidic water. Organic acids aid the process.
Attrition The wearing down of broken particles into rounder, smaller particles.

Other processes include mass movements, wind erosion, weathering, deposition by rivers and, increasingly, human activities.

Weathering includes the impact of salt crystals, freeze-thaw, and biological weathering.

THE DEVELOPMENT OF CLIFFS AND WAVE CUT PLATFORMS

Cliffs change over time as they are eroded and weathered. Steep cliffs are replaced by lower angle cliffs, and an increasingly long wave cut platform **(Figure 2.56)**. The 'new' cliff is affected by processes such as mass movement and weathering rather than marine processes.

Figure 2.56 Cliffs and wave cut platforms

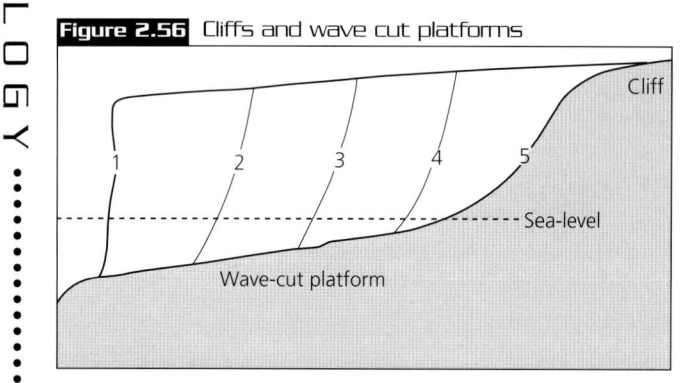

Figure 2.57 Rates of erosion

Location	Geology	Erosion (m /100 years)
Holdeness	Glacial Drift	120
Cromer, Norfolk	Glacial Drift	96
Folkestone	Clay	28
Isle of Thanet	Chalk	7 – 22
Seaford Head	Chalk	126
Beachy Head	Chalk	106
Barton, Hants.	Barton Beds	58

Erosion is highest when there is:
- frequent storm waves;
- easily erodable material.

Questions

48 Describe how a stack **(Figure 2.58)** is formed.

49 Suggest reasons why rates of erosion are given in metres per century rather than cm/year.

COASTAL DEPOSITION

Essential requirements for deposition include:
- a large supply of material;
- long shore drift;
- an irregular, indented coastline e.g. river mouths.

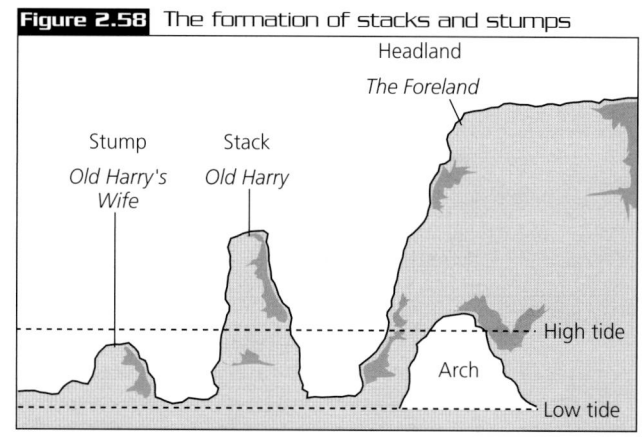

Figure 2.58 The formation of stacks and stumps

Sources of material include:
- material eroded from cliffs and headlands;
- off-shore supplies;
- river sediments;
- beach deposits **(Figure 2.59)**.

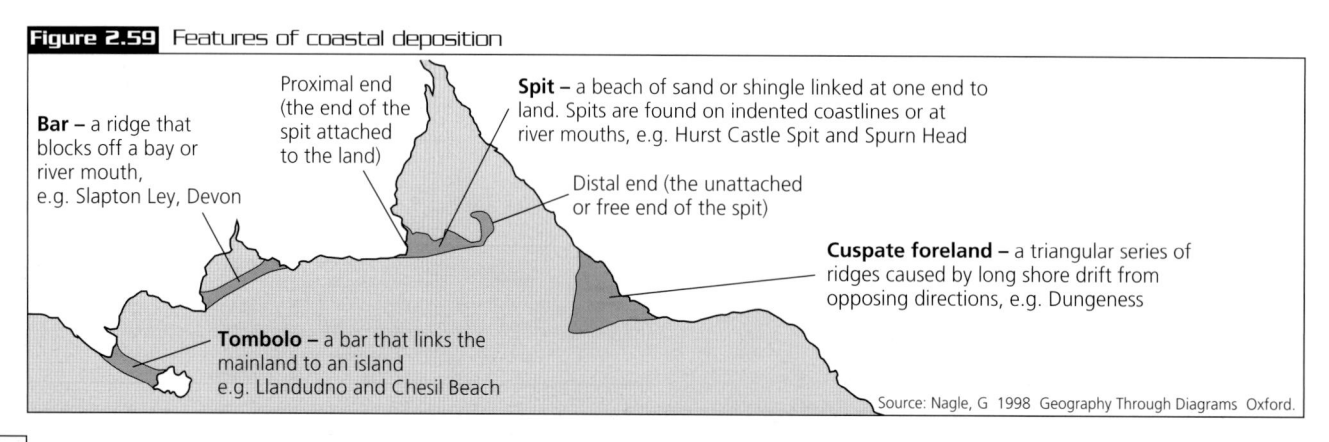

Figure 2.59 Features of coastal deposition

Bar – a ridge that blocks off a bay or river mouth, e.g. Slapton Ley, Devon

Proximal end (the end of the spit attached to the land)

Spit – a beach of sand or shingle linked at one end to land. Spits are found on indented coastlines or at river mouths, e.g. Hurst Castle Spit and Spurn Head

Distal end (the unattached or free end of the spit)

Tombolo – a bar that links the mainland to an island e.g. Llandudno and Chesil Beach

Cuspate foreland – a triangular series of ridges caused by long shore drift from opposing directions, e.g. Dungeness

Source: Nagle, G 1998 Geography Through Diagrams Oxford.

COASTAL MANAGEMENT

Coastal environments are very active landscapes. Because people live and work in coastal areas it is important that coastal areas are managed, so that lives and properties are protected from coastal processes. There are many problems related to coastal areas. Some are completely natural while some are man-made, or have become worse as a result of human interference. These problems include:

- coastal flooding;
- removal of beaches by long shore drift;
- cliff erosion;
- sand dune erosion;
- pollution of coastal waters.

POSSIBLE SOLUTIONS

The cost of protecting Britain's coastline was about £60 million in the early 1990s. Since then government cuts have reduced this. Part of the problem is that southern and eastern England are slowly sinking while sea level is rising. Thus the risk of flooding and the cost of protection are rising. **Managed retreat** allows nature to take its course: erosion in some areas, deposition in others. Benefits include less money spent and the creation of natural environments. However, in many places it is just not possible to allow the coast to be eroded. This is because there are too many people or too many businesses that would be affected. In these cases coastal protection schemes need to be used. Some of these are quite simple, such as groynes, whereas others are more elaborate.

There are many ways of trying to manage these problems. For example, **groynes (Figure 2.60)** can prevent long shore drift from removing a beach by interrupting the natural flow of sediment. However, by trapping sediment they deprive another area, down drift, of beach replenishment. Without its beach a coast is increasingly vulnerable to erosion. For example, the cliffs at Barton on Sea were easily eroded following the construction of groynes along the coast at Bournemouth.

A number of ways of stabilising dunes exist:

- planting marram grass;
- building walkways or 'duckboards' to reduce trampling;
- planting fences and brushwood to trap sand;
- land use zoning to keep areas from pressure.

More complex forms of hard engineering **(Figure 2.61)** are used when the problems of coastal environments are more intense.

KEY TERMS AND DEFINITIONS

Bar – a ridge that blocks off a bay or river mouth such as Slapton Ley, Devon.

Tombolo – a bar that links the mainland to an island such as Llandudno and Chesil Beach.

Spit – a beach of sand or shingle linked at one end to land. They are found on indented coastlines or at river mouths such as Hurst Castle Spit and Spurn Head.

Cuspate foreland – a triangular series of ridges caused by longshore drift from opposing directions such as at Dungeness.

Figure 2.60 Groynes

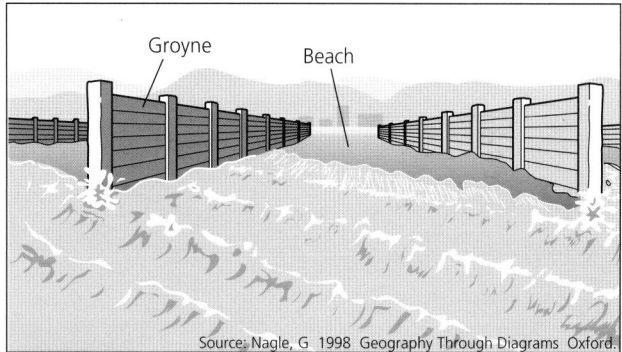

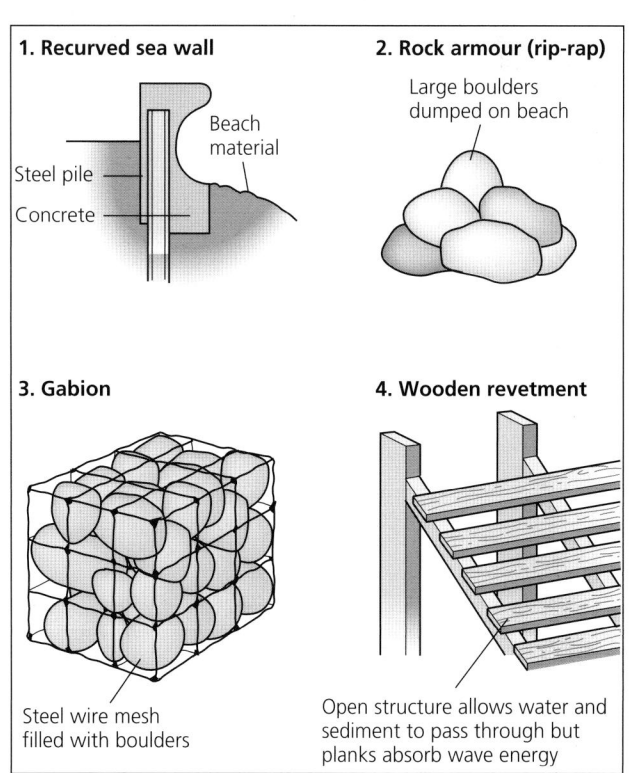

Figure 2.61 Hard engineering

1. Recurved sea wall — Steel pile, Concrete, Beach material
2. Rock armour (rip-rap) — Large boulders dumped on beach
3. Gabion — Steel wire mesh filled with boulders
4. Wooden revetment — Open structure allows water and sediment to pass through but planks absorb wave energy

CASE STUDY: MANAGING LULWORTH COVE – A TOURIST HONEYPOT

Lulworth Cove is a tourist *honeypot* **(Figure 2.62)**. It attracts more than 500 000 visitors each year. Over 200 000 walk the footpath from Lulworth Cove to Durdle Door. 25% of visitors come in August and 16% in July. Between 50% and 60% of visitors visit the Heritage Centre. The car park can hold 1200 cars and 20 coaches. The village has five hotels and a youth hostel. The camp site has 420 fixed caravans and spaces for 32 touring caravans and 150 tents. The village contains five souvenir shops, a number of cafes and food stalls, two public houses, and a restaurant.

Figure 2.62 Lulworth Cove

Lulworth Cove is a unique and very important landscape. Because of its rich landscape and the large number of visitors it attracts each year Lulworth Cove requires management and careful planning.

The large number of visitors does have a positive impact on the area. For example:

- a large number of local people are employed directly and indirectly through tourism;
- money generated by tourism is reinvested in the area.

Nevertheless, there are problems related to tourism. These include:

- the large car park which scars the landscape **(Figure 2.63)**;
- a large caravan site which also ruins the landscape;
- footpath erosion;
- litter and sewage.

To try and improve the tourist experience and reduce the impact of tourism a number of schemes have been carried out. They include:

Figure 2.63 The car park, Lulworth Cove

- footpath management **(Figure 2.64)**, such as rerouting of paths, reseeding of devegetated areas, improved signposting, reinforced footpaths (covered with gravel) around pressure points such as Stair Hole, steps, and improved access;
- education through information boards, leaflets, guided walks and tours, and displays.

In addition, the Lulworth Estate has opened a number of paths from the coast inland, and has also opened Lulworth Castle grounds in an attempt to reduce visitor pressure at Lulworth Cove.

Despite these achievements there are still many issues that need to be investigated and schemes implemented. These include:

- either screen the car park or resite it;
- improved screening of the caravan park;
- improve water quality;
- control unregulated parking;
- investigate the erosion of cliff tops;
- improve information boards.

Figure 2.64 Footpath management, Lulworth Cove

Weather and climate

3

World climatic regions

KEY TERMS AND DEFINITIONS

climate refers to the state of the atmosphere e.g. temperature, rainfall, winds, humidity, cloud cover, pressure etc., over a period of not less than thirty years. It refers not just to the averages of these variables but to the extremes as well.

weather refers to the state of the atmosphere at any particular moment in time. Generally, we look at the weather over a period of a few days. The same variables as for climate are considered.

microclimate refers to the distinct climate associated with small areas such as a city, a woodland, a coastal area or even a school.

WEATHER FACTS

- The wettest place on earth is Tutuneudo in Columbia which receives 11,770mm per year.
- In Cherrapungi in India over 1870mm of rain fell in one month in 1861.
- The warmest place on Earth is Aziz Iyah in Libya where shade temperatures have been recorded at 58°C (136°F).
- The coldest place inhabited is Oymyakon in Siberia which can reach −68°C (−90°F).
- Wind speeds in Antarctica can reach 320 km per hour.
- In 1921 in Colorado, USA, 1930mm of snow fell in one day.

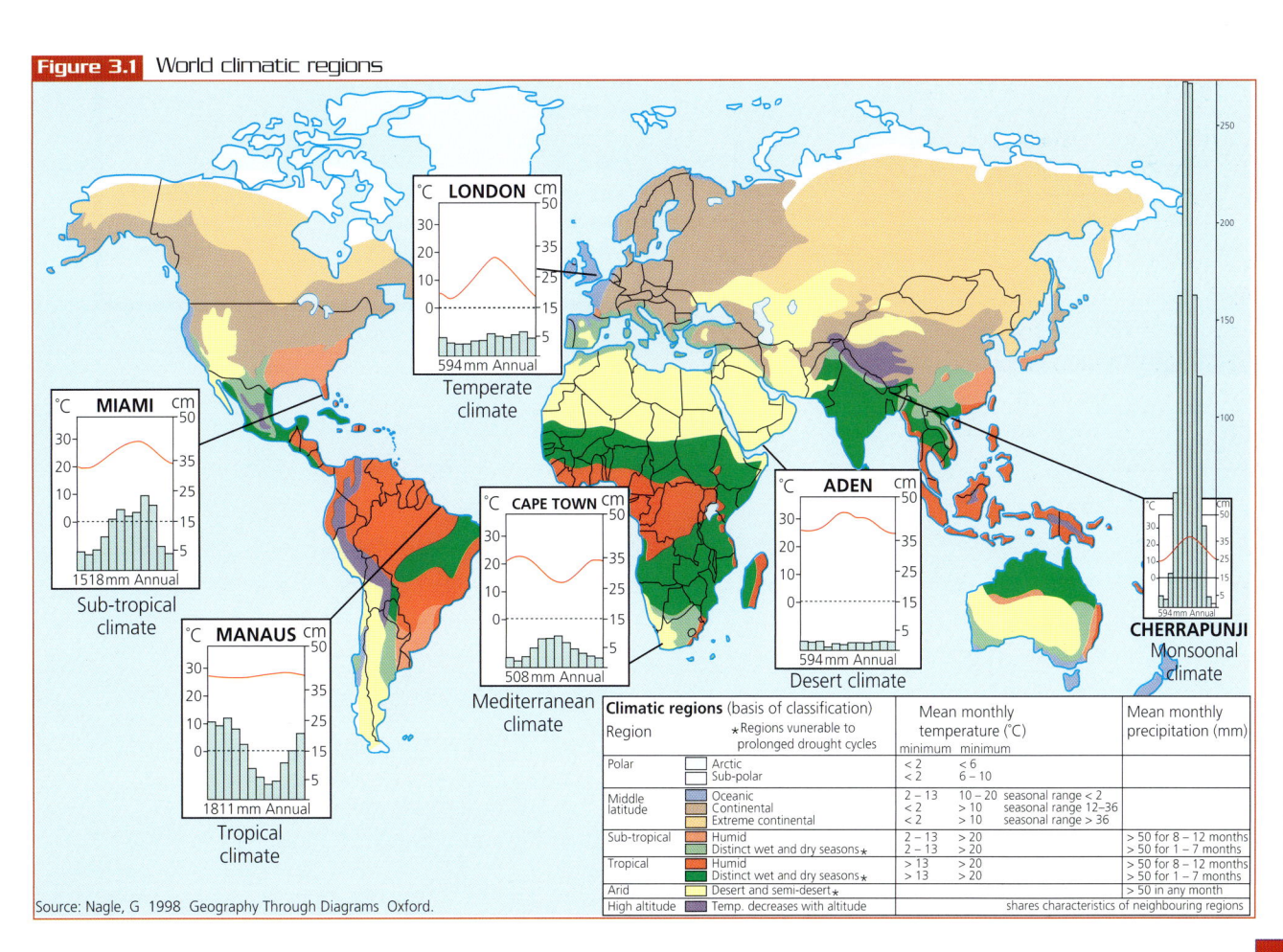

Figure 3.1 World climatic regions

Climatic regions (basis of classification)		Mean monthly temperature (°C)		Mean monthly precipitation (mm)
Region	*Regions vulnerable to prolonged drought cycles	minimum	minimum	
Polar	Arctic	< 2	< 6	
	Sub-polar	< 2	6 – 10	
Middle latitude	Oceanic	2 – 13	10 – 20 seasonal range < 2	
	Continental	< 2	> 10 seasonal range 12–36	
	Extreme continental	< 2	> 10 seasonal range > 36	
Sub-tropical	Humid	2 – 13	> 20	> 50 for 8 – 12 months
	Distinct wet and dry seasons*	2 – 13	> 20	> 50 for 1 – 7 months
Tropical	Humid	> 13	> 20	> 50 for 8 – 12 months
	Distinct wet and dry seasons*	> 13	> 20	> 50 for 1 – 7 months
Arid	Desert and semi-desert*			> 50 in any month
High altitude	Temp. decreases with altitude		shares characteristics of neighbouring regions	

Source: Nagle, G 1998 Geography Through Diagrams Oxford.

41

3

READING A CLIMATE GRAPH

A climate graph shows variations in rainfall and temperature over a year. When studying climate graphs it is important to look out for a number of key facts: total rainfall; seasonality – the season(s) in which most of the rain occurs; maximum temperature; minimum temperature; range of temperature (maximum minus minimum); length of time (if any) below freezing.

DESCRIBING A CLIMATE GRAPH

The climate graph for Shannon shows a maximum temperature in summer of 20°C and a minimum of 2°C in winter. The average temperature varies, and none of the seasons fall below freezing point so there is a year round growing season. Rainfall is high, 929mm, falling throughout the year but mostly in winter **(Figure 3.2)**.

Questions

1. Using **Figure 3.1** state what type of climate is found in the following places:
   the British Isles,
   Siberia,
   North East Brazil,
   Central Australia
   Cape Town.
2. Using an atlas identify the areas that have:
   a a Mediterranean climate,
   b a mountainous climate.

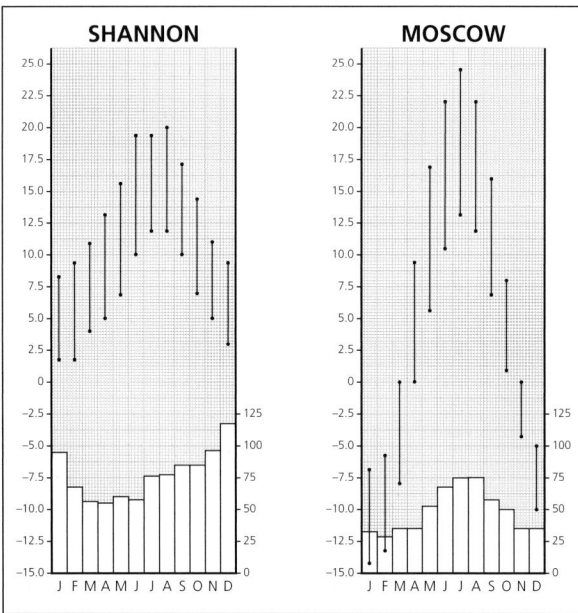

	Shannon	Moscow
Max temp	20°C	24°C
Min temp	2°C	−14°C
Range	18°C	38°C
No. of months below freezing	0	5
No. of months above 6°C	Max 12 Min 6	7 5
Rainfall amount distribution type	929mm Winter max All rain	577mm Summer Rain in summer Snow in winter

Figure 3.2 Climate graphs for Moscow and Shannon

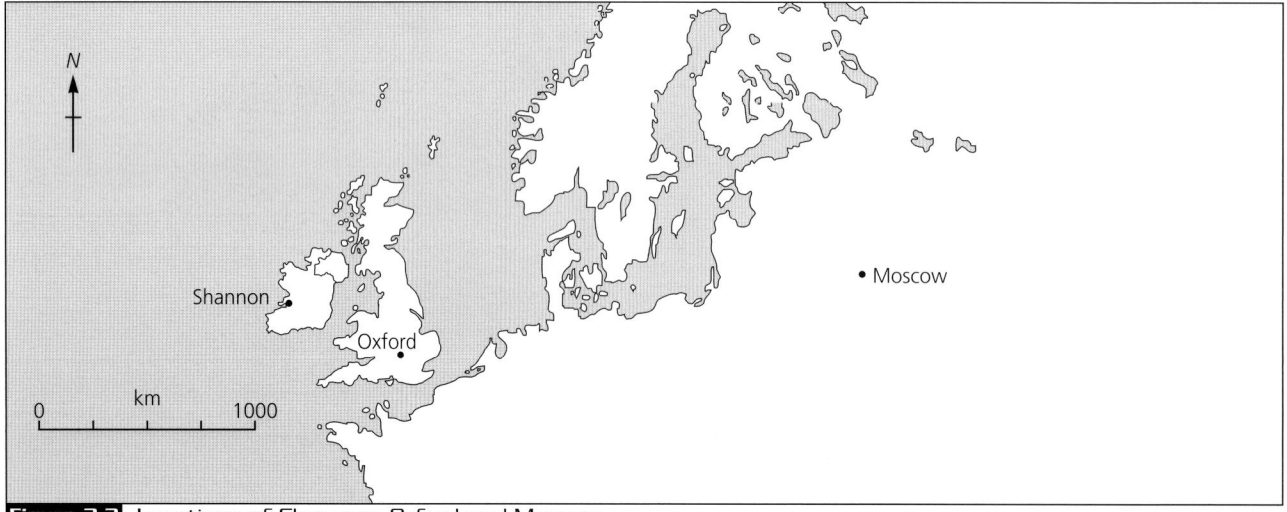

Figure 3.3 Locations of Shannon, Oxford and Moscow

	J	F	M	A	M	J	J	A	S	O	N	D	Yr
Mean temp (°C)	5.7	3.7	8.1	8.4	11.2	15.6	19	16.7	13.1	10.2	10.4	6.7	10.7
Max temp (°C)	8.5	6.7	11.7	12.5	15.4	20.5	24.8	21.1	16.5	14.1	12.7	9.6	14.5
Min temp (°C)	3.3	1.3	5.3	5	7.6	11	13.8	13	10.4	6.9	8.4	3.9	7.5
Rainfall (mm)	81.2	62.4	41.9	52	84.5	13.5	54.2	52.5	62.6	67.4	55.7	74.6	702.5

Figure 3.4 Climate data for Oxford

Questions

3 Use Figure 3.5 to plot the figures for the climate in Oxford in 1995. Describe the patterns you have drawn using the descriptions of Moscow and Shannon as a guide.

FACTORS AFFECTING TEMPERATURE

- Latitude: areas closer to the Equator receive more heat than areas closer to the Poles because:
  1. incoming solar radiation (*insolation*) is concentrated near the equator, but dispersed over a wide area near the Poles
  2. insolation near the Poles passes through a greater amount of atmosphere so more of it is reflected back out to space **(Figure 3.5)**.
- Altitude: temperatures decrease with altitude. On average it drops about 10°C over 1000m. This is because air at higher altitudes is thinner and less dense.
- Distance from the sea: it takes more energy to heat up water than land. This is known as the **specific heat capacity**. However, it takes longer for water to lose heat by night. Thus, the land is warmer than the sea by day, but colder by night. Places close to the sea are cool by day, but mild by night. With increasing distance from the sea this effect is reduced **(Figure 3.8)**.
- Prevailing winds: these are the most frequent winds in an area. Their impact depends upon where they come from. The south west winds that affect the British Isles bring warm air from the Atlantic whereas north east winds from the Arctic bring bitterly cold conditions **(Figure 3.6)**.
- Aspect: this is the direction a place faces. Aspect is very important, especially on a local scale. In the British Isles south facing places are warmer than north and east facing places **(Figure 3.7)**.

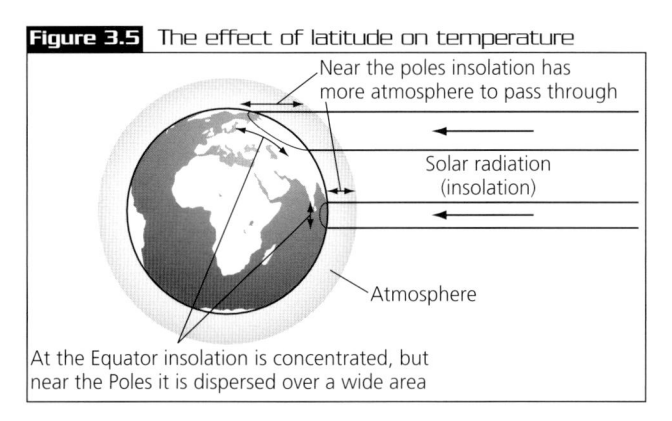

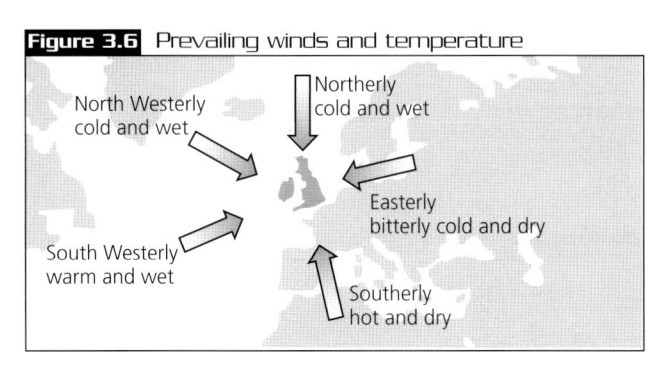

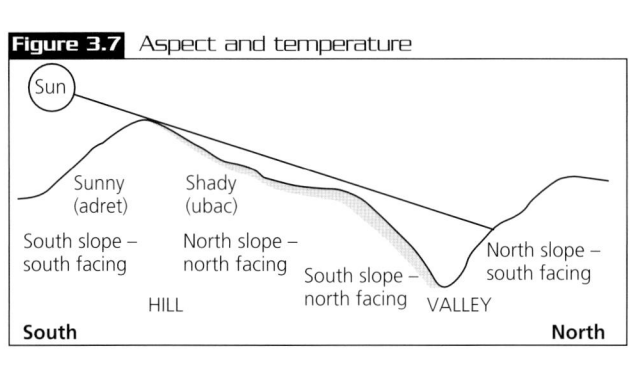

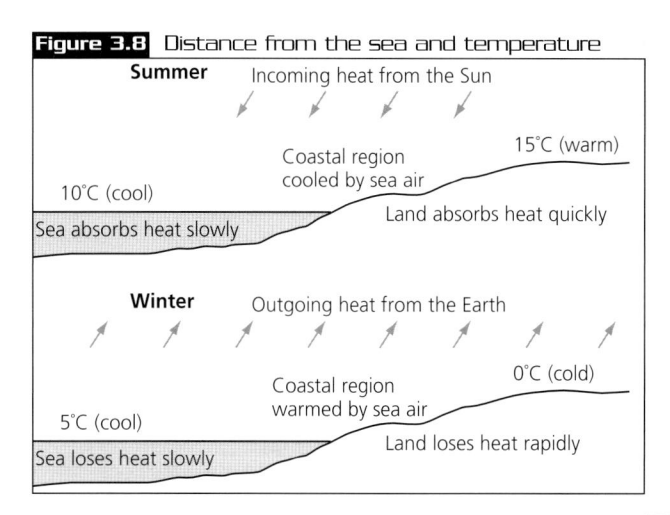

Figure 3.5 The effect of latitude on temperature

Figure 3.6 Prevailing winds and temperature

Figure 3.7 Aspect and temperature

Figure 3.8 Distance from the sea and temperature

TYPES OF RAINFALL

Precipitation refers to the ways in which moisture in the atmosphere is returned to the earth. The most common types of precipitation are rain and snow but there is also rime (frozen fog), dew and fog.

CONVECTIONAL RAIN

When the land is very hot it heats the air above it. This air then rises. As it rises, it cools and condensation occurs forming clouds and then rain **(Figure 3.9)**. It is common in equatorial areas. In Britain it is most common in the summer, especially in the South East, the hottest part of the British Isles.

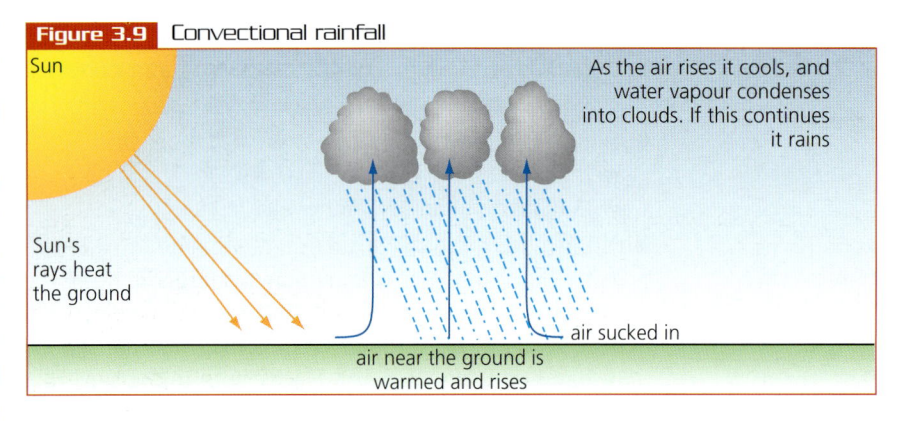

Figure 3.9 Convectional rainfall

Questions

4. Define the following terms: specific heat capacity, aspect, insolation.
5. State two reasons why the British Isles is warmer than Finland.
6. Briefly explain why Moscow has a more extreme temperature range than Shannon. although they are both on approximately the same line of latitude – Shannon 52°N, Moscow 55°N.

FRONTAL OR CYCLONIC RAIN

When warm air meets cold air, the warm air is forced to rise over the cold, denser air. This is known as a front. As the warm air continues to rise it cools, condenses and forms rain **(Figure 3.10)**.

RELIEF OR OROGRAPHIC RAIN

In some places air may be forced to rise over a mountain. As the air rises it cools, condenses and forms rain **(Figure 3.11)**. On the windward (up wind) side of the mountain, rainfall is high, but on the leeward side (down wind) rainfall is lower.

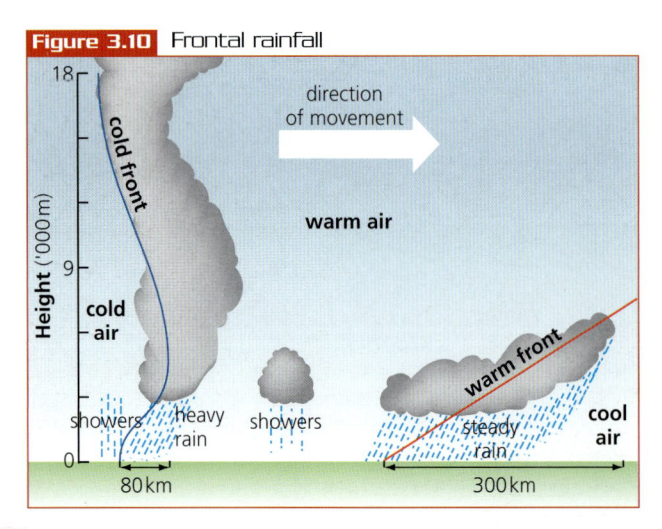

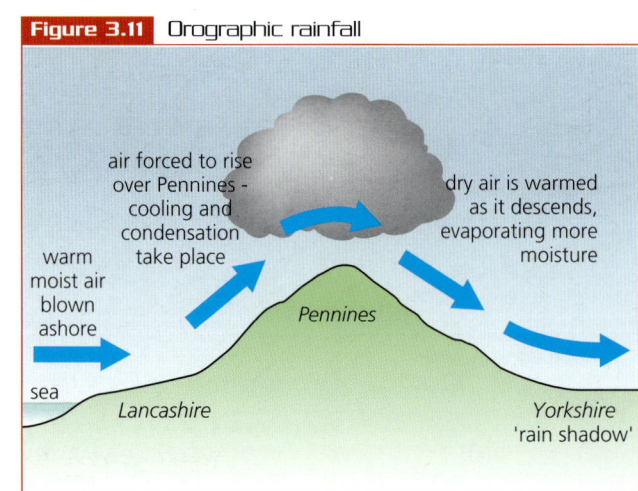

Figure 3.10 Frontal rainfall

Figure 3.11 Orographic rainfall

RAINFALL IN BRITAIN

Rainfall in Britain is very variable in terms of the amount, type and seasonal nature The heaviest rainfall (over 2000 mm) is over mountainous areas such as Wales and the Scottish Highlands. In general, rainfall is heavier in the west than the east. This is due to the movement of fronts from west to east, dumping more of their rain in the highground of the west. The South East and East Anglia have some convectional rainfall mostly in Summer.

WEATHER MAPS

A weather map is a map which provides a snapshot of the weather conditions over an area for a particular time. It tells us about temperature, precipitation, wind speed, wind direction, cloud cover, air pressure and the presence of any weather fronts. These elements are shown for selected weather stations on **Figure 3.12**. An isobar is a line of equal air pressure. *The closer the isobars are to each other, the greater wind speed; the further the isobars are away from each other the less the wind speed.*

THE FORMATION OF A DEPRESSION

Air masses are very large bodies of air that can often cover thousands of kilometres squared. Air masses vary in temperature and moisture content. When cold and warm air masses meet, the warm air mass rises above the cold one because it is less dense. As the warm air rises a centre of low pressure is formed. At the warm front cold air is replaced by warm air. At the cold front warm air is replaced by cold air.

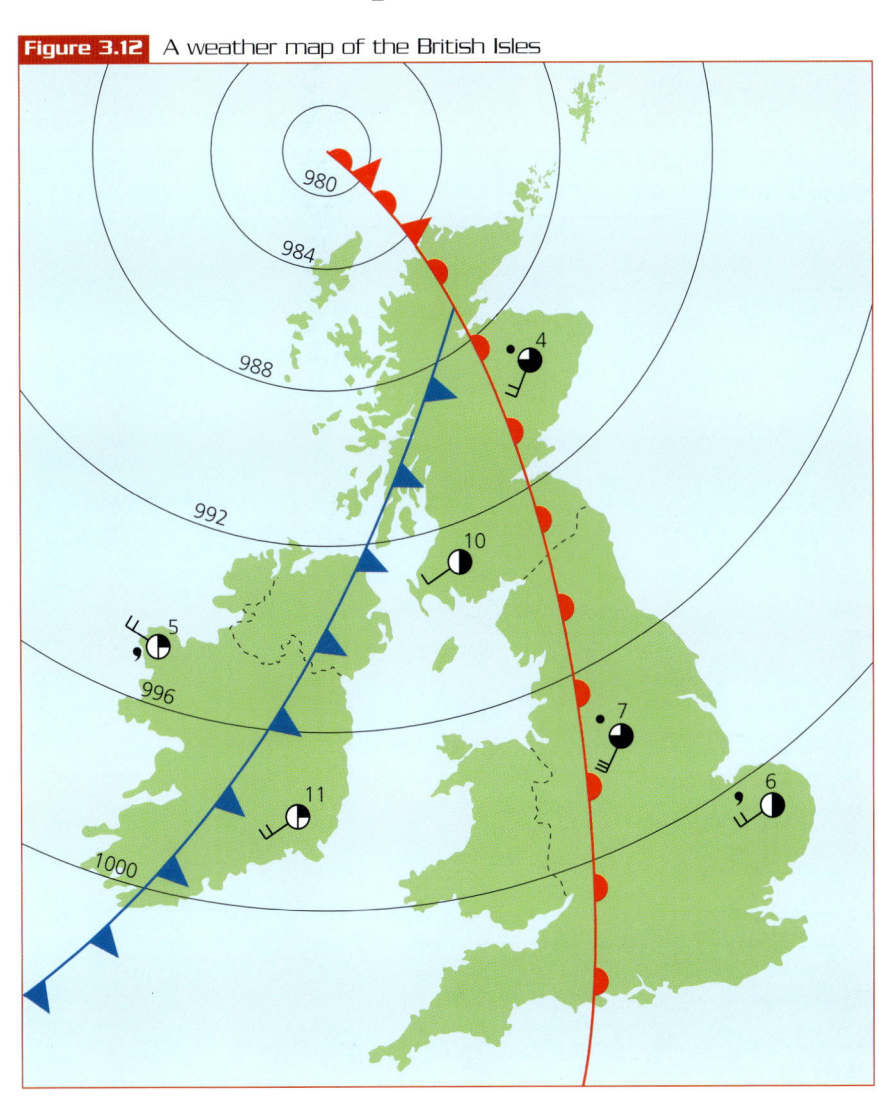

Figure 3.12 A weather map of the British Isles

Questions

7. Describe the weather at
   i north-east Scotland (ahead of the warm front)
   ii south-east Ireland (in the warm sector), and
   iii north-west Ireland (after the cold front)?
8. What is an isobar?
9. What is the wind speed and wind direction in East Anglia?
10. What type of precipitation occurs at
    i north-east Scotland, and
    ii north-west Ireland?
11. Define the terms: *cold front, warm front, air mass, low pressure*

WEATHER SATELLITES AND DEPRESSIONS

The satellite map and the weather chart show a low pressure system (depression) centred off Brittany. The satellite was taken at 0614 GMT on the 3rd February 1994 and the weather map shows the situation at noon on the same day.

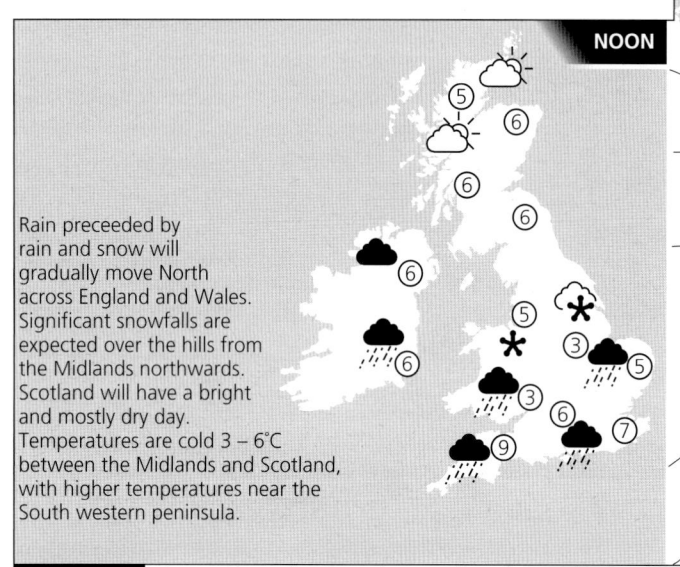

Rain preceeded by rain and snow will gradually move North across England and Wales. Significant snowfalls are expected over the hills from the Midlands northwards. Scotland will have a bright and mostly dry day. Temperatures are cold 3 – 6°C between the Midlands and Scotland, with higher temperatures near the South western peninsula.

Figure 3.13 A weather chart and map showing a depression

Figure 3.14 A satellite map showing the same depression

Figure 3.15 The impact of weather on human activities – tourists in Oxford

HIGH PRESSURE SYSTEMS

High pressure systems or **anticyclones** act very differently compared with low pressure systems or **depressions**. Whereas depressions produce wet, windy weather high pressure systems produce hot, sunny, dry calm days in summer and cold, sharp, crisp days in winter. Nights are cold in winter as the lack of cloud cover allows heat to escape. Frost and fog are common in winter and autumn. Winds in a high pressure system blow out from the centre of high pressure in a clockwise direction. By contrast, in a low pressure system winds blow into the centre of low pressure in an anti-clockwise direction. The winds are light hence the isobars on a high pressure weather chart are circular and spaced far apart.

Figures 3.16 and 3.17 (page 48) show a high pressure system. The weather forecast for the day stated: 'Wales and western England will have a glorious summer's day with unbroken sunshine. Central and eastern counties will start dull and cloudy, but by mid-morning the sun will break through to give a sunny afternoon. Eastern coastal areas will be cooler with a brisk wind off the North sea. Northern Ireland and western Scotland will have a dry and sunny day.

Questions

12 Describe how the low pressure system A shown on the weather map (figure 3.13) appears on the satellite map (figure 3.14).
13 Describe the pattern of isobars as shown on the weather map.
14 What is the isobar interval of the map?
15 What is the pressure of the system A in Mb?
16 Describe the differences in cloud cover between the far north of Scotland and the Midlands. Suggest reasons for these differences.
17 Why are the temperatures in Devon, Cornwall and Scotland higher than those in the Midlands?

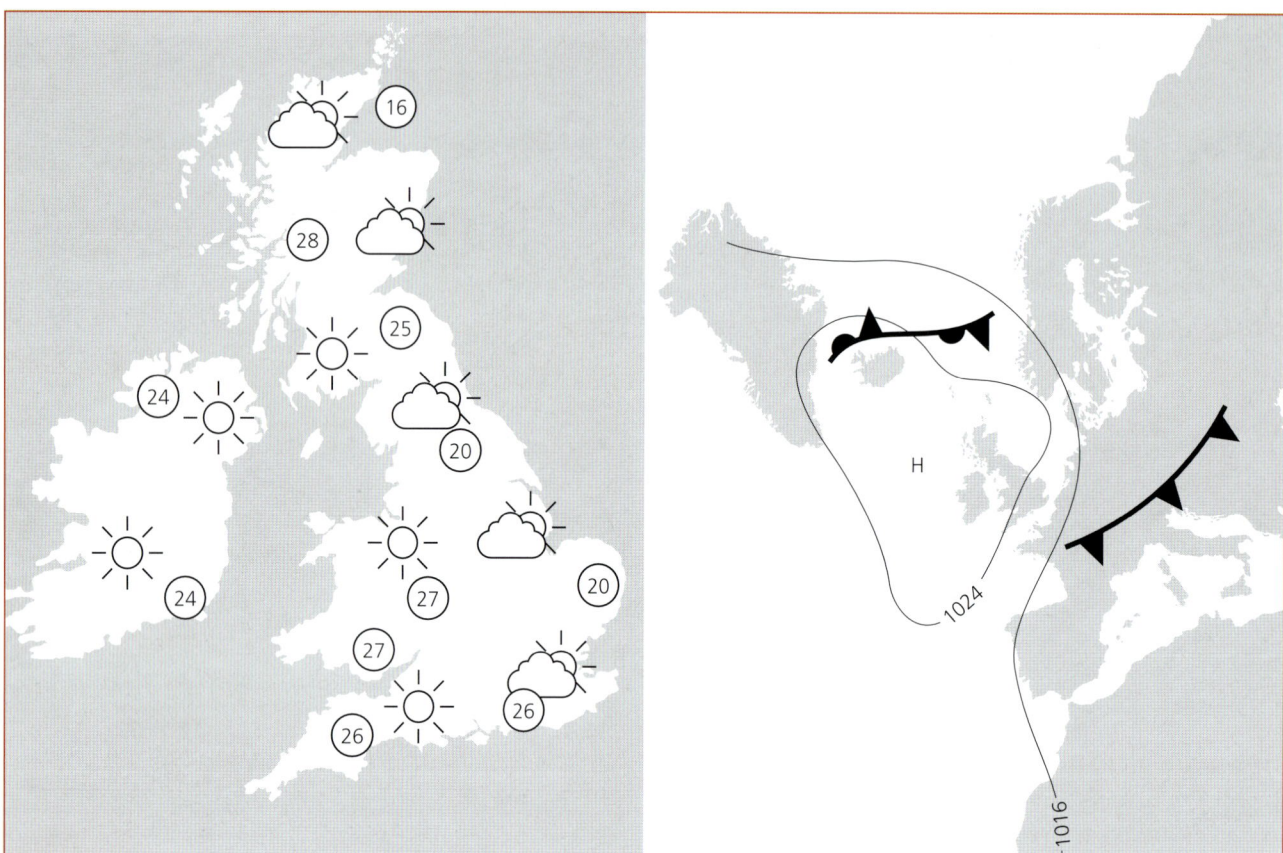

Figure 3.16 A high pressure chart and map

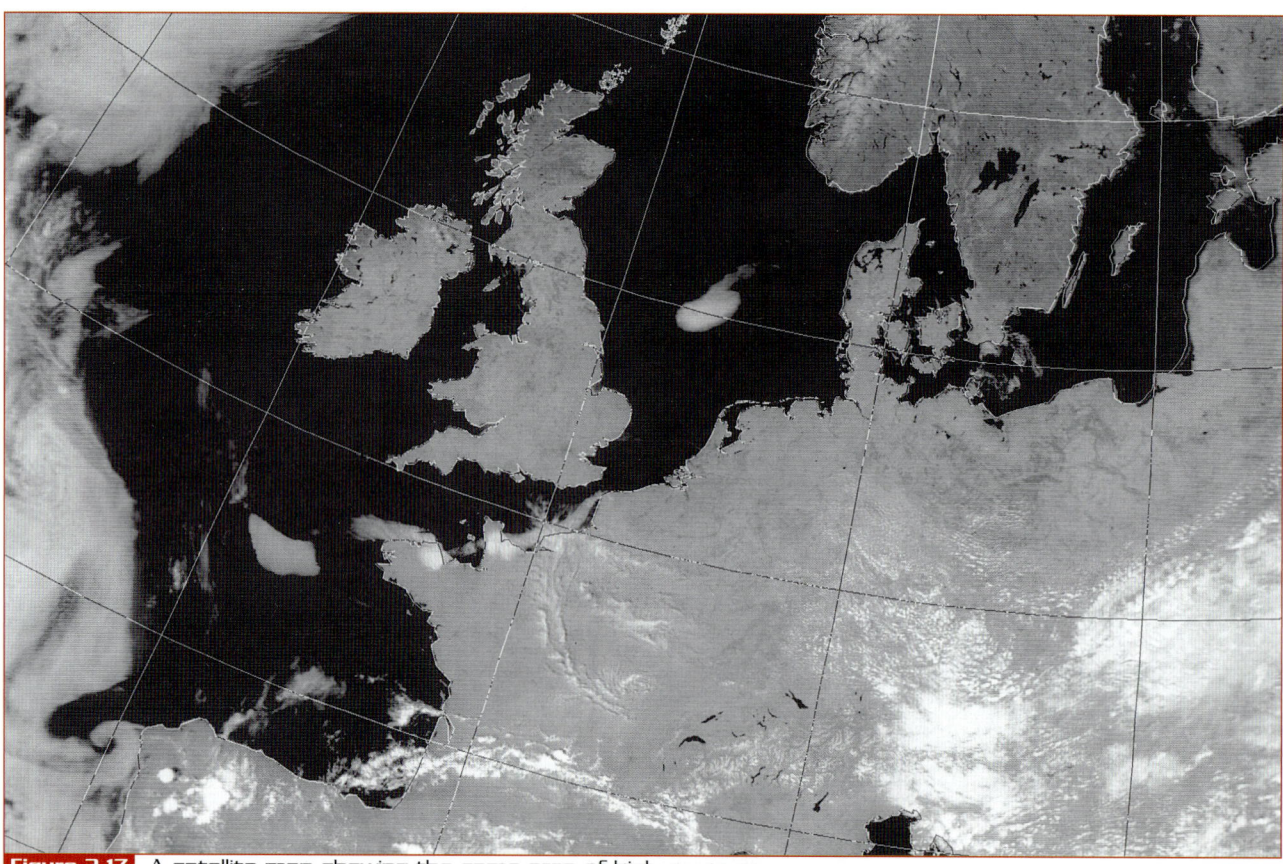

Figure 3.17 A satellite map showing the same area of high pressure

WEATHER AND CLIMATE

3

48

Questions

18 Study the weather chart and the satellite image which show high pressure systems based over the British Isles. Describe the weather conditions in south-west England.

19 a Which three places on **Figure 3.17** have the lowest temperatures?

b Suggest at least **two** reasons why temperatures there might be lower than elsewhere.

20 What does the pattern of isobars tell us about wind speed?

21 What time of year do you think this image was taken? Give **two** reasons for your answer.

Figure 3.18 The concentration of vehicles and buildings causes an urban heat island

URBAN MICROCLIMATES

Urban climates occur as a result of extra sources of heat released from industry, commercial and residential buildings. Concrete, glass, bricks and tarmac all act very differently from soil and vegetation. Some of these – notably dark bricks – absorb large quantities of heat and release them slowly by night. In addition, pollutants help trap radiation in urban areas. Consequently, urban microclimates can be very different from rural ones **(Figure 3.19)**.

Figure 3.19 The urban heat island

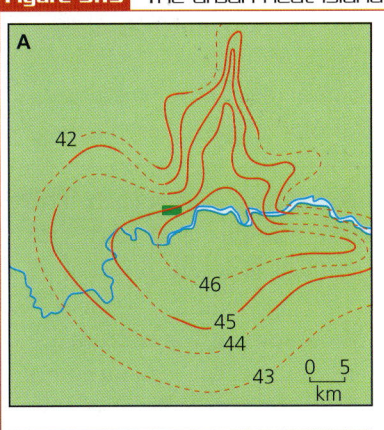

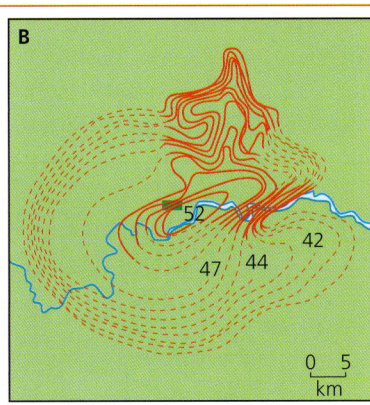

Urban heat-island effects in London, England (after Chandler 1965). The location of Hyde Park is indicated by the small shaded area nearly in the centre of the diagram. Broken lines indicate some uncertainty of position. Diagrams show temperature distributions in °F as follows:

A minimum temperature 30 April 1959
B minimum temperature 14 May 1959
C maximum temperature 3 June 1959
D minimum temperature 2 August 1959

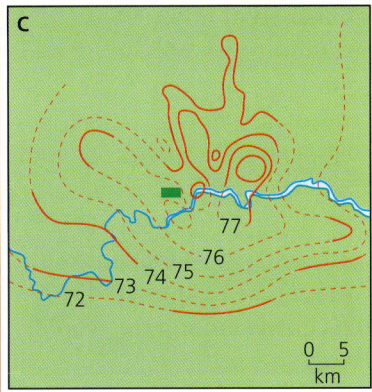

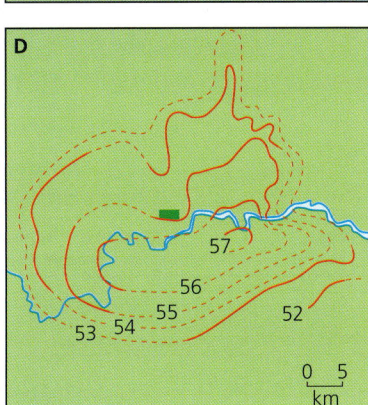

The contrast between urban and rural climates is greatest under calm high pressure conditions. The typical heat profile of an urban heat island shows the *maximum* at the city centre, a *plateau* across the suburbs and a *temperature cliff* between the suburban and rural area. Small scale variations within the urban heat island occur with the distribution of industries, open space, rivers, canals and so on.

The heat island is a feature which is shown by **isotherms** (lines of equal temperature). These show that the urban area is warmer than the surrounding rural area, especially by dawn during anticyclonic conditions.

The heat island effect is caused by a number of factors:
- heat produced by human activity such as industry and commerce;
- bricks retain heat by day and release it by night;
- the urban atmosphere (if cloudy) may prevent heat from escaping.

In urban areas there is a relative lack of moisture, due to:
- lack of vegetation;
- high drainage density (sewers and drains) which removes water.

Hence little energy is used for evapotranspiration, thus more is available to heat the atmosphere. This is in addition to the manmade sources of heating such as industries, cars, and people.

Questions

22 Why are microclimates, such as urban heat islands, best observed during high pressure (anticyclonic) weather conditions?

When air flow over an urban area is disrupted, winds are deflected over buildings. Large buildings can produce eddying (Figure 3.20).

INVESTIGATING MICROCLIMATE

It is quite straightforward to test for small-scale variations in climate around a house or a school. For example we could see if north facing areas are colder than south facing places (i.e. test the importance of **aspect**) or whether rainfall varies around a school due to differences in vegetation and obstructions (walls, buildings etc).

To test these ideas we must first make a map of the area to be tested. Different areas may be used to test different ideas. For example an exposed flat roof (often the top of a science block or sports pavilion) can be used to check rainfall variability in a small area. Place at least a dozen rain gauges in contrasting locations – next to a wall, an exposed site, close to a grill, on the east and west sides (or north and south) of an obstruction. Record the rainfall totals in each gauge clearly.

Using the school grounds place rain gauges in areas of different vegetation – close to rose bushes, deciduous vegetation, coniferous vegetation, grass and shrubs. You will need at least five in each. This experiment shows whether the type and density of vegetation effects the amount of interception of rainfall.

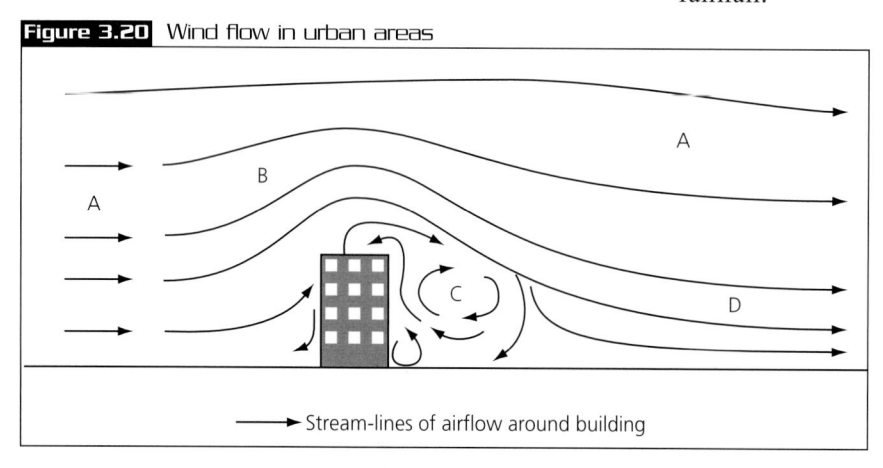

Maximum and minimum thermometers can be placed on north and south facing walls and also in areas of different vegetation types. Maximum and minimum temperatures are recorded each day.

Temperature varies throughout the day with vegetation and aspect. Temperatures should be recorded hourly so that an accurate picture can be built up of the microclimate around the school.

Figure 3.20 Wind flow in urban areas

→ Stream-lines of airflow around building

Questions

23 Study the data presented in **Figure 3.21**. Describe the variations in the amount of rainfall found under the apple tree, the magnolia bush and in the open. Suggest reasons for the differences you have noted. How might the results differ if the survey had been carried out in winter. Again, suggest reasons for your answer.

24 Look at **Figure 3.22**. Describe how the temperature of the west facing wall and the east facing wall have varied over the day. How might the results have differed if the day had been cloudy?

Figure 3.21 Rainfall under different types of vegetation

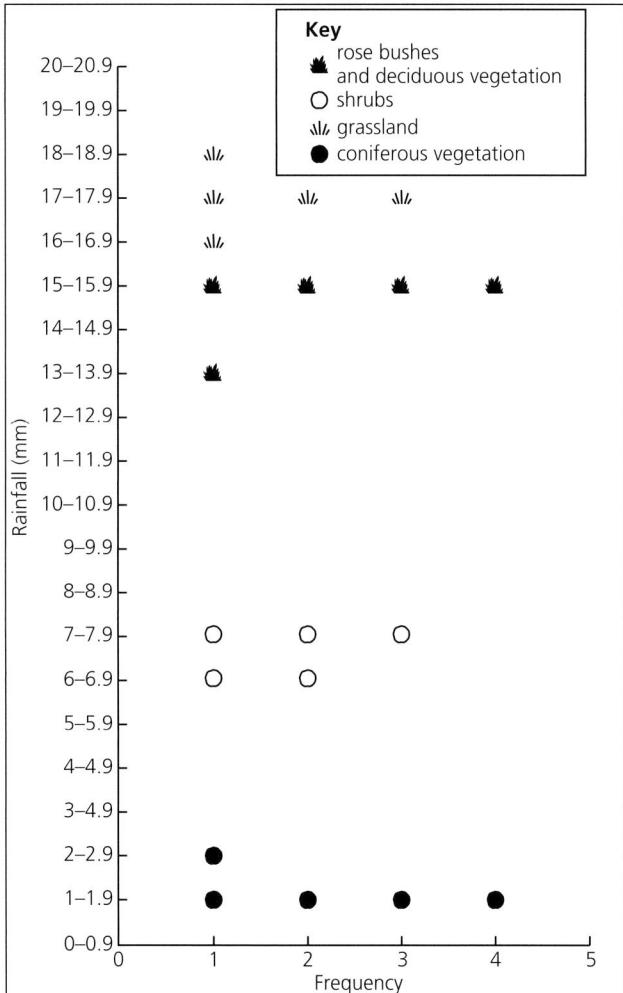

Key:
- rose bushes and deciduous vegetation
- shrubs
- grassland
- coniferous vegetation

Figure 3.22 Temperature variations on a west and east facing wall

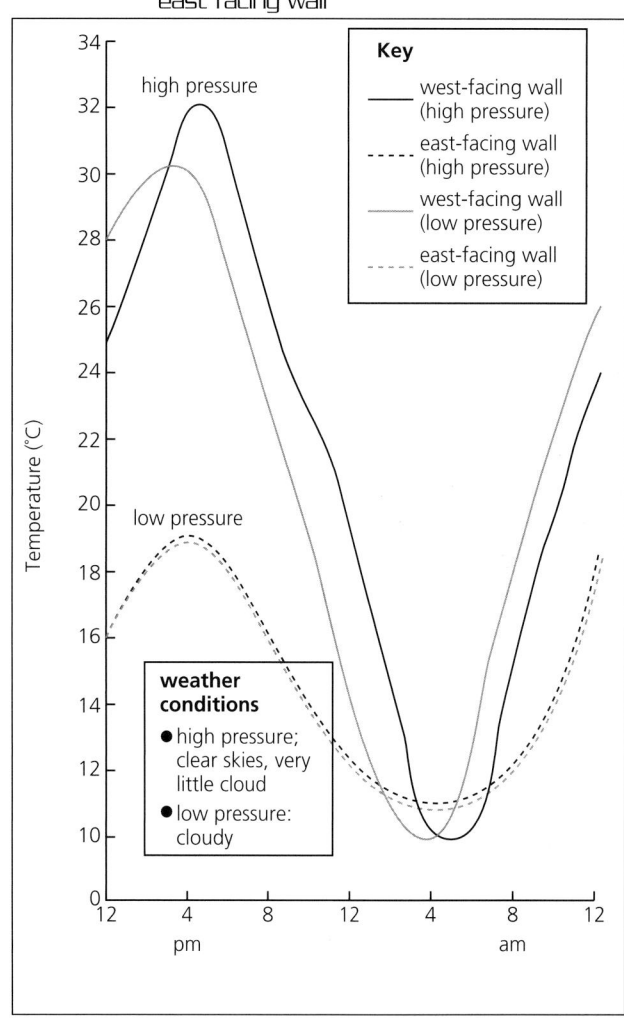

Key:
- west-facing wall (high pressure)
- east-facing wall (high pressure)
- west-facing wall (low pressure)
- east-facing wall (low pressure)

weather conditions
- high pressure; clear skies, very little cloud
- low pressure: cloudy

Ecosystems

4

An ecosystem is the interaction of plants and animals within their environment. The environment contains living and non-living features known as **biotic** and **abiotic** elements. At a world scale the links between the ecosystems and climate are very strong, however in reality most ecosystems have been heavily affected by human activities, especially farming, urbanisation and transport. For example, the world map of ecosystems suggests (Figure 4.1) that the UK contains large areas of temperate deciduous forests whereas in reality most of these have been cut down to make way for farmland. Even when forests have been created in Britain they are more likely to be coniferous evergreen forests than deciduous ones – this is because evergreen trees grow faster and provide an economic return faster than a deciduous forest.

Function of ecosystems

Ecosystems consist of two types of components – abiotic elements and biotic elements. Abiotic elements include the non-living parts such as air, water, heat, soils, nutrients, rock and sediments; whereas biotic elements are the living elements such as plants and animals (Figure 4.3).

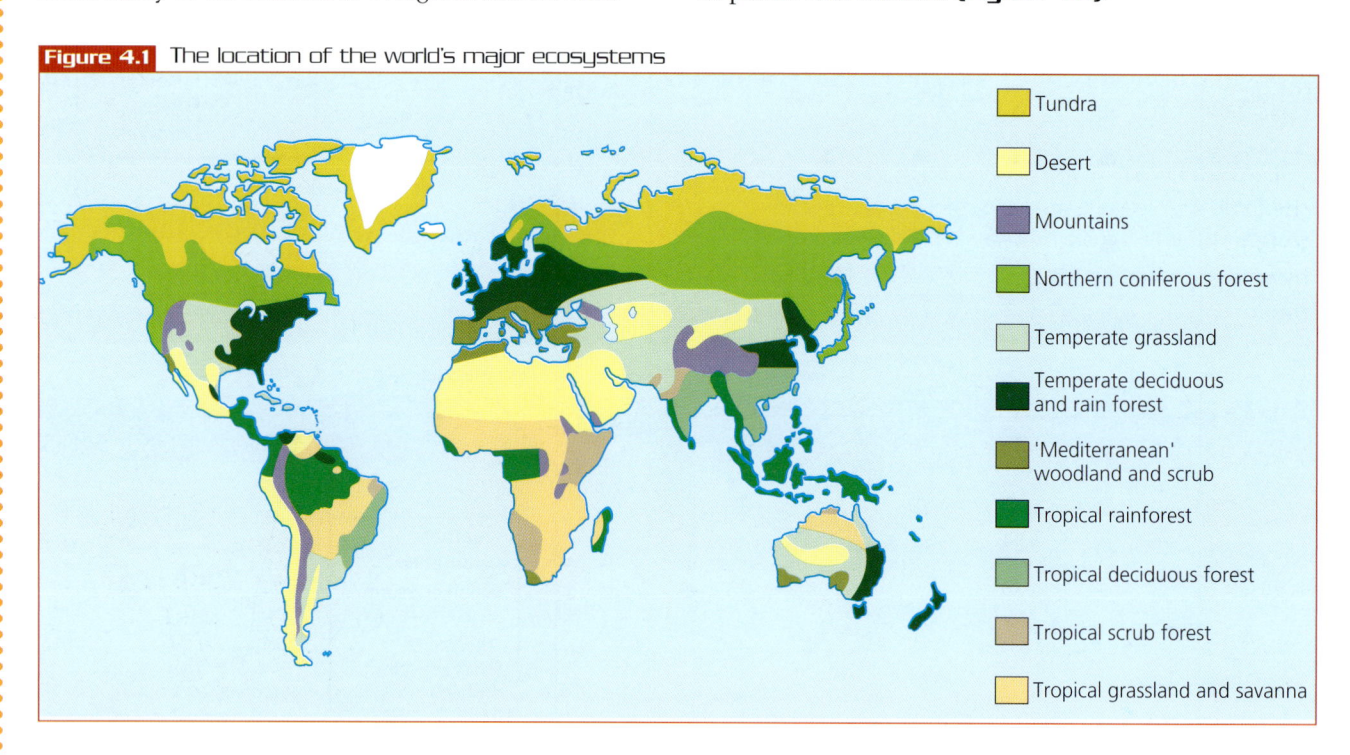

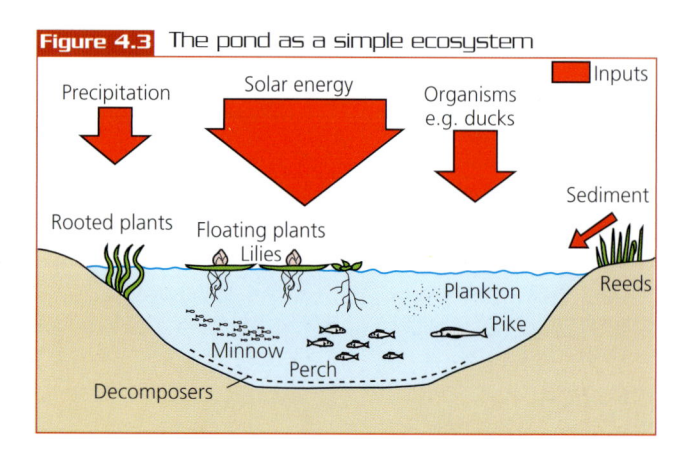

Figure 4.1 The location of the world's major ecosystems

- Tundra
- Desert
- Mountains
- Northern coniferous forest
- Temperate grassland
- Temperate deciduous and rain forest
- 'Mediterranean' woodland and scrub
- Tropical rainforest
- Tropical deciduous forest
- Tropical scrub forest
- Tropical grassland and savanna

Figure 4.2 Rhinos are important in Savannah ecosystems

Figure 4.3 The pond as a simple ecosystem

Inputs: Precipitation, Solar energy, Organisms e.g. ducks, Sediment

Rooted plants, Floating plants, Lilies, Plankton, Reeds, Minnow, Pike, Perch, Decomposers

52

Figure 4.4 A food web from Wytham Woods

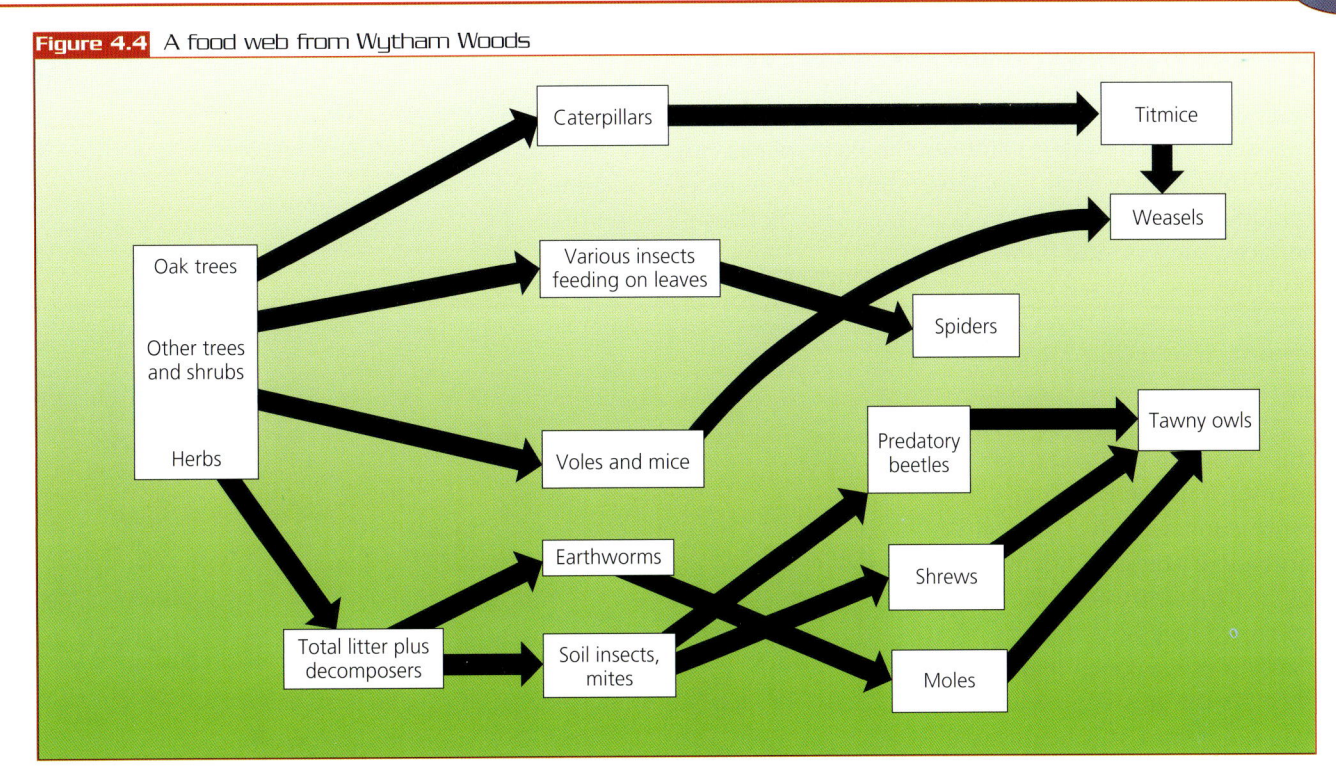

Ecosystems are ecological systems which are driven by solar energy and the available water and nutrients. Plants use solar energy and convert it to food energy by the process of photosynthesis. Animals get their energy by eating plants or other animals. This transfer of energy from solar to plant material to animals is known as the food chain. A simple food chain is shown in **Figure 4.4**. The amount of plant growth each year is known as **productivity**. Plant growth increases when conditions are light, warm, moist and nutrients are freely available – thus productivity varies across the globe as shown in **Figure 4.5**.

Figure 4.5 World annual plant growth

Ecosystem	Mean NPP (kg/m2/yr.)	Mean biomass (kg/m2)	NPP/biomass
Tropical Rain Forest	2.2	45	
Savanna	0.9	4	
Mediterranean woodland	0.5	6	
Desert	0.003	0.002	
Temperate Grassland	0.6	1.6	
Temperate deciduous forest	1.2	32.5	
Boreal coniferous forest	0.8	20	
Tundra and mountain	0.14	0.6	
Open ocean	0.12	0.003	
Continental shelf	0.36	0.001	
Estuaries	1.5	1	

NPP (net primary productivity) is a measure of annual plant growth
Biomass is a measure of total plant growth over many years (so in the case of trees, for example, it includes bark and branches as well as leaves)

Questions

1. Study Figure 4.5 which shows world variation in annual plant growth. Complete column 3 by dividing the value in column 1 by that in column 2. Which is the most productive ecosystem in terms of NPP/biomass?

2. Using an atlas or the diagrams on page 43 explain why plant productivity in the tropical rainforest is greater than in the tundra.

3. Briefly explain why plant growth in hot deserts is less than in tropical rainforests.

4 Managing sand dunes

Sand dunes are very popular environments with tourists. They are also very fragile environments and need to be managed carefully. As plants grow they change their local environment in a number of small but important ways. These changes are especially noticeable when their surfaces, such as sand dunes, building sites and salt marshes are involved. These changes in an ecosystem over time are known as *succession*.

At low tide sand is blow across the exposed beach and may become trapped against an obstruction such as a piece of driftwood. The sand builds up against the driftwood and is colonised by grasses such as marram or sea couch **(Figure 4.6)**. As the grasses grow they trap more sand, this helps grasses to grow and so a new dune begins to form. The older dunes further back from the sea, receive less sand and so the marram there stops growing. As the marram has added organic matter to the soil (its roots help to form humus) other plants such as heather and gorse are able to grow there instead of marram. Thus there is a change in plant cover with the distance from the sea because there is a change in the local environment **(Figure 4.7)**. In addition to the natural changes, beaches are heavily affected by human activities – at Studland Beach in Dorset, for example.

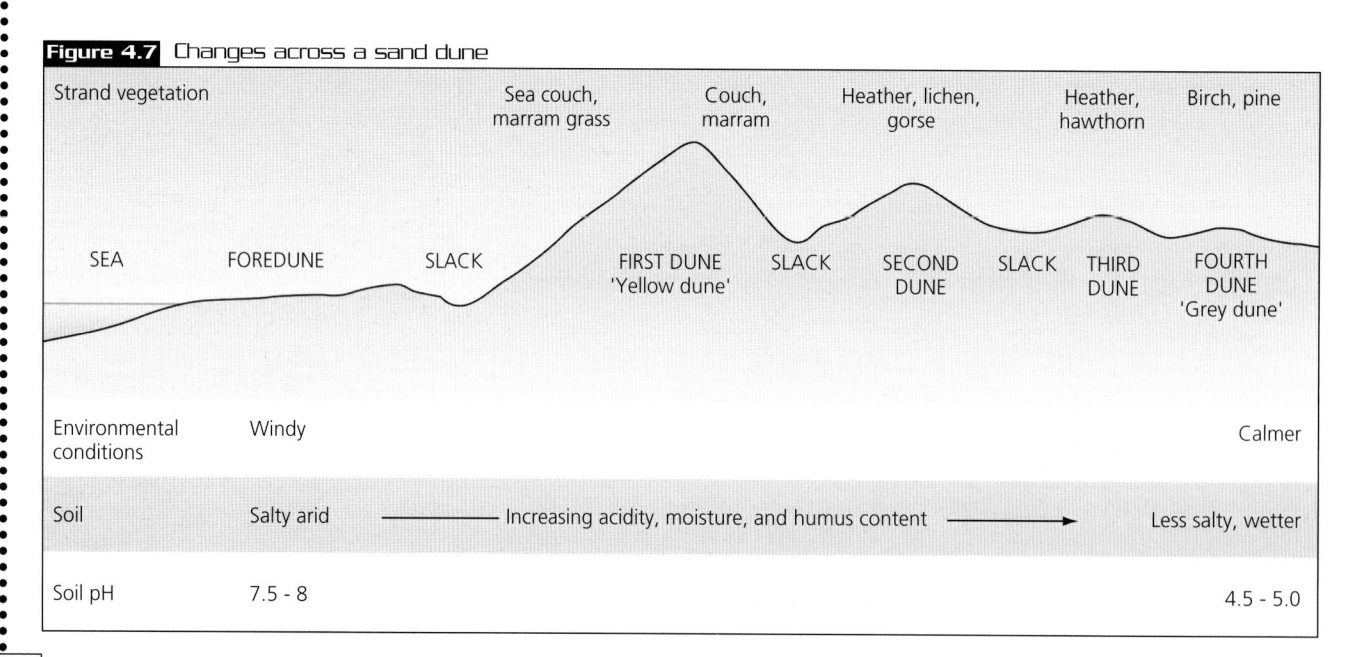

Figure 4.6 Sand dune formation

Figure 4.7 Changes across a sand dune

Strand vegetation			Sea couch, marram grass	Couch, marram	Heather, lichen, gorse		Heather, hawthorn	Birch, pine
SEA	FOREDUNE	SLACK	FIRST DUNE 'Yellow dune'	SLACK	SECOND DUNE	SLACK	THIRD DUNE	FOURTH DUNE 'Grey dune'
Environmental conditions	Windy							Calmer
Soil	Salty arid		———— Increasing acidity, moisture, and humus content ————▶					Less salty, wetter
Soil pH	7.5 - 8							4.5 - 5.0

Figure 4.8 Studland Beach

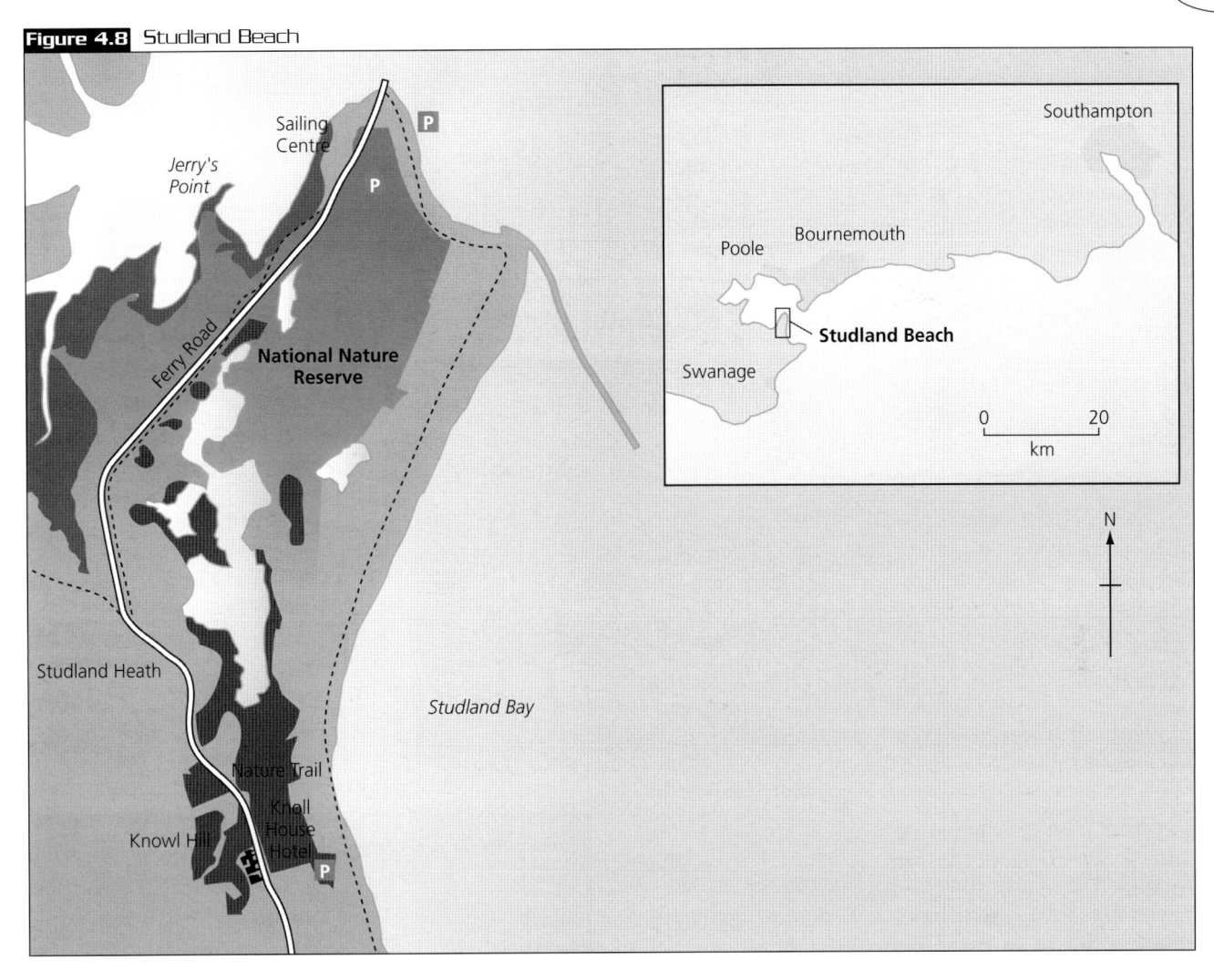

STUDLAND SAND DUNES AND BEACH

Studland Beach is a National Nature Reserve run by the National Trust (Figure 4.8). The number of visitors is controlled by price and car parking spaces available. There are many problems for the staff to deal with on the Beach. These include:

- **vehicle congestion** – during busy periods up to 1,000 cars parked on the Ferry Road;
- **visitor congestion** – especially in July and August, when 95% come just for the beach and only 5% venture into the Nature Reserve;
- **large volume of litter** – 12-13 tonnes a week;
- **lost children** – often up to 30 a day;
- **erosion** – of the sand dunes (Figure 4.9).

Figure 4.9 Sand dune erosion

Figure 4.10 Visitors to Studland Beach

Number of cars using the car parks
1992   138 430
1993   142 643
1994   158 949
1995   178 228
1996   150 880

The spread of visitors
Up to June   33%   49 668
July and August   58%   87 699
September   9%   13 513

Visitor numbers Over **1 000 000** per year.

Parking spaces About 3500 in National Trust parks 1000 on the roadside of Ferry road. 300 on the verges around the village.

Total number of cars per year in National Trust parks **135 000–210 000**
Foot passengers during the High Season on the Ferry **8000**.
Estimated numbers of visitors to the beach on busy day **20 000–25 000**

Questions

4. Choose a suitable method to show the data shown in **Figure 4.10**. Describe and explain what you have shown.
5. What are the implications of the concentration of visitors in July and August for managing the beach at Studland?
6. Briefly explain **three** problems that result from human activities on Studland Dunes and Beach. Describe **two** methods of tackling these problems.

Soils

Soils consist of weathered rock, organic matter, air and water. Soils vary considerably even over a small distance due to variations in rock age, position on a slope, drainage and human activities. Natural soils contain **horizons**: these are the layers within soil and vary in terms of pH, colour, and mineral content.

Soils on chalk and limestone are usually very shallow **(Figure 4.11)**. When chalk and limestone is weathered the eroded material is removed in solution – this means that the soils which develop consist of organic matter and impurities of rock. By contrast in other rocks weathering can produce soils up to 2m deep. In some tropical areas they can even be as deep as 100m, this is because the soils of these areas were not eroded by glaciers 20 000 years ago but have developed over the last two million years.

Soils also vary with the climate: if the amount of rainfall is greater than evapotranspiration, water drains down removing **(leaching)** matter from the top and depositing it near the bottom of the soil. However in dry areas such as grasslands and deserts, water drawn up to the surface, is evaporated and leaves behind soluble materials.

Figure 4.11 A soil profile showing clearly defined horizons

Questions

7 Define the following terms:
horizon,
gley,
leaching.

8 What do the following letters stand for on soil horizons: Oh, Ap, Ea, Bh, Cg?

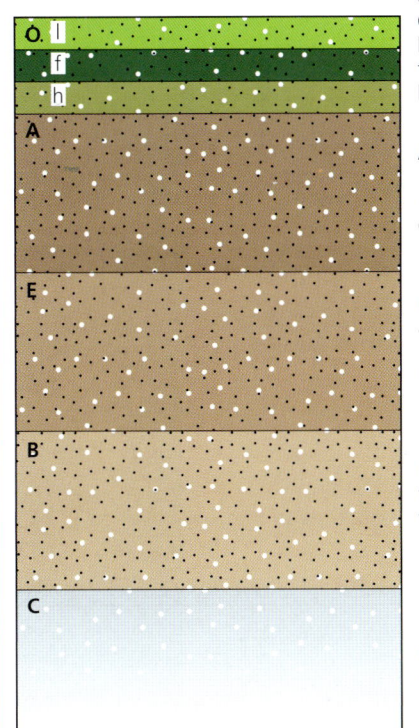

Figure 4.12 Soil horizons

SOIL HORIZONS

O Organic horizon
l   Undecomposed litter (plant remains)
f   partly decomposed litter
h   humus (decayed plant remains)

A Mineral horizon
h   humus
p   ploughed, as in a field or a garden
g   gleyed or waterlogged

E Leached horizon
a   strongly leached, ash coloured horizon, as in a podzol
b   weakly leached, light brown horizon, as in a brown earth

B Deposited horizon
fe iron deposited
t   clay deposited
h   humus deposited

C Bedrock or parent material
g   gleyed

Soils are also influenced by drainage – soils that are waterlogged are known as **gleyed** soils. They may dry out in summer to give a blue grey speckled colour.

Soil horizons are the layers within a soil **(Figure 4.12)**. The top layer of vegetation is referred to as the Organic (O) horizon. Beneath this is the mixed mineral-organic layer (A horizon). It is generally a dark colour due to the organic matter. An **Ap** horizon is one that has been mixed by **ploughing**. In some soils **leaching** takes place. This removes material from the horizon. Consequently the layer is much lighter in colour. The B horizon is the **deposited** horizon. This contains material that has been removed, such as iron (fe) humus (h) and clay (t). Sometimes the B horizon is weathered (w). At the base of the horizon is the **parent material** or **bedrock**. Horizons that are waterlogged are given the letter **g** (for **gleyed** or waterlogged).

DECIDUOUS WOODLAND – WYTHAM WOODS, NEAR OXFORD

Wytham Woods is near Oxford **(Figure 4.13)** and is owned and managed by the University of Oxford and has been intensively studied since the 1940s. The vegetation there is deciduous woodland

Figure 4.13 Wytham Woods

(Figure 4.14) – trees shed their leaves in winter to conserve nutrients and moisture and to reduce the risk of damage from snow or ice. The vegetation is layered, trees form the canopy (top layer) and there are also shrubs such as Elder trees and Holly as well as ground and field vegetation such as primroses, bluebells and grasses.

Deciduous woodlands are very productive ecosystems because of the high summer temperatures and long hours of daylight. Wytham has a summer temperature of 15-20°C and up to sixteen hours of sunlight in June. Rainfall is moderate, about 600 mm, and winters are mild at about 5°C. Soils in this ecosystem are quite fertile and are called brown earths. However because they are fertile they have been valuable for agriculture and so many deciduous woodland areas have been cut down to make way for farming **(Figure 4.15)**.

Figure 4.14 Vegetation associated with deciduous forests

Questions

9 Explain why deciduous woodlands are productive ecosystems.
10 Why are there so few large areas of deciduous woodland in the British Isles?
11 Study Figure 4.1. Describe the distribution of woodlands as shown on the map.
12 Why are there no areas of deciduous woodland in the southern hemisphere?

Figure 4.15 Farming close to Wytham Woods

Figure 4.16 Vegetation of rainforests

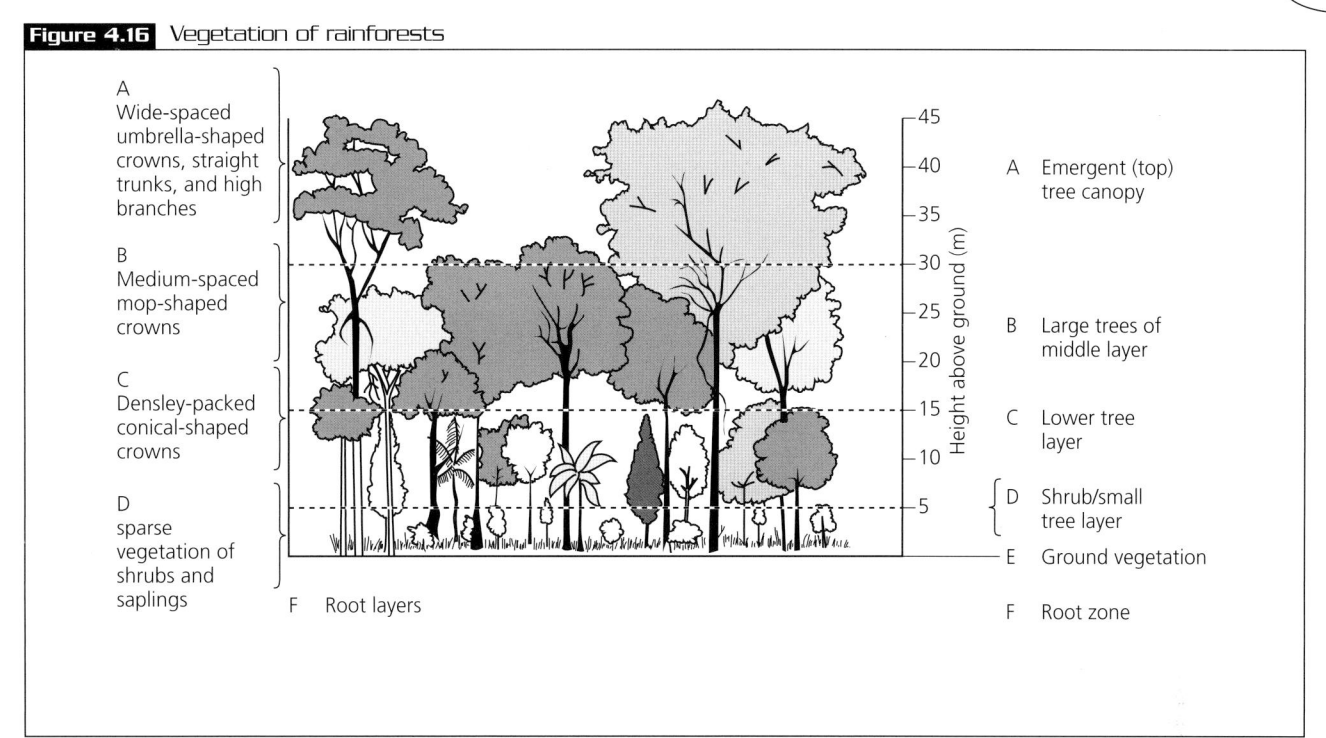

A Wide-spaced umbrella-shaped crowns, straight trunks, and high branches

B Medium-spaced mop-shaped crowns

C Densley-packed conical-shaped crowns

D sparse vegetation of shrubs and saplings

F Root layers

A Emergent (top) tree canopy

B Large trees of middle layer

C Lower tree layer

D Shrub/small tree layer

E Ground vegetation

F Root zone

Tropical rainforests

The tropical rainforest is one of the world's most luxuriant ecosystems (**Figure 4.16**) and also one of the most threatened (**Figure 4.17**). The rainforest has been described as a 'desert covered by trees' because its soil is very infertile. The key to understanding the rainforest is the speed with which plants take nutrients out of the soil.

The vegetation of the rainforest is very diverse – plants are found at five levels and there may be up to three hundred species of tree in just one hectare (the size of a football pitch), including mahogany, teak and yellow wood. The rainforest climate is hot and wet throughout the year, temperatures remain high due to its equatorial location. Rainfall is also high, over 2000 mm per annum and it falls in heavy convectional storms. As a result the growing season is year round.

Figure 4.17 Pressures on the rainforest

Figure 4.18 The advantages of the rainforest

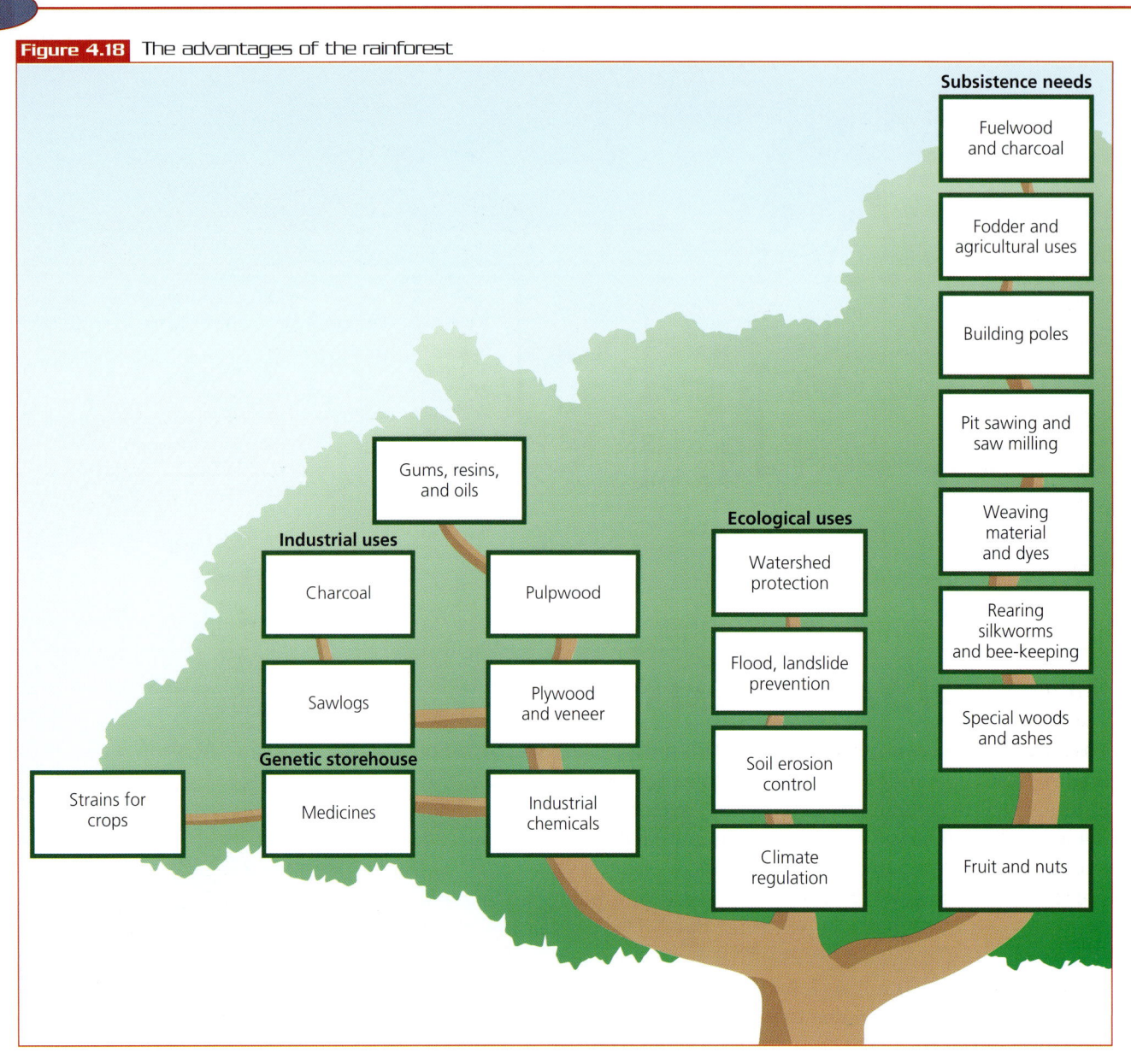

Subsistence needs
- Fuelwood and charcoal
- Fodder and agricultural uses
- Building poles
- Pit sawing and saw milling
- Weaving material and dyes
- Rearing silkworms and bee-keeping
- Special woods and ashes
- Fruit and nuts

Industrial uses
- Gums, resins, and oils
- Charcoal
- Pulpwood
- Sawlogs
- Plywood and veneer

Ecological uses
- Watershed protection
- Flood, landslide prevention
- Soil erosion control
- Climate regulation

Genetic storehouse
- Strains for crops
- Medicines
- Industrial chemicals

Tropical soils are deep and, owing to the high rainfall, clay, salts and other nutrients have been leached away under the hot wet conditions of the rainforest. Vegetation is broken down rapidly and nutrients are released back into the soil. Because of the year long growing season and the large number of plants there is great competition for nutrients. As soon as they are released in leaf decay they are absorbed by growing plants. Rainforest areas are under great pressure from farming (ranching and plantations), mining, forestry and urbanisation. The destruction of rainforests removes a great natural resource **(Figure 4.18)** and even when shifting cultivation occurs the rainforest takes a long time to recover. It is now believed that the practice of shifting cultivation gradually reduces the fertility of the soil **(Figure 4.19)**.

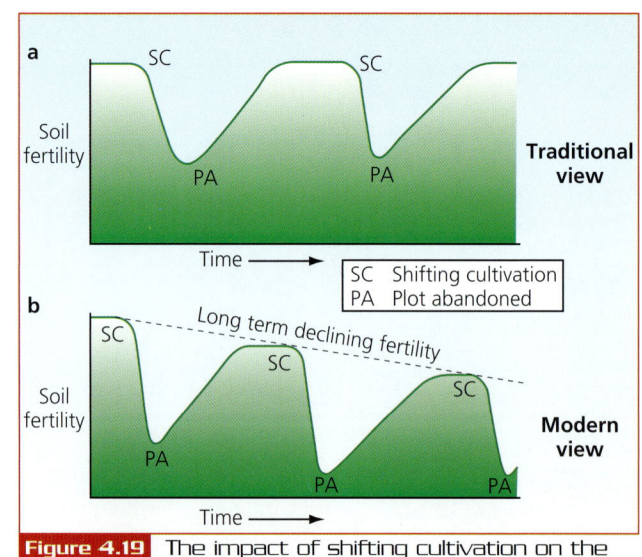

a Traditional view
b Modern view — Long term declining fertility

SC Shifting cultivation
PA Plot abandoned

Figure 4.19 The impact of shifting cultivation on the rainforest

DESTRUCTION OF THE RAINFOREST

Current rates of deforestation are:
- Latin America   20 million acres
- Africa   11 million acres
- Asia   9 million acres

The main conflicts include:
- Cattle ranching   South America
- Banana plantations   Costa Rica, South America
- Coffee plantations   Africa
- Logging   All over
- Farming   All over
- Mining   South America, Asia, Africa
- Rubber plantations   Indonesia

Questions

13 Why is the rainforest described as 'a desert covered by trees'?

14 **Figure 4.18** shows some of the benefits of the rainforest. Briefly describe the value of preserving the rainforest.

15 **Figure 4.19** shows the changes that occur in a rainforest after it has been burnt. Describe the changes in the vegetation and soil fertility following burning, farming and the abandoning of the plot.

Urban ecosystems

Urban ecosystems are very varied – in the city centre there are many tall buildings and little soil or nutrients available **(Figure 4.20)**. Such an environment is very stressful for most plants and animals, however there are some 'cliff dwellers' such as pigeons, sparrows and kestrels which can tolerate these conditions and thrive there. Many have changed their diets so they also eat discarded food. Mammals are less common in city centres although rats and mice are found again living off people's leftovers. By contrast the suburbs contain a variety of ecosystems. There is more soil present, a denser covering of vegetation and a greater variety of trees and shrubs **(Figure 4.21)**, consequently there is a large food supply to support birds and mammals. Common mammals include hedgehogs and foxes while breeding birds are attracted by nest boxes and bird tables.

Figure 4.20 A wall as an ecosystem

Figure 4.21 A suburban ecosystem

Advantages:

- **Warmth** – more animals and plants can survive in winter.
- **Food** – birds, squirrels and small mammals do not die of starvation or thirst in winter.
- **Trees** – a greater number of trees give nest sites, food and shelter to many animals.
- **Shelter** – buildings or bat boxes give safer breeding places.
- **Light** – birds breed for longer because of artificial light.
- **Lack of pesticides** – fewer bees, butterflies and other insects are killed.

Disadvantages:

- **Lack of soil** – large areas are covered with roads and buildings.
- **Pollution**.
- **Water** – drought due to the rapid run off and evaporation; waterlogging because of soil compaction.
- **Damage** – due to mowing, trampling and vandalism.
- **Lack of nutrients** – removal of debris prevents natural recycling.
- **Wind** – areas where buildings cause excessive turbulence.

Figure 4.22 Advantages and disadvantages of urban living

Questions

16. Why is the city centre a stressful place for plants and animals?
17. Why are cliff dwellers well suited to city centres?
18. Why are suburbs ecologically varied?
19. **Figure 4.22** lists some of the advantages and disadvantages of urban ecosystems. Suggest how these advantages and disadvantages vary between a city centre and a suburb.

Agricultural ecosystems

Agricultural ecosystems are very different from natural ones. In a natural ecosystem such as a deciduous woodland there are a variety of species and a number of complex food webs. By contrast in an agricultural ecosystem there are very few species and in some cases there might only be one (monoculture) and the food web is very simple. In most agricultural ecosystems humans consume the plants (such as rice or potatoes) or people eat the animals that eat the plants. Natural ecosystems are also more productive; this is partly because there are more layers of vegetation and also because the vegetation is there throughout the year.

Agriculture has replaced most of the natural forest in Britain, and with it much of the **biodiversity** (genetic diversity). The decline of plants and animals continues. The chemical control of weeds in arable crops is a major cause in the decline of wildlife. Other agricultural practises which have led to a reduction in biological diversity include:

- an increase in arable agriculture (crops) **(Figure 4.23)**;
- an increase in the inputs of inorganic **fertilisers** and **pesticides**;
- the **intensification** of pasture management.

Other changes that farming may cause include genetic modification, irrigation, drainage (of excess water), and the removal of nutrients and vegetation during harvest.

However, in some cases farmers are helping the environment by using traditional methods, and farming the land less intensively. This is mostly done on a small-scale and does not make up for the damage that has been done.

Figure 4.23 An arable ecosystem

	Natural	Agricultural
Foodweb	Complex; several layers	Simple; mostly one or two layers
Biomass (living matter)	Large; mixed plant and animal diversity	Small; mostly plant
Biological diversity (biodiversity)	High	Low – often monoculture
Productivity	High	Lower
Modification	Limited	Large-scale – inputs of feed, seed, water, fertilisers, energy fuel; outputs of products, waste, etc.

Figure 4.24 A comparison between natural and agricultural ecosystems

Questions

20. Draw a simple diagram to show a food chain, in which there is just grass, cattle and people. Identify the primary producer, herbivore and consumer in the diagram you draw.
21. State **three** ways in which agricultural ecosystems differ from urban ones.
22. Make two lists – one for natural ecosystems and one for agricultural ecosystems – and place each of the following characteristics under one or the other list:
    - plants all the same age;
    - large diversity of species;
    - artificial fertilisers (nutrients);
    - many layers of species;
    - complex food chains;
    - top consumers are wild animals;
    - top consumers are people;
    - natural soils;
    - altered soils.

Population

5

KEY TERMS AND DEFINITIONS

Population distribution refers to where people live.

Population density refers to how many people there are in an area – it is normally given as the number of people per square km.

Population distribution

Population distribution refers to where people live (Figure 5.1). On a global scale:

- 75% of the population live within 1000 km of the sea;
- over 90% live in the northern hemisphere.

The most favoured locations include:

- fertile valleys, such as the River Nile and the River Ganges;
- a regular supply of water such as in the British Isles;
- a climate which is not too extreme;
- good communications, such as along the M4 corridor in Britain.

Areas of low population density include deserts (too dry and hot or cold!), mountains (too steep and cold), high latitudes (too cold and short growing seasons) and rainforests (infertile soils).

Figure 5.2 The world's largest countries by size and population

Population (millions)		Area (thousand km^2)	
China	1131	CIS	22 098
India	871	China	9326
CIS	282	Canada	9221
USA	251	USA	9167
Indonesia	188	Brazil	8457
Brazil	153	Australia	7618
Pakistan	126	India	2973
Japan	124	Argentina	2737
Bangladesh	119	Sudan	2376
Mexico	90	Algeria	2382

Figure 5.1 The global distribution of population

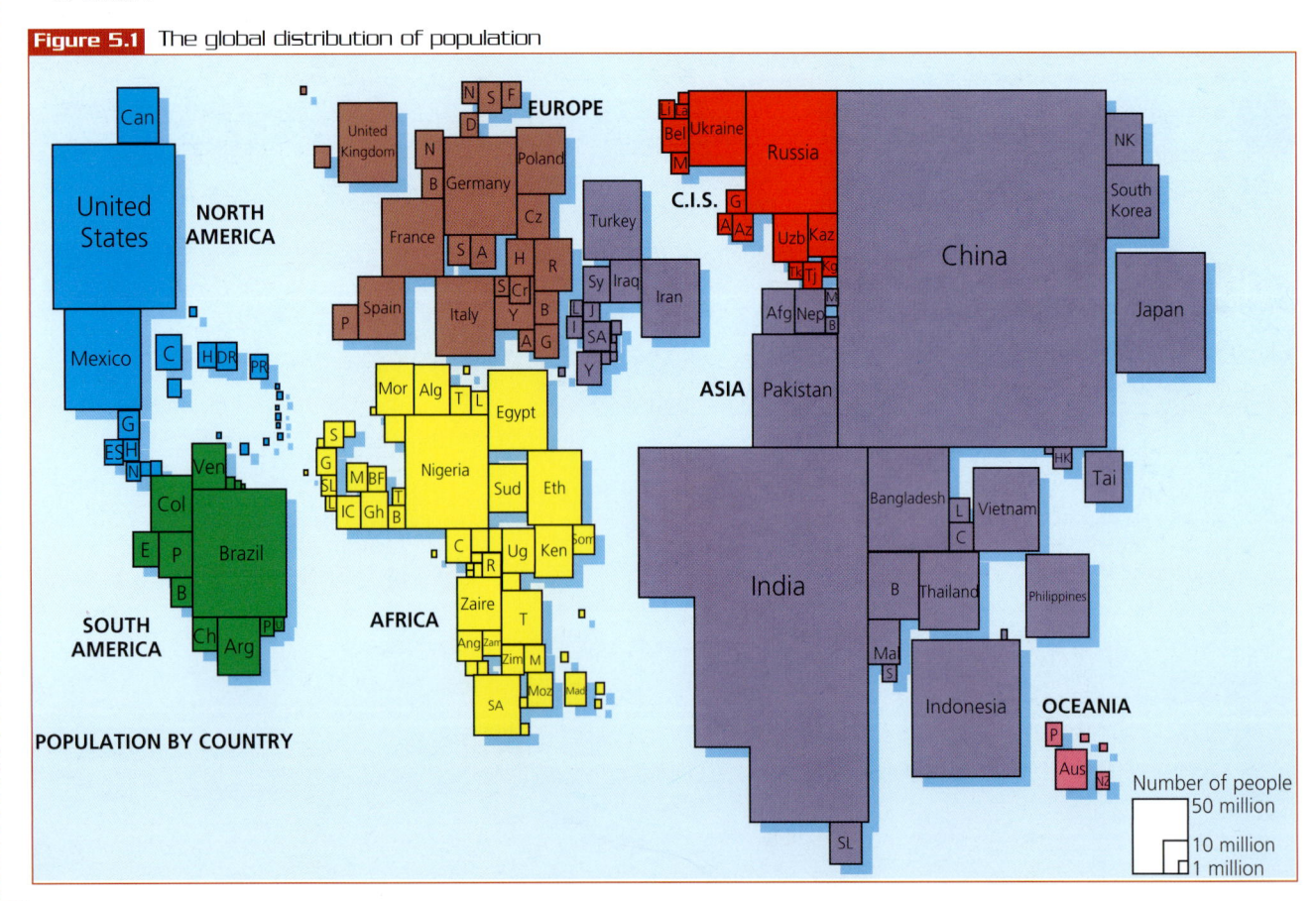

64

Population density

Population density refers to the number of people per square km. The same factors affect population density as affect population distribution, namely a supply of water, fertile soils, raw materials, good communications and so on. At a global scale we can identify three major areas of high population density (with over 200 people per km square) – South East Asia, North East USA and Western Europe. Smaller areas include, for example, south east Brazil, the Mexican plateau, California, the Nile Valley and Java.

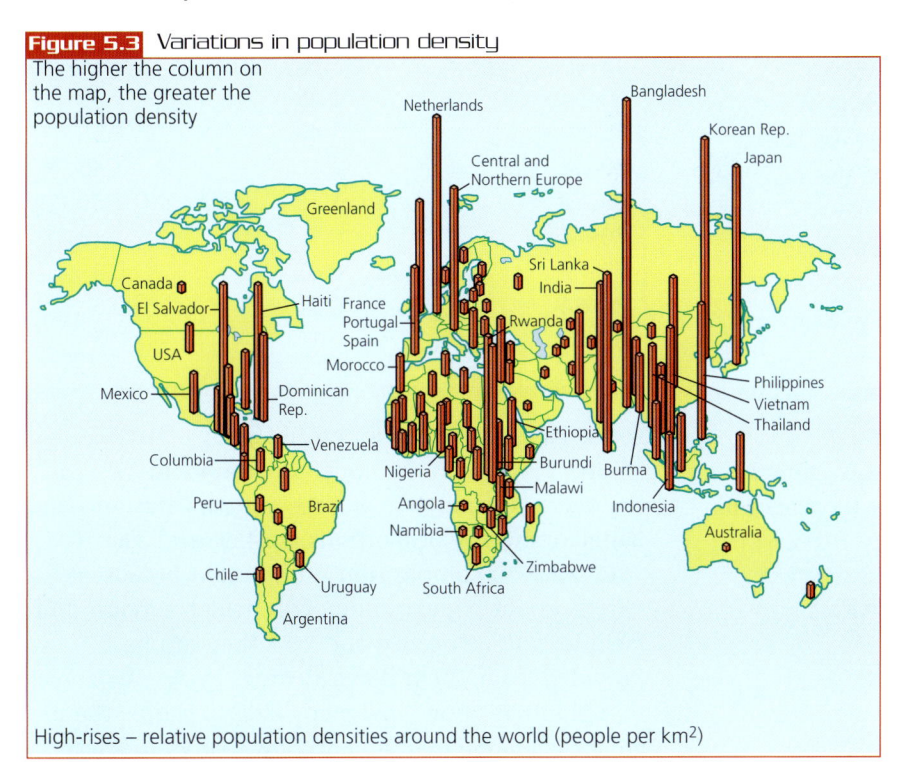

Figure 5.3 Variations in population density

The higher the column on the map, the greater the population density

High-rises – relative population densities around the world (people per km²)

Questions

1. Why do most people live:
   a. within 1,000 km of the sea?
   b. below 500m?
   c. in the northern hemisphere?

2. Study the tables which show the world's largest countries by population and by size.
   a. Which countries are among the largest in population size and also the largest in area?
   b. What does this suggest about their population density?
   c. Which countries have a large population but a small land area? What does this tell us about population density in these countries?
   d. Which countries have a large land area but do not have a large population size? What does this suggest about average population density in these countries?

Figure 5.4 Population density (people per km sq.)

Australia	2.4
Bangladesh	909
Brazil	19
Canada	3.3
Egypt	64
El Salvador	277
Japan	332
Korea	457
Malta	1146
Netherlands	457
New Zealand	13
Russia	8.7
Singapore	4902
Taiwan	586
UK	241
USA	28

Questions

Study the data provided in **Figure 5.4**. Arrange the countries in two groups – one with high population density and the other with low population density.

3. What are the characteristics of countries with high population densities? (You may need to look at an atlas to help you). How does this contrast with the characteristics of the less densely populated countries?

   Using an atlas, find a map that shows world variations in population density. Population density is usually shown by a choropleth. This is a type of map which shows all areas with similar characteristics (in this case similar population densities) by means of colour shading.

4. State **two advantages** of the choropleth map over the bar charts shown in this page.

   State **two advantages** of the bar chart over the choropleth.

5. For any country with a **high** population density and any country with a **low** population density briefly explain why it has a high or low population density. Use an atlas to help you.

5
Population pyramids and population composition

Population composition refers to any characteristic of the population such as age, sex, ethnicity, language, occupational structure, and religion.

Population pyramids tell us a great deal of information about the age and sex (composition) of a population. For example:

- a wide base suggests a high birth rate;
- a narrow base tells us that the birth rate has fallen;
- straight or near vertical sides tell us that the death rate is low;
- sides that narrow inwards from the bottom show a high death rate;
- large amounts of males around 20–34 year groups suggest high rates of in-migration;
- a small amount of young people indicates high rates of out-migration.

In the UK 19% of the population are aged under the age of 15 years and 16% are aged over the age of 65 years. This is different for ethnic groups. Among Whites 19% are in the under-15 group and 21% in the over 60-group. By contrast, among Pakistanis and Bangladeshis the proportions are 45% and 3%.

Population composition is important because it tells us about population growth, which services and facilities will be needed and how they can be provided for in 20 or 30 years time.

If planners know how many elderly people there are, how many children, and how many homeless, they can make projections into the future. How many schools are needed? How many hospitals and clinics are required? Is there enough money to pay for all this? Will taxes have to be increased?

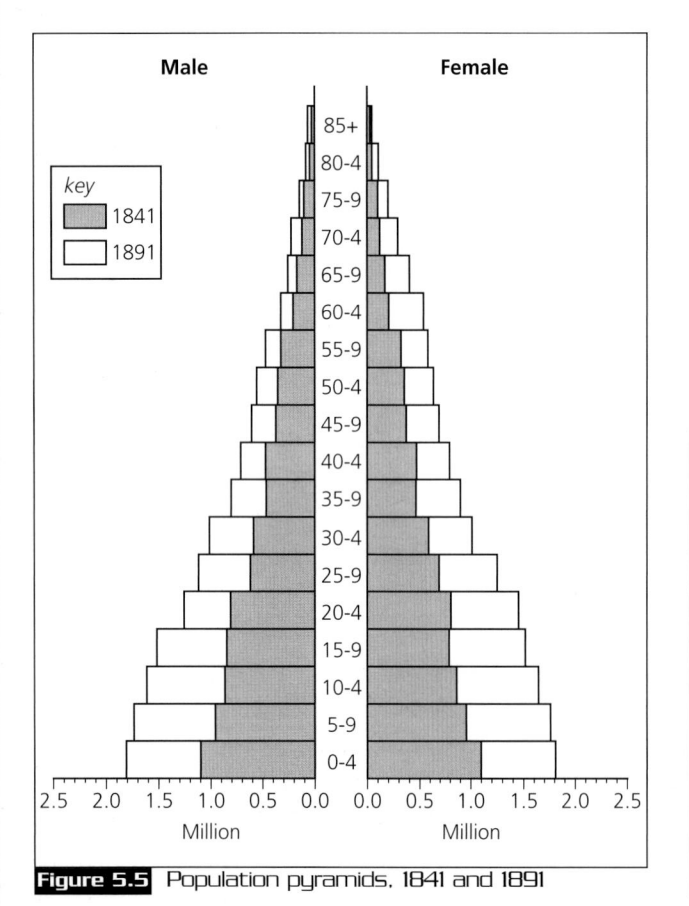

Figure 5.6 Approximate population figures for UK 1991

Age group	Male	Female
0–4	2.0	1.9
5–9	2.1	2.0
10–14	1.9	1.8
15–19	1.75	1.6
20–24	1.8	1.85
25–29	1.6	1.6
30–34	1.5	1.4
35–39	1.45	1.35
40–44	1.5	1.4
45–49	1.6	1.5
50–54	1.45	1.45
55–59	1.45	1.5
60–64	1.4	1.45
65–69	1.15	1.35
70–74	0.7	1.15
75–79	0.45	0.8
80–84	0.3	0.5
85+	0.15	0.3

Figure 5.5 Population pyramids, 1841 and 1891

Questions

6. **Figure 5.5** which shows population pyramids for the UK in 1841 and 1891.
   On a copy of this add the data for the UK's population in 1991.

7. Write a short paragraph describing how the UK's population structure has changed between 1841 and 1991. You should refer to:
   - the birth rate;
   - the death rate;
   - the proportion of elderly people;
   - the number of young people.

Birth and death rates

The **birth rate** is the number of births per 1000 people. **Figure 5.7** shows global variations in the birth rate. The highest birth rates are found in Malawi (55 per thousand), Uganda and Afghanistan (52 per thousand), Guinea, Niger, and Yemen (51 per thousand), and Ivory Coast and Rwanda (50 per thousand). The lowest birth rates are found in Denmark, Germany and Italy (11 per thousand), and in Japan, Switzerland, Belgium, Austria and Luxembourg.

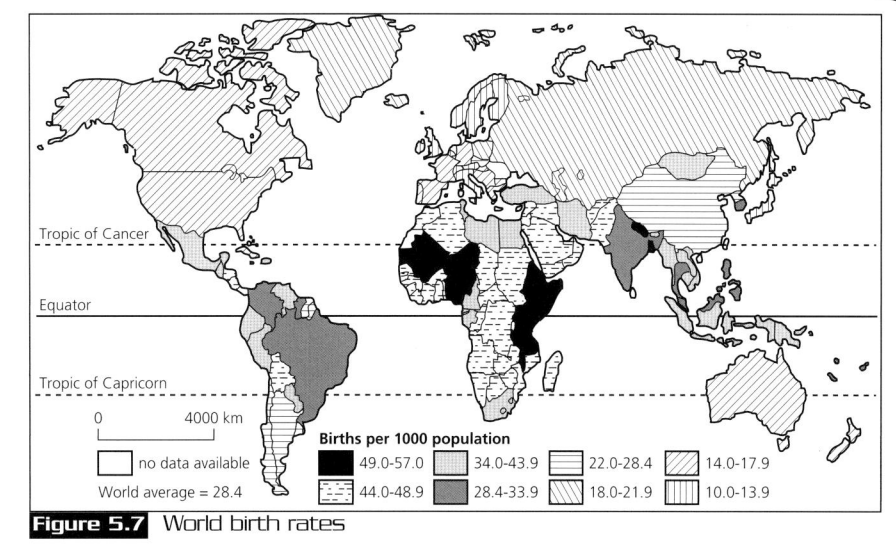

The **death rate** is the number of deaths per 1000 population. **Figure 5.8** shows global variations in the death rate. Among countries with the highest death rate are Sierra Leone and Afghanistan (22 per thousand), Guinea Bissau (21 per thousand) and Benin, Gambia, and Guinea (20 per thousand). By contrast countries with a very low death rate include Costa Rica (4 per thousand) and Panama, Mexico, Malaysia, Jordan, the Bahamas and Taiwan (5 per thousand).

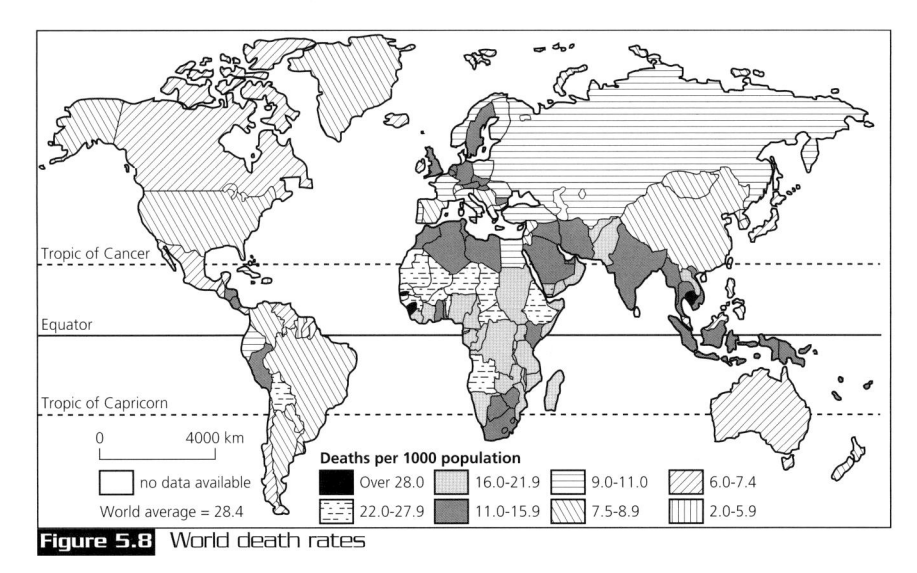

Figure 5.7 World birth rates

Births per 1000 population
- 49.0-57.0
- 44.0-48.9
- 34.0-43.9
- 28.4-33.9
- 22.0-28.4
- 18.0-21.9
- 14.0-17.9
- 10.0-13.9

World average = 28.4

Figure 5.8 World death rates

Deaths per 1000 population
- Over 28.0
- 22.0-27.9
- 16.0-21.9
- 11.0-15.9
- 9.0-11.0
- 7.5-8.9
- 6.0-7.4
- 2.0-5.9

World average = 28.4

Figure 5.9 Birth and death rates

Why are birth rates high? Parents want children:

- to help work on a farm
- to look after the parents when they are old
- to continue the family name
- to replace other children who have died.

Why are death rates high? This is due to a number of related factors, including:

- a lack of clean water
- a shortage of food
- poor hygiene and sanitation
- overcrowding
- diseases such as TB and measles being passed from person to person
- poverty.

Questions

8. Describe the pattern of birth rates as shown on **Figure 5.7**.
9. Describe the pattern of death rates as shown on **Figure 5.8**.
10. Explain any **two** reasons why the birth rate comes down, and any **two** reasons why death rates fall.

The Demographic Transition Model (DTM)

The DTM describes how birth rates and death rates change over time (Figure 5.10). It is divided into five stages:

Stage 1 High and variable
- Birth rates and death rates are high and variable
- population growth fluctuates
- there are no countries now at this stage although some tribes such as the Kalahari bush people and the Amazonian Indians show these patterns
- the UK was at this stage until about 1750.

Stage 2 Early expanding
- The birth rate remains high but the death rate comes down rapidly
- population growth is rapid
- countries such as Afghanistan, Sudan and Libya are at this stage
- the UK passed through this stage by 1850.

Stage 3 Late expanding
- The birth rate drops and the death rate remains low
- population growth continues but at a slower rate
- Brazil and Argentina are at this stage
- the UK passed through this stage around 1950.

Stage 4 Low and variable
- Birth rates and death rates are low and variable
- population growth fluctuates
- the UK and most developed countries are now at this stage.

Stage 5 Low and declining
- The birth rate is lower than the death rate
- the death rate increases due to the **ageing** of the population
- the population declines – Sweden and Japan are in this stage or are about to enter this stage.

Questions

11 a Describe the population pyramid associated with Stage 1 of the DTM.

b Describe the population pyramid associated with Stage 4 of the DTM.

c Why has the population pyramid changed over the course of the DTM.

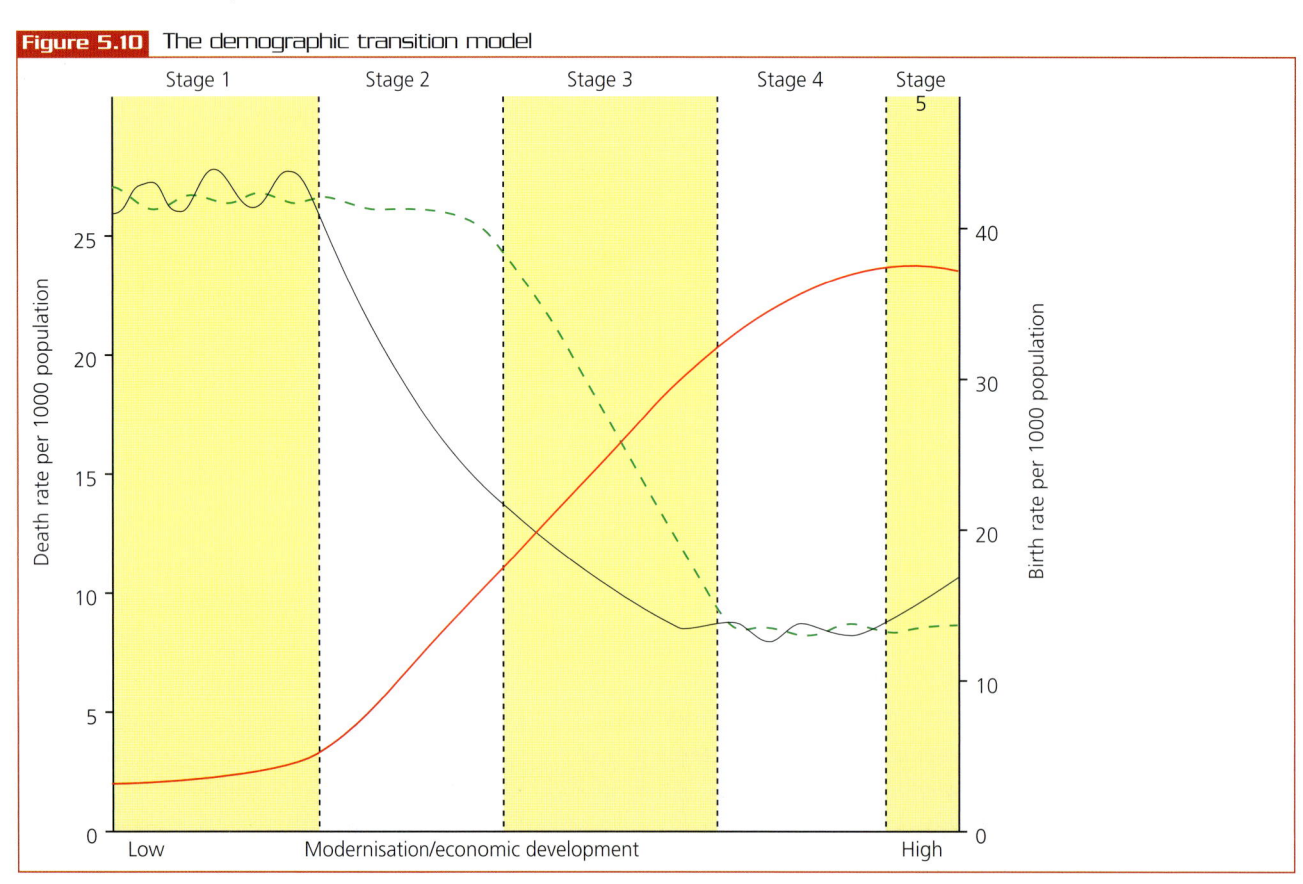

Figure 5.10 The demographic transition model

Population growth

The world's population is growing very rapidly **(Figure 5.11)**. Most of this growth is quite recent. Up to 95% of population growth is taking place in less economically developed countries (LEDCs). However, the world's population is expected to **stabilise** at about 12 billion. **Zero population growth (ZPG)** is a term used when the birth rate is as low as the death rate, and the population stops increasing.

Population growth creates great pressures on governments to provide for their people; increased pressure on the environment; increased risk of famine and malnutrition; greater differences between the richer countries and the poorer countries.

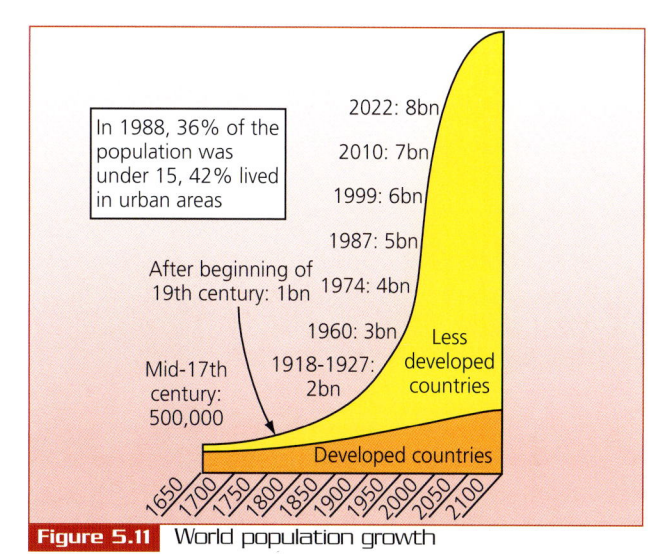

POPULATION AND RESOURCES

In 1798 Thomas Malthus predicted that population growth would be greater than the growth in food and resources **(Figure 5.12)**. He said that food supply grew at a steady pace such as 1, 2, 3, 4, 5 and so on. By contrast, population grew at an increasing pace such as 1, 2, 4, 8, 16 and so on. If there was no attempt to reduce population growth the result would be war, famine and disease.

According to Malthus population growth could be reduced by delaying the age of marriage. His views may seem strange to us today but he was a vicar and was writing long before the widespread availability of contraceptives.

However, Esther Boserup, writing in the 1960s, stated that people have the resources, namely knowledge and technology, to increase food production. When the need arises someone will find a solution.

Since Malthus's time there have been many ways in which people have increased food production. These include:

- draining marshlands;
- reclaiming land from the sea;
- cross breeding of cattle;
- high yielding varieties of plants;
- terracing on steep slopes;
- growing crops in green houses;
- using more sophisticated irrigation techniques;
- making new foods such as soya;
- making artificial fertilisers;
- farming native species of crops and animals;
- fish farming.

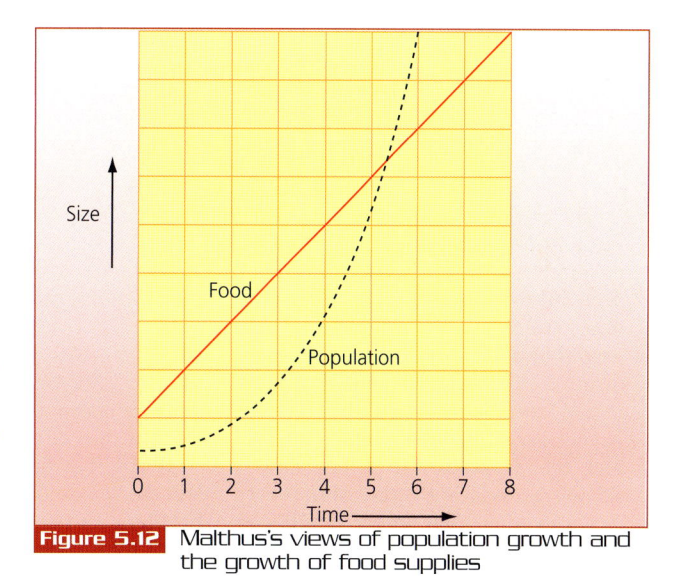

Figure 5.11 World population growth

In 1988, 36% of the population was under 15, 42% lived in urban areas

- 2022: 8bn
- 2010: 7bn
- 1999: 6bn
- 1987: 5bn
- After beginning of 19th century: 1bn
- 1974: 4bn
- 1960: 3bn
- 1918–1927: 2bn
- Mid-17th century: 500,000

Less developed countries
Developed countries

Figure 5.12 Malthus's views of population growth and the growth of food supplies

Questions

12 Study **Figure 5.11** and state the world's population size in 1650, 1850, 1920, and 1970. What does this tell you about population growth?

13 Study **Figure 5.11**. Describe the growth of the world's population. To what extent is population growth occurring in

a developed countries?

b developing countries?

Family planning in developing countries

World-wide, for every 100 men, there are 105 women. In India, the average fell to 93 women for every 100 men. UNICEF stated that 'there is no more shameful statistic than the fact that some 40 to 50 million girls and women are 'missing from the Indian population'.

Questions

14 What do you think is meant by the term human rights? What evidence is there that human rights in India is not the same for all people?

15 Using a dictionary find out the meaning of the term 'dowry'.

16 What is meant by the term 'sex selective abortion'? What evidence is there for sex selective abortions and female infanticide in India?

India's population explosion has been described as a 'nightmare'. In 1951, India had a population of 361 million. In 1995 it reached almost one billion, and is growing fast. By 2050 it should overtake China's population. While states such as Kerala and Tamil Nadu, with their high literacy rates, have great success in bringing fertility down, in the poor northern states, population continues to boom. The social pressure to have sons is intense. Nevertheless there are signs of hope. Fertility in India has dropped by more than 40% since 1970. If present rates are maintained, population stability – what is called 'replacement fertility' will be reached as early as 2016 **(Figure 5.14)**. However, as a very large proportion of the billion people are young, India's population will rise steeply over the next few decades.

Figure 5.13 Population growth in India

Figure 5.14 Population growth in India

India has 40 million fewer women than it would have, if the sexual balance had been left to nature. Most were aborted: many were killed after birth. The arrival of a daughter can be a financial disaster. A male heir is needed to carry on the family name. A girl, by contrast, is considered 'another families wealth' and the demands for a big dowry, though forbidden by the Anti-Dowry Act, can often ruin poorer families or those with several daughters.

The dowry threat induces many families to forestall the problem in almost barbaric ways. In parts of poor states like Bihar, there are still said to be midwives who specialise in strangling girl babies at birth. Elsewhere, women go to a respectable clinic for the test used to check for genetic defects, but in India almost invariably to check the baby's sex. If it is a girl, abortion often follows soon afterwards. The government says that in a study of 8000 abortions carried out after tests in Bombay, 7999 of the foetuses were female. In this way, India's traditional imbalance between the sexes has got worse: in 1901 there were 972 females for every 1000 males, but 90 years on, there were only 927 **(Figure 5.16)**. In 1994 sex determination tests were banned by law but they continue.

If a girl is born her prospects are still poor compared to those of her brothers. In the country, even if boys go to school the girls are likely to be kept behind to help at the house – which helps to account for the fact that the female literacy rate is just 40%, compared to 65% among males. The woes continue into adulthood with dowry burden and related terrors. The United Nations Children's Fund (UNICEF) reported that 5000 Indian women every year are burnt to death by their in-laws in revenge for their families failure to provide sufficient dowry.

Historically the position of women in a Hindu society was grim, from uncertain birth to fiery death in sati on the funeral pyre of the lord and master. Sati was abolished in the 19th century (though a case of an attempted sati was reported in Rajasthan in September 1997) but in other respects the position of women has hardly advanced at all.

Figure 5.16 Population composition in India

Figure 5.15 Parents are paid to have the daughters of India lost (Independent 3 October 1997)

Population change in the UK

Population change occurs due to differences in birth rates, death rates and migration. If birth rates are greater than death rates, a population would increase. Similarly, if death rates were higher than birth rates the population of a place would fall.

MIGRATION

Migration is the permanent change of residence with a complete change of friends and social connections. Thus it does not include commuting (a daily movement to work), seasonal movements, or moving house in the same neighbourhood. Migrations are commonly divided into a number of types:

- forced or voluntary;
- long distance or short distance;
- international or internal.

Migration is often explained by push factors and pull factors. **Push factors** are the negative features which make a person want to leave an area, such as unemployment, low wages and natural hazards. **Pull factors** on the other hand are the attractions (whether real or just imagined) that exist somewhere else, such as better wages, more jobs and good schools. Migration also varies with age **(Figure 5.17)** and with levels of education (more qualified people are more likely to travel further).

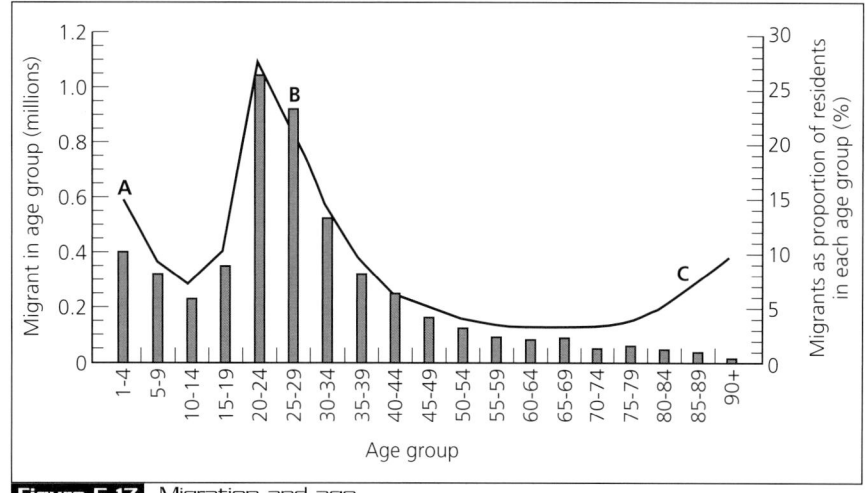

Figure 5.17 Migration and age

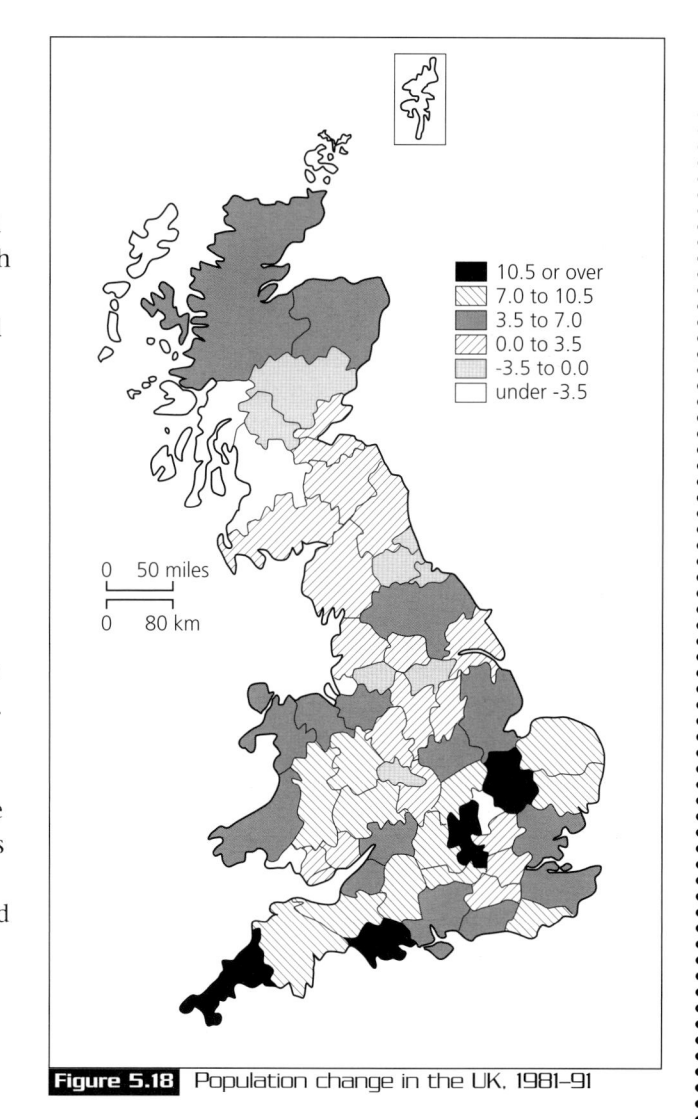

POPULATION CHANGE IN THE UK

Between 1981 and 1991 the fastest growth rates were found in East Anglia, the south of Britain, and Wales. Large cities lost populations while at the same time people moved to small towns and cities and rural areas **(Figure 5.18)**. **Natural change** (the difference between birth rates and death rates) is higher in areas with a younger population and fewer elderly people. Hence, the highest rates of *natural increase* were found in counties stretching from Berkshire to Cambridgeshire and Leicestershire due to low death rates and high birth rates. By contrast, some retirement resorts along the South Coast have very low levels of natural change.

Figure 5.18 Population change in the UK, 1981–91

Migration in the UK

Up to 10% of Britain's population moves address each year. In Oxfordshire it is as high as 13% whereas in parts of South Wales it is as low as 7%. Over half the people moving move less than 5 km from their old address and two thirds move less than 10 km. The very young and the elderly tend to travel over much shorter distances.

The main pattern of migration is that of flows **between** neighbouring regions. Of the rest, most involve migration to or from London and the South East and migration to the South West (for retirement).

AGE OF MIGRANTS

Migration is dominated by young adults, especially in the 20–29 year groups. These account for almost 40% of all migrants. However, there are important regional contrasts. For example London's migrants are mostly aged 25-9, whereas rural areas and south coast counties have a much higher proportion of 45+ year olds. Large cities attract young people while rural areas are losing them. Areas which attract populations aged 30-44 (and their children) are the suburban areas, e.g. Oxfordshire and Cheshire, and parts with strong economic growth.

BRITAIN'S AGEING POPULATION

Regional variations in the age structure occur because of migration:

- there are fewer under 45 year olds in rural areas (out-migration of school leavers to urban areas);
- movement of over 45 year olds away from conurbations (crowded and expensive);
- suburban pull for people with young families.

The distribution of the elderly in Britain is very uneven (**Figure 5.19**), and the very elderly are growing in number rapidly. In 1901 the proportion of elderly was about 5%. By 1971 the elderly accounted for 16.4% of the population but by 1991 this had risen to 18.4%. The proportion of the very old (over 75 years) has been more dramatic – 4.7% in 1971 rising to 7% in 1991, an increase from 2.6 million to 4 million.

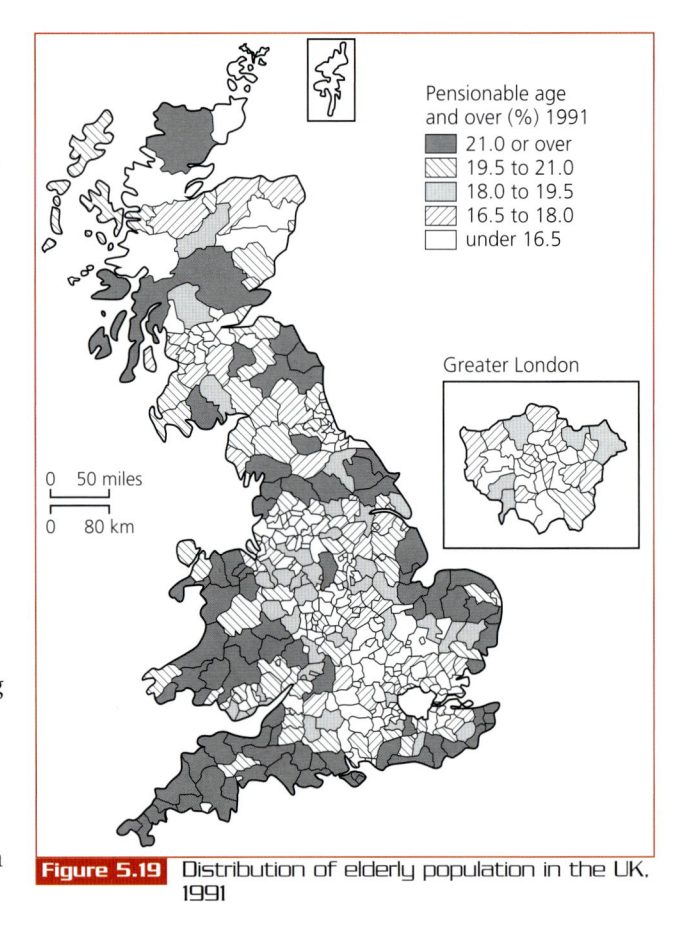

Figure 5.19 Distribution of elderly population in the UK, 1991

Pensionable age and over (%) 1991
- 21.0 or over
- 19.5 to 21.0
- 18.0 to 19.5
- 16.5 to 18.0
- under 16.5

Questions

17. Describe how migration varies with age. How do you explain the three peaks (A, B, and C) shown on **Figure 5.17**?
18. Describe the distribution of the elderly population in the UK, as shown in **Figure 5.19**. Suggest reasons to explain the distribution you have drawn.
19. Carry out a survey in your class. Find out where each person was born and where they have lived. Plot the results on a map of the world and an enlarged map of the UK. How do your results compare with the 'theory' of migration, i.e. that most migration is short-distance, within the same country or region, and for reasons of employment?

Settlement

6

Rural settlement

The site of a settlement is the land on which it is built. When early settlers established settlements they had to make a choice as to whether they built on a dry point (in a wet area), a wet point (in a dry area), south facing slopes to get more sunlight, defendable slopes and whether the site had good soils – thus south facing hilltops free from flooding were very much favoured (**Figure 6.2**). For example in Figure 6.1 Stonesfield (square 3917) is a defendable site on south facing slopes above the River Evenlode. There is also woodland nearby which had been useful for building and penning in animals.

Village shapes also vary (**Figure 6.1**). Some are linear, stretched out along a road, while others are cross-shaped (cruciform) owing to the roads meeting. The exact shape depends on the angle of the roads

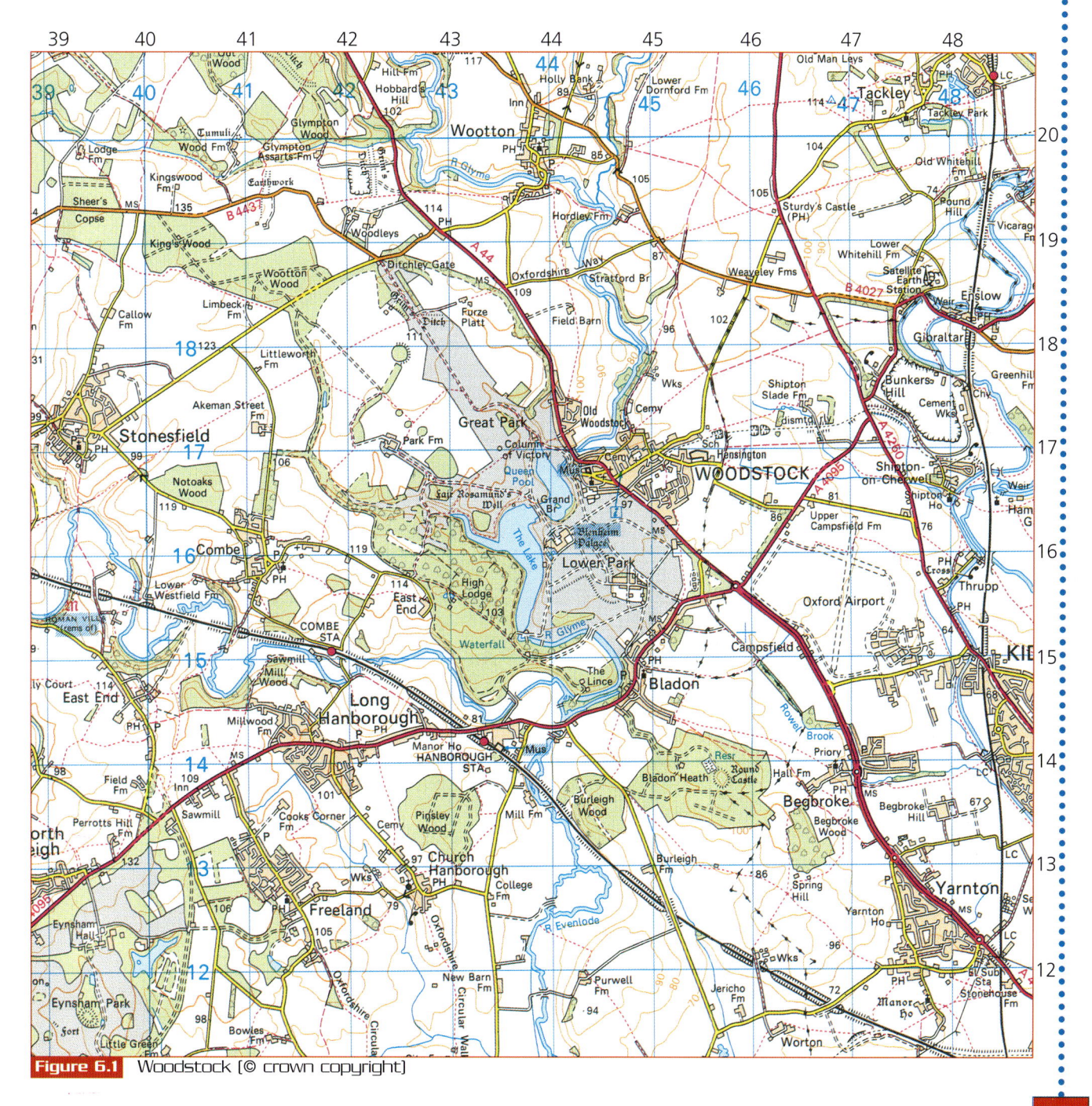

Figure 6.1 Woodstock (© crown copyright)

73

6 SETTLEMENT

and the amount of infilling (recent building). In some cases the village may be built around a village green.

Villages also provide a function, people live and work there. In the past many people worked in farming; now far fewer people work on farms but rural areas are still important places for people to live. As people live there, certain services are provided. Some of these can be shown on ordnance survey maps – such as schools, churches, public houses, railway stations and post offices. Not all services however, are shown, so OS maps are useful but do not tell us the whole story.

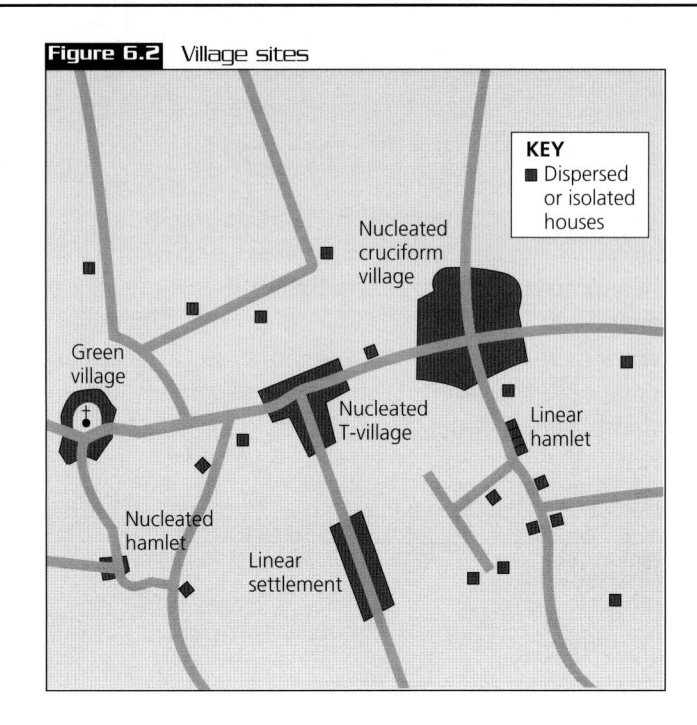

Figure 6.2 Village sites

KEY
■ Dispersed or isolated houses

- Nucleated cruciform village
- Green village
- Nucleated T-village
- Linear hamlet
- Nucleated hamlet
- Linear settlement

Questions

Study the map extract and answer the following questions:

1. Give the four figure square reference for Church Hanborough and Yarnton.
2. What is the shape of Church Hanborough and Yarnton?
3. How have main roads affected the shapes of Bladon and Begbroke?
4. Describe the site of Combe and Wooton.
5. What functions are found in Woodstock?

Settlement	Population Size	Actual No. of Services	Area on Map	No. of Services on Map	Hamlet, Village or Market Town
Wootton	553	7			
Tackley	888	18			
Stonesfield	1454	16			
Combe	782	10			
Woodstock	2604	103			
Bladon	644	10			
Long Hanborough	2444	18			
Church Hanborough	220	4			
Begbroke	710	10			
North Leigh	1769	20			
Freeland	1385	10			
Yarnton	2386	39			

Figure 6.3 Settlement hierarchy from the Woodstock area

74

A hamlet is a very small settlement with only a few functions, whereas a village is a large settlement with more functions **(Figure 6.4)**. Market Towns are even larger and offer a greater range of functions. Not only do the number of functions differ but so too do the type of functions. Hamlets usually offer only low order goods or convenience goods such as newspapers, bread and chocolate **(Figure 6.6)**. These are sold in small shops or sub-post offices. By contrast market towns offer high order goods or comparison goods as well as the convenience goods – these include electrical shops, supermarkets and restaurants. Some of the shops may be specialist shops **(Figure 6.7)**.

The range of a good refers to the distance people are prepared to travel to obtain that good or service. For lower order goods the range is not very far; by contrast people will often shop around for more expensive high order goods. The sphere of influence is the area a settlement serves. A hamlet serves only a small area, whereas a market town serves a much larger area.

Figure 6.4 Settlement hierarchy

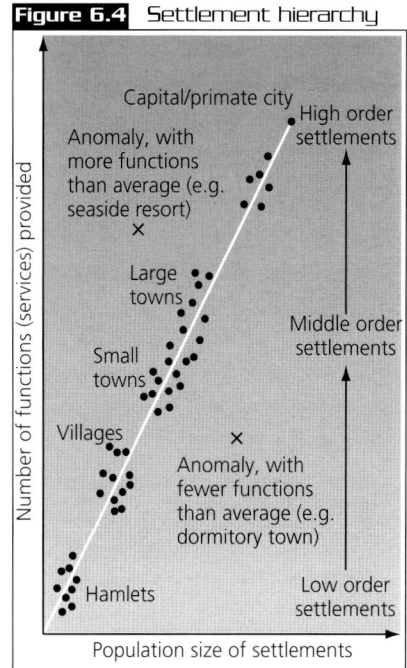

Figure 6.5 Services associated with selected settlements

Hamlet	Village	Small market town
General store	General store	General store
Post office	Post office	Post office
Pub	Pub	Pub
	Garage	Garage
	Grocer	Grocer
	Primary school	Primary school, bike shop, chemist, electrical, TV/radio, furniture, hairdresser, video shop, restaurant

Questions

Study **Figure 6.5** which shows some of the typical functions to be found in a hamlet, a village and a market town.

6 a Categorise each function as either high order goods or lower order goods.

  b What proportion of functions in each settlement can be described as being high order and low order?

7 Conduct a survey in your class – find out where (and how far) people in your class go to buy:
- a magazine;
- a bar of chocolate or a fizzy drink;
- a new CD;
- a pair of jeans.

Work out the average distance people travel for each of these goods, what can you conclude about the range of these goods?

Figure 6.6 Low order goods in Combe

Figure 6.7 High order goods in Woodstock

6 The growth of urban areas

Urbanisation is an increase in the percentage of people living in urban areas. **Urban growth** is an increase in the number of people living in urban areas. The reasons for urbanisation are varied, although most people move in search of work. Not only do towns provide employment, it is easier to provide schools, hospitals, and services to people who are concentrated in small areas.

Life in the growing urban areas was difficult – in London for example, life expectancy in 1900 was just 15 years in the East End and 12 year old boys in poor areas were, on average, 15 cm shorter than boys from wealthy areas. Many of Charles Dickens's novels capture the poverty and brutality of nineteenth Century London (Figure 6.8). In fact the health of Britain's working population was so poor that Britain's industries began to decline and the Army had to reject forty per cent of all recruits because they were physically and/or mentally unfit. To improve the health of the workforce wealthy industrialists, and later the Government, provided better housing, with running water and less crowded conditions. Gradually the health of the population, and the economy, improved.

Urban areas did not grow very rapidly in the nineteenth century because transport was limited. London, for example, remained very compact until the 1870s but as transport developed cities expanded rapidly (Figure 6.9). First the railways and then the tubes allowed London to shoot out in all directions; at a later stage buses allowed the areas between the railway lines to be infilled. This growth of the city at the edges is known as **suburbanisation**.

In the early twentieth century the Government provided **subsidies** (financial help) to local governments and to house builders to build new homes. These developments caused cities to spread rapidly and provided people with bigger healthier homes, complete with gardens – a far cry from the congestion in the squalid inner cities. However, people had to commute to work – good agricultural land was lost and some of the poorer people found the cost of living in suburban areas too high. Thus the growth of large cities was causing problems; to stop cities from growing outwards (**urban sprawl**) many cities used green belts.

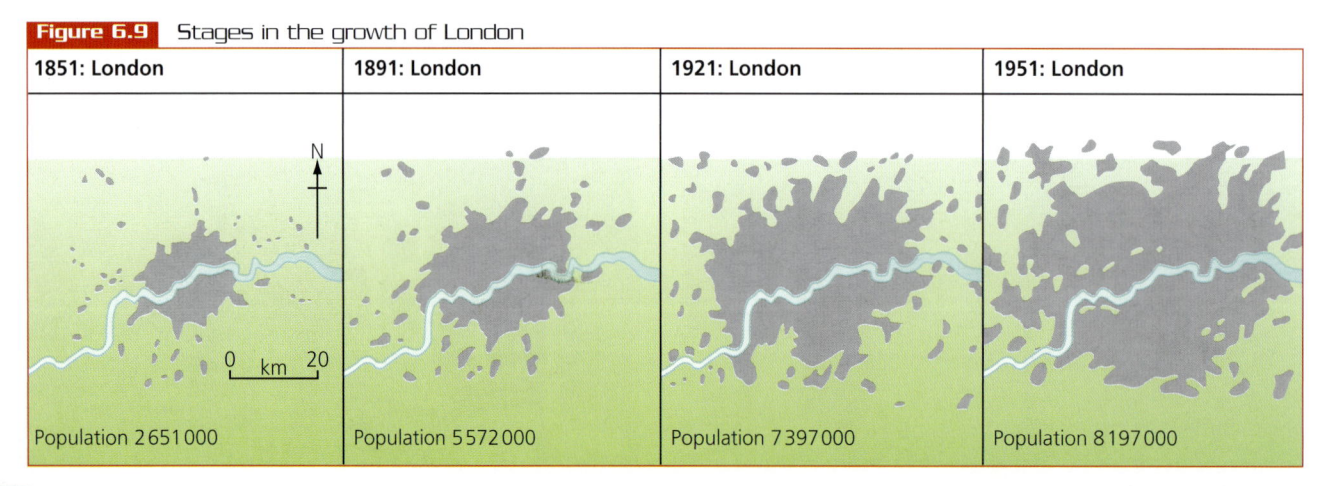

Figure 6.8 Dickens's description of London

> ... a maze of close, narrow and muddy streets ... tottering housefronts, projecting over the pavement, dismantled walls that seem to totter as he passes, chimneys half crushed half hesitating to fall ... Crazy wooden galleries common to the backs of half-a-dozen houses, with holes from which to look upon the slime beneath; windows broken and patched, with poles thrust out, on which to dry the linen that is never there; rooms so small, so filthy and squalor which they shelter; wooden chambers thrusting themselves out above the mud, and threatening to fall in – as some have done; dirt-besmeared walls and decaying foundations; every repulsive lineament of poverty, every loathsome indication of filth, rot and garbage.

Figure 6.9 Stages in the growth of London

1851: London	1891: London	1921: London	1951: London
Population 2 651 000	Population 5 572 000	Population 7 397 000	Population 8 197 000

1 CONCENTRIC ZONE MODEL (BURGESS, 1925)

- model based on Chicago in the 1920s
- the city is gowing spacially due to immigration and natural increase
- the area around the CBD has the lowest status and highest density housing
- residents move outwards with increasing social class and their homes are taken by new migrants

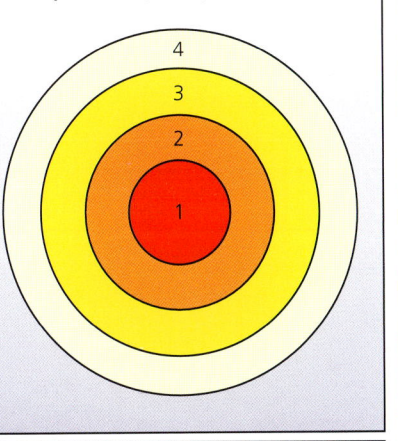

Key for diagrams 1 and 2
1 CBD (central business district)
2 Zone in transition light manufacturing
3 Low-class residential
4 Medium-class residential
5 High-class residential
6 Outlying business district

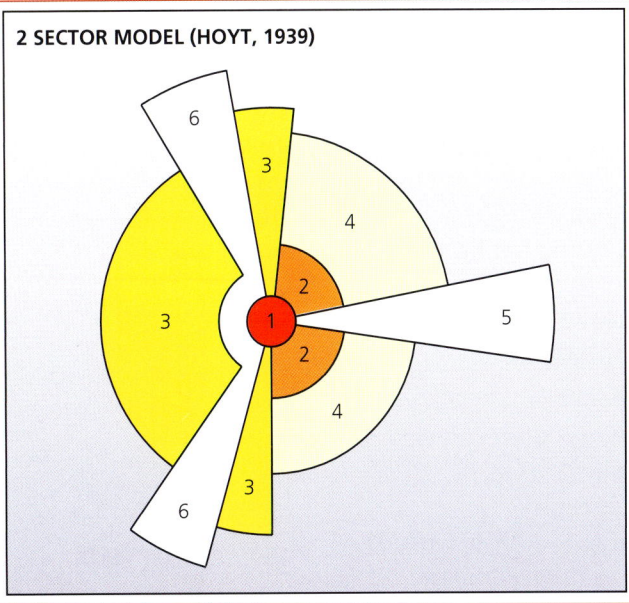

2 SECTOR MODEL (HOYT, 1939)

Figure 6.10 Simple models of urban areas

In general the quality of houses in the suburbs improves towards the edge of town, hence most cities share a basic plan or form which includes:

- a central business district – the commercial core of the city containing most of the shops and offices;
- a zone or ring of industrial warehousing and storage facilities and some poorer quality housing, some of which can be very old Victorian housing. This area is usually called the inner city;
- suburban developments which improve in quality away from the city centre.

Two typical models are shown in **Figure 6.10** – one uses concentric rings around the CBD, the other sectors or wedges. Although neither of these is a perfect match for any town, they do provide some useful general points.

Figure 6.11 Nineteenth century housing in central London

Figure 6.12 Suburban housing, Mitcham in Surrey

Questions

8. Briefly explain why both transport developments and housing subsidies were needed for urbanisation.
9. **Figure 6.11** shows a former inner city area near central London. Describe the type of housing as shown in the diagram. State as many differences as you can between **Figure 6.11** and **Figure 6.12**. Use terms such as tenement, detached, spacious, high density and low density. (Use a dictionary to find out the meaning of any terms you do not understand.)
10. Make a copy of the shape of London or else another urban area you have studied. On your map mark the CBD, an area of high class housing, an area of manufacturing and warehousing, the main transport routes, high density terraced housing and low density suburban housing.

THE GROWTH OF MEXICO CITY

Mexico City is Mexico's largest city **(Figure 6.13)**. It has a population of about eighteen million people, whereas Mexico's second largest city has only a population of two million people. Population growth in Mexico City has been very rapid **(Figure 6.14)**. In 1900 it was only about 370,000 but by 1930 it had grown to one million. Such rapid growth causes a number of problems including:

- housing shortages;
- poor quality housing;
- poor standards of living for many people;
- overcrowding of people in industries leads to pollution.

People migrate to Mexico City for a number of reasons but the main one is the search for employment. Many of the rural areas in Mexico are very poor and there are few jobs available so young people move to Mexico City for casual work. Because the migrants are young (usually under thirty years) the city's birth rate is high and the death rate is low. Such population growth causes great problems for the city planners: to provide sufficient housing, employment, schools, water and sanitation.

Unemployment is wide-spread and for those with jobs many are low paid, unskilled, informal jobs such as cleaning, selling food and shoe shining. The very poor make ends meet by scavenging through rubbish heaps – this is very dangerous, especially as hazardous waste is dumped illegally by many firms. Moreover Mexico City is experiencing water shortages. The **aquifer** (water bearing rock) beneath Mexico City is sinking. In addition hazardous waste is seeping into the aquifer and contaminating it. As Mexico City uses up more and more water there is less water for irrigation in surrounding areas and farming suffers.

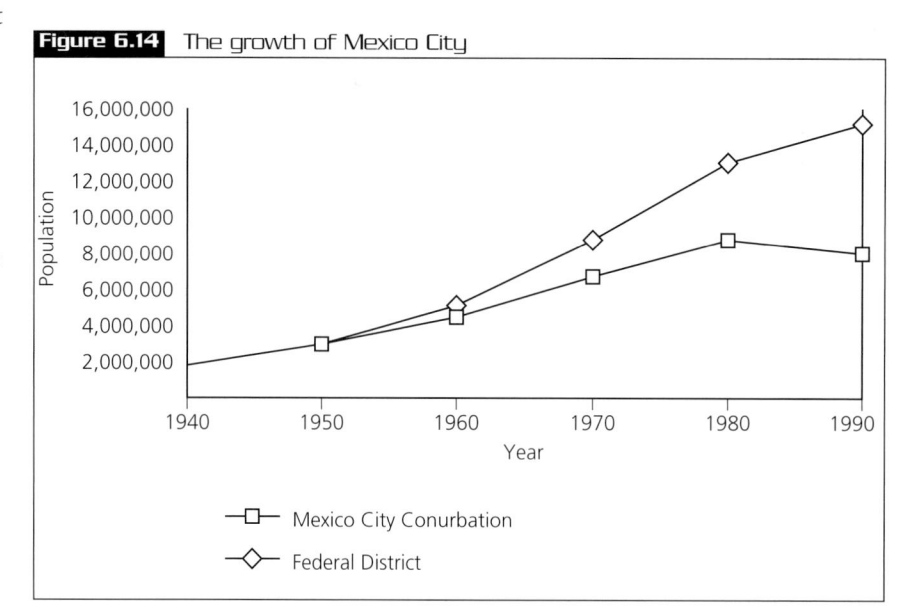

Figure 6.13 Slum housing in Mexico City

Figure 6.14 The growth of Mexico City

A model of Mexico City's land use shows that the historic core and modern CBD are surrounded by poor housing **(Figure 6.15)**. In addition there are wedges or spines of rich and poor, however the pattern is not as clear as the model shown in **Figure 6.16**, mainly because of the large size of Mexico City.

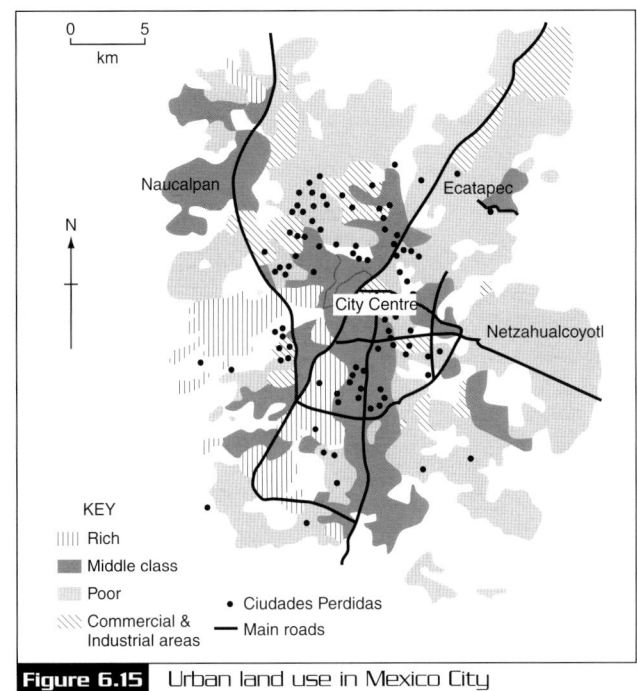

Figure 6.15 Urban land use in Mexico City

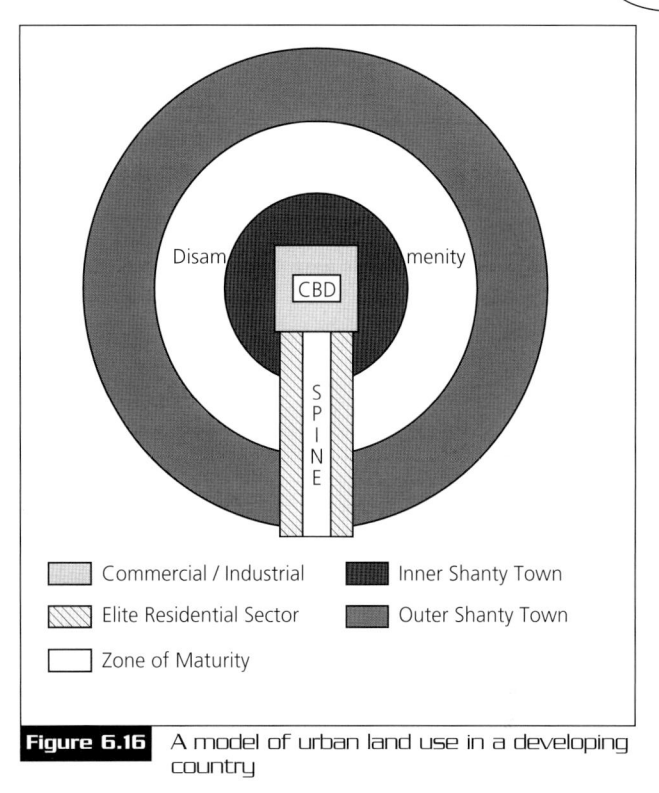

Figure 6.16 A model of urban land use in a developing country

Question

11 Using the data in **Figure 6.17** show how the proportion of population living in Mexico's urban and rural areas has changed over time.

Figure 6.17 Urbanisation in Mexico

Year	Percentage Urban	Percentage Rural
1900	28.3	71.7
1910	28.7	71.3
1921	31.2	68.8
1930	33.5	66.5
1940	35.0	65.0
1950	42.6	57.4
1960	50.7	49.3
1970	58.7	41.3
1980	66.3	33.7
1990	71.3	28.7

Question

12a Compare the distribution of households with low incomes to those with high incomes.

b In which areas are households with the fewest (i) toilets? (ii) use of firewood/coal?

Figure 6.18 Distribution of low income households in Mexico City and the distribution of houses without toilet facilities

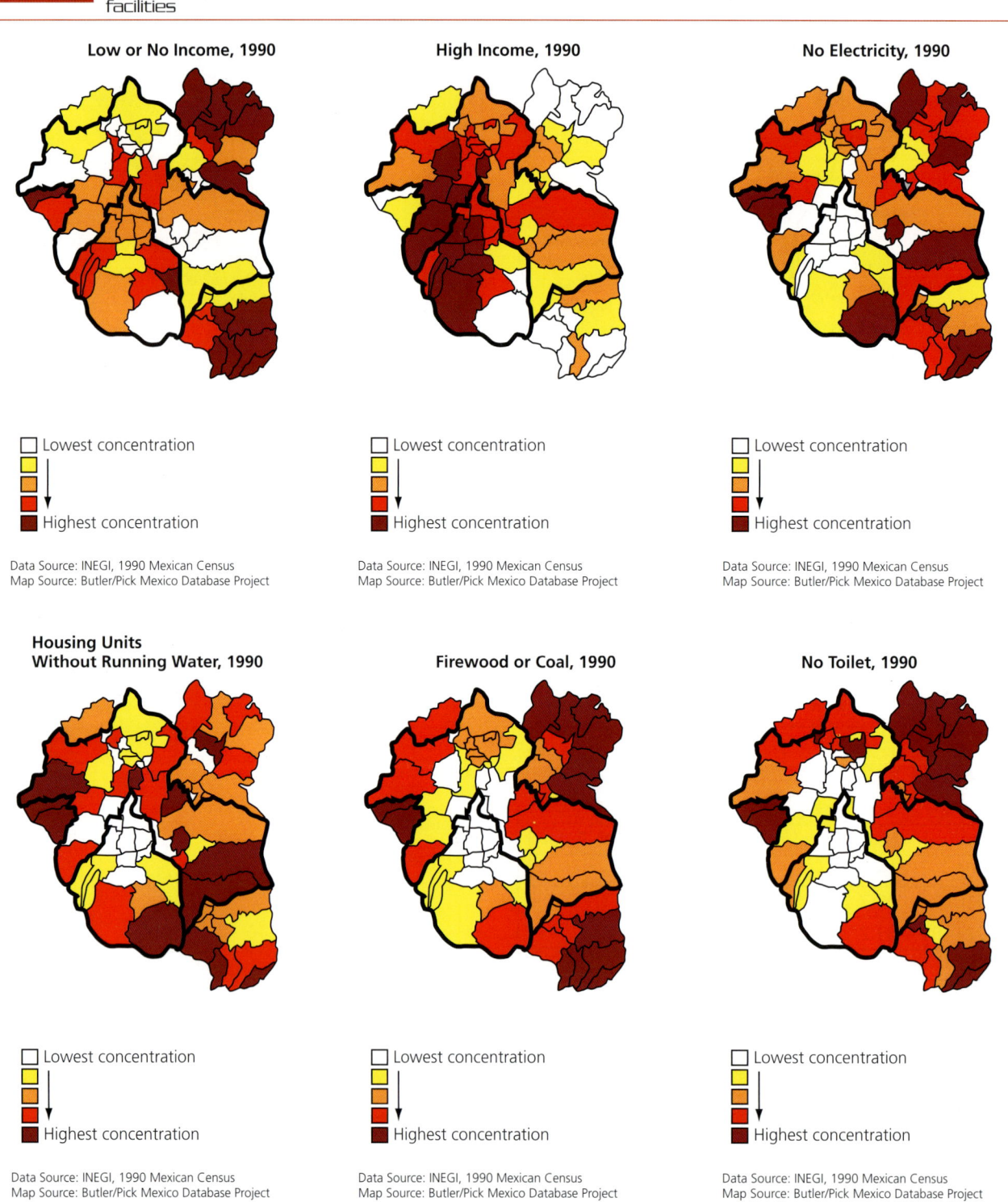

Low or No Income, 1990

☐ Lowest concentration
☐
☐ ↓
☐
■ Highest concentration

Data Source: INEGI, 1990 Mexican Census
Map Source: Butler/Pick Mexico Database Project

High Income, 1990

☐ Lowest concentration
☐
☐ ↓
☐
■ Highest concentration

Data Source: INEGI, 1990 Mexican Census
Map Source: Butler/Pick Mexico Database Project

No Electricity, 1990

☐ Lowest concentration
☐
☐ ↓
☐
■ Highest concentration

Data Source: INEGI, 1990 Mexican Census
Map Source: Butler/Pick Mexico Database Project

Housing Units Without Running Water, 1990

☐ Lowest concentration
☐
☐ ↓
☐
■ Highest concentration

Data Source: INEGI, 1990 Mexican Census
Map Source: Butler/Pick Mexico Database Project

Firewood or Coal, 1990

☐ Lowest concentration
☐
☐ ↓
☐
■ Highest concentration

Data Source: INEGI, 1990 Mexican Census
Map Source: Butler/Pick Mexico Database Project

No Toilet, 1990

☐ Lowest concentration
☐
☐ ↓
☐
■ Highest concentration

Data Source: INEGI, 1990 Mexican Census
Map Source: Butler/Pick Mexico Database Project

Managing urban problems

Given the large number of people, industries, shops, offices, cars, buses and so on that are found in urban areas it is important to manage them. Moreover as urban areas change it is vital that problems are tackled and that solutions can be found. Urban problems are very varied and include:

- suburbanisation covering large areas of valuable farmland (urban sprawl);
- congestion in city centres;
- air pollution in city centres;
- declining inner city areas due to the decline of the manufacturing industry;
- ageing houses lacking in modern facilities;
- overcrowding in large urban areas leading to very high land prices;
- shortgages of land;
- the decline of city centres as out of town retailing and greenfield sites prove more attractive.

To manage these problems planners have used a variety of techniques. **Green belts** have been established to prevent urban sprawl, preserve agricultural land and promote recreation. To reduce overcrowding in the cities **new towns**, **expanded towns** and **overspill towns** have been developed to house people and to provide jobs for them (a new town is a town or city that has been developed from a very small village, whereas an expanded town is one that was already quite large and where growth has been directed. An overspill town by contrast, is one close to a large urban area that gains from commuting).

There are many conflicts in city centres due to the interests of businesses, shoppers, tourists, retailers, residents, universities, students, transport companies and the emergency services. Most city centres now have a **city centre manager** whose job is to improve the city centre environment, reduce crime, attract investment, increase accessibility and advertise the city centre. The results have been very successful – in Oxford, for example, crime in the city centre is down, there is a new traffic scheme, investment is increasing and the environment has been approved, mostly as a result of the pedestrianisation of main roads. A number of town centres in Britain have been losing customers and businesses to out of town areas, this is because city centres are crowded, the land is expensive and parking is restricted. By contrast **greenfield** sites on the edge of town have plenty of space, the cost of land is lower and parking is free and the area is often very accessible, especially due to dual carriageways.

In other parts of the city the problems are more difficult – **inner city areas** have lost large numbers of jobs, mostly in manufacturing, and the areas have declined. Investment in transport and infrastructure can regenerate areas such as London Docklands, but it is very expensive. Some inner city areas have been redeveloped and houses have been cleared to make way for car parks, administrative offices, colleges. The people who used to live there have been moved to out of town estates. Such estates have not always been very successful, especially if there are few jobs available.

On a small scale some urban areas have been upgraded by a process called **gentrification**. Inner city properties may be attractive to young professional people – when they move into an area they may improve the condition of their house, for example by putting in double glazed windows, or new central heating or a new roof; this increases the value of the property. If a large number of young professionals (sometimes called **Yuppies** – young upwardly mobile professionals or **Dinkies** – double income no kids) move into an area, services may be attracted, such as wine bars, restaurants and food stores – this may help to revitalise part of the inner city.

Questions

13 How do the urban problems in the city centre differ from those in the inner city?

14 a For an urban area you have studied, identify the urban problems that exist?

b In what ways have planners tried to manage these problems?

Economic activities

7

Economic activities are often defined as being either primary, secondary, tertiary or quaternary. **Primary industries** include farming, fishing, forestry, mining and quarrying. They extract raw materials from the ground. By contrast **secondary industries** or **manufacturing industries** change the raw materials into finished or semi-finished products. For example, the conversion of coal and iron ore into iron and steel. **Tertiary industries** are also called services. These are very varied and include transport, retailing, banking, medical services, and education services. Finally, **quaternary industries** refer to **research and development**. These are brain intensive industries which provide information and expertise.

A triangular graph shows the employment characteristics of a country. The three sides are used to show employment in primary, secondary and tertiary industries **(Figure 7.1)**. As the quaternary sector employs so few people it is not shown on the triangular graph.

In most countries primary industries have declined, whereas tertiary industries have increased steadily over time. By contrast, manufacturing industries increased for a while and then decreased **(Figure 7.2)**.

Figure 7.1 Triangular graph

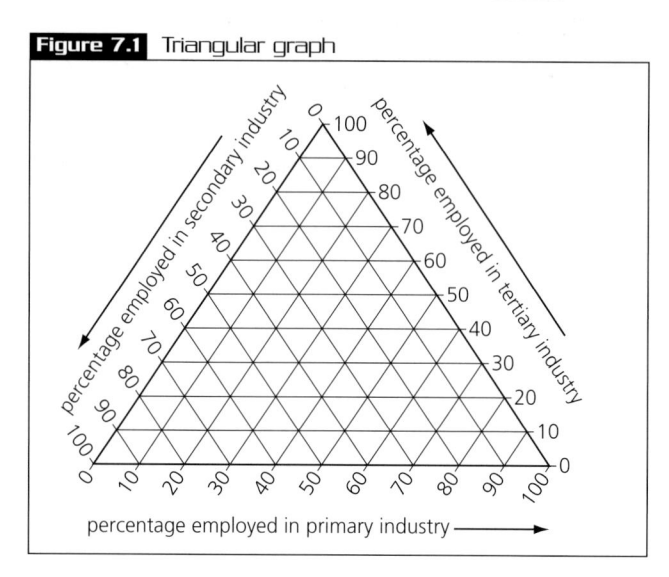

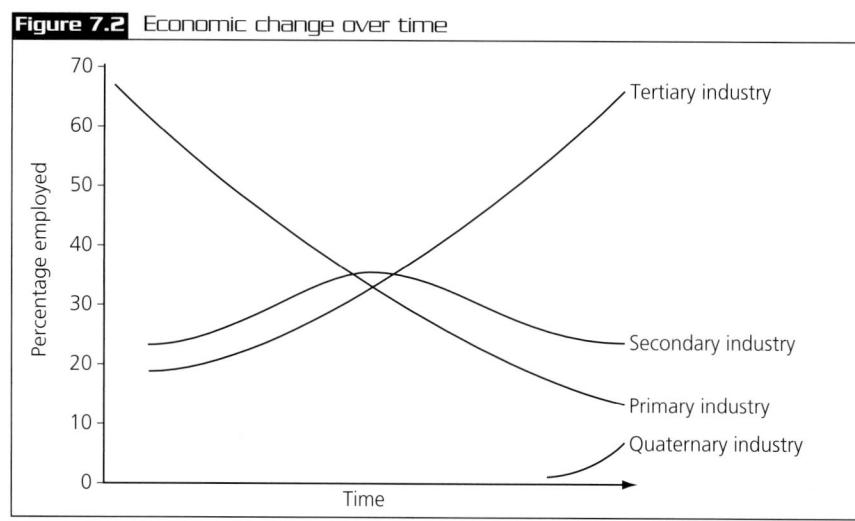

Figure 7.2 Economic change over time

Figure 7.3 Employment by economic sector

	Agriculture		Industry		Services	
	(1965)	(1990–92)	(1965)	(1990–92)	(1965)	(1990–92)
Singapore	6	0	27	35	67	65
Mexico	49	23	22	29	29	48
Brazil	49	25	20	25	31	47
China	81	73	8	14	11	13
Egypt	55	42	15	21	30	37
India	73	62	12	11	15	27
Korea	55	17	15	36	30	47
UK	—	3	—	28	—	70
USA	—	3	—	25	—	72
Germany	—	3	—	39	—	58

Questions

1 a Make a copy of the triangular graph. Plot the points for the countries listed in **Figure 7.3**. Some of them have already been drawn for you. For those countries which have two sets of data, join the two points with a line, as indicated.

b Describe the main results that you have drawn. What conclusions can you make about the economic structure of the countries listed?

Farming

KEY TERMS AND DEFINITIONS

Intensive – where there are large inputs of labour or investment per unit area.

Extensive – where there are low inputs of money or labour or investment per unit area.

Commercial Farming – where farmers farm to sell the produce and make a profit.

Subsistence Farming – where farmers grow food for their own needs.

Pastoral Farming – the rearing of animals.

Arable Farming – the growing of crops.

Mixed Farming – a mixture of arable and pastoral.

Figure 7.4 Dairy farming in Britain is becoming less profitable for most farmers

Figure 7.5 Factors affecting agriculture

Physical		
Climate	Precipitation – amount – intensity	If there is too much rain arable crops cannot be grown
	Temperature – growing season (> 6°C) – ground frozen (0°C)	When the ground is frozen seeds cannot germinate
Soil	Fertility Depth	On thin soils only grass will grow
Pests	locusts, disease etc.	
Slope	Gradient	On steep slopes it is difficult to use machinery
Relief	Altitude	On high ground it is too cold for farming
Human		
Political	Land ownership Government policies War	People who own their land have more control over what they do Governments create high levels of demand for certain foods, such as cereals in the EU
Economic	Farm size – field size and shape Demand for goods Technology – HYVs, fertilisers, irrigation Infrastructure – roads, communications, Advertising	The bigger the farm the more likely it is to use machinery Machinery is best suited to regular, square fields

FARMING TYPES IN BRITAIN

In Britain there is a very clear cut pattern to farming **(Figure 7.6)**. Arable farming tends to occur in the east of the country, pastoral farming is more likely in the west of the country, while market gardening is found close to large urban areas.

- **Sheep farming in the Lake District** – many physical factors influence this type of farming: **Low summer temperatures** and **cold winter temperatures** prevent the growing of arable crops. The **high rainfall** is too great for most arable crops and also leaches the soil making it **infertile**. **Hilly, rocky, stony ground** is difficult for machinery. As well as the physical factors there are human factors too – the area is quite **remote** from the main markets, there is **falling demand** for red meat and wool products and young people are leaving remote rural areas. This is because the returns from farming are generally very poor.

- Arable farming in East Anglia – the physical environment in East Anglia is very different from that of the Lake District. Summers are very **warm**, often over 20°C which allow the groups to ripen. The **rainfall** is much lower and much of it occurs in spring and summer when the plants are growing. The soils are deep, thick, boulder clays which, when drained, are very **fertile**. The land is also very **flat** which makes the use of machinery quite easy. In addition human factors favour arable farming; there is support from the EU for arable farmers, there is **increased demand** from consumers for cereal products and the area is close to ports for export of finished goods.

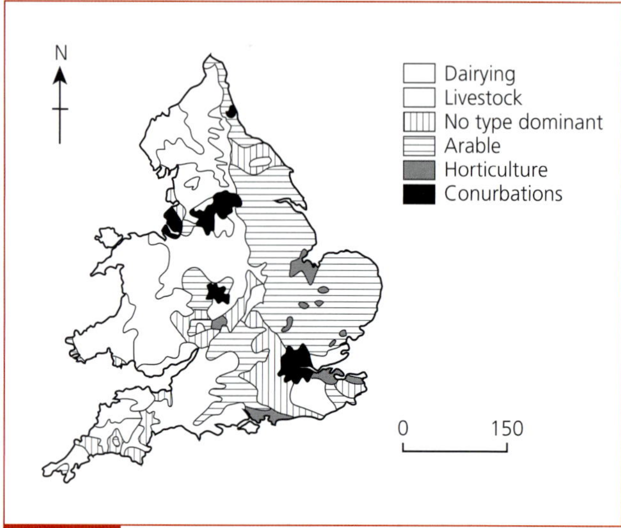

Figure 7.6 Farming in England and Wales

Market gardening is a form of highly intensive, highly specialised farming. Many of the crops are grown under **greenhouses** so that temperatures can be controlled. The physical environment is highly artificial but very favourable for the crops. Human factors are also important, as there is a high level of *demand* for these goods and in most urban areas there are large numbers of relatively well off people who are prepared to pay for them.

Figure 7.7 Farming types in Britain

UK Region	Agricultural land as a percentage of land	Arable land as a percentage of agricultural land
UK average	71.2	34.2
North	63.9	25.2
Yorkshire & Humberside	64.5	56.9
East Midlands	70.0	72.0
East Anglia	68.7	86.5
South East	51.1	67.2
South West	69.8	41.2
North West	57.2	30.8
Wales	77.9	12.8
Scotland	72.5	16.4
Northern Ireland	76.5	23.3

Questions

2. Make a copy of Figure 7.5. Where an explanation has **not** been provided suggest how and why the factor influences farming.

3. Study **Figure 7.7**. Which three areas of the UK have the highest amount of agricultural land?
   a. Which three areas of the UK have the highest amount of arable land?
   b. Using an atlas suggest reasons to explain the distribution of arable land – think about rainfall, summer temperatures, slope angle, length of growing season and soil type.

Industrial Change in Bradford

In the late nineteenth century and early twentieth century Bradford was one of the world's most important centres for textile manufacturing **(Figure 7.8)**. However, nowadays Bradford's importance as a textile centre is almost non-existent.

Bradford's first manufacturing revolution occurred in the nineteenth century based on textile and engineering industries, making Bradford the wool capital of the world. The reasons for its growth are varied: from the seventeenth century onwards the woollen and linen industry used local skills, local water power from upland streams and local coal, while soft water and high humidity aided the processes of dyeing and spinning. The transport network, the canal and later the railways, was very good, as was proximity to ports. This aided the import of raw cotton and the export of finished goods. In the nineteenth century there were over one hundred mills in the city and it was the fastest growing industrial city in Britain.

However, in the twentieth century the textile industry declined dramatically, for a number of reasons:

- The home market was very static and in some cases even declined **(Figure 7.9)**;
- there was increased competition from lower cost producers overseas;
- the industry was unable to respond quickly to changes in fashion;
- many of the factories were too small and inefficient, lacking flexibility and ability. Finally new products, such as synthetic fibres, led to a decline in the demand for textile products: the main cotton producers now include China, India, Pakistan and Korea.

The decline of textiles has had a heavy impact on Bradford. Bradford has long had high unemployment, urban decay and industrial dereliction. However in recent years there have been attempts to tackle these problems and the change has been spectacular. Many of the derelict mills have become the new locations for industrial growth in Bradford. Bradford has been described as 'Silicon Dale' and is one of Britain's top tourist destinations, attracting more visitors each year than Bournemouth **(Figure 7.10)**!

Figure 7.8 Bradford's textile industry in its heyday

Figure 7.9 Bradford's industry suffering terminal decline

Figure 7.10 The location of Bradford

Road distances (Miles) from Bradford					
Haworth	11	Birmingham	126	Liverpool	73
Ilkley	14	Cardiff	230	London	200
Saltaire	4.5	Edinburgh	214	Manchester	40
Keighley	10	Glasgow	208	Newcastle	103
Shipley	4	Hull	67		
Bingley	6	Leeds	11		

Bradford has been classified by the European Union (the EU) as a Declining Industrial Area and as such has been able to collect over £20 million in grants. Many of the abandoned warehouses in the inner city have been upgraded and redeveloped for industrial growth, for example the Merchant's House built in 1902 has been redeveloped to cater for small and medium sized firms.

TOURISM IN BRADFORD

In the early 18th Century the town of Bradford was still quite small. However, by 1851 its population had grown to over 100,000 people. Merchants from other parts of the country and Europe gradually settled in the area and their investment and wealth led to the construction of many fine buildings. The lavish properties in Little Germany are a relict of Bradford's rich industrial heritage.

Saltaire is a Victorian model industrial village built between 1851 and 1873 **(Figure 7.11)**. It was developed by the wool baron Sir Titus Salt. It is located about 8km from Bradford and was built to house the textile mill and work force. When first built the village included the Mill, a school, hospital and alms house, two churches, a Sunday school, bath and wash houses, a park, a railway station and a dining hall. Compared to conditions in the inner city slums this was a luxury – a revolution in housing and industrial practice. Now the Mill houses the largest collection of work by the Bradford born artist David Hockney. The Mill is now one of the most popular tourist attractions in Bradford.

Although Bradford has always been connected with wool and textiles it is now noted for its financial and commercial sectors as well as its tourism.

Bradford's tourism developed out of the economic collapse of the 1970s. The traditional industries lost over 60,000 jobs causing **unemployment** to increase to 16%. In addition Bradford was losing out to other West Yorkshire towns and cities on account of its poor image and high levels of **social deprivation**. In 1979 Bradford Metropolitan District Council created Britain's first **Economic Development Unit** (EDU) in order to create new jobs by encouraging new firms and expanding those that already existed. The EDU planned to develop Bradford as the first inland industrial district to become a successful tourist destination. In its favour Bradford had a good range of hotel accommodation which was well used during the week but not used at weekends. In addition there were a variety of attractions such as Haworth, home of the Bronte sisters, the Victorian industrial heritage including Saltaire and its presence close to the Yorkshire Dales **(Figure 7.12)**. In 1982 Bradford won an award for its outstanding contribution to the growth of UK tourism. By 1984 30,000 people a year were taking holidays in the district. Promoting its Asian heritage 'Flavours of Asia' was launched in 1987. The idea of sampling the rich and exotic culture of the Indian sub-continent without leaving Britain proved very attractive and gave a major boost to the Asian business sector. Almost 20% of Asian businesses are in the food sector. Many developed simple street cafes catering for the mill workers. After the 'Flavours of Asia' campaign eighteen new restaurants opened and existing curry houses reported an increase in business. Panorama Stores, one of the largest Asian food supermarkets in Europe, saw an increase of 20% in business with nearly one thousand new visitors each week.

Bradford now attracts six million national and international visitors each year and tourism accounts for some £64 million of the local economy.

Figure 7.11 The model village at Saltaire

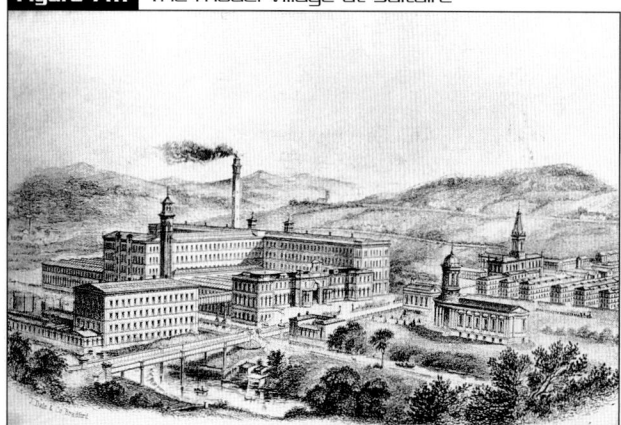

Figure 7.12 The Yorkshire Dales

Figure 7.13 Promoting Bradford

What has Bradford got to offer? Big city, big outdoors, big hearted – that's what visitors like best about Bradford. Yorkshire's friendliest city where you can go from city centre to wild unspoiled moors in less than fifteen minutes, following the footsteps of the Brontes, explore Emmerdale Farm country, taste the 'Flavours of Asia' and take home luxury fabrics at bargain prices.

The attractions include Saltaire village, Salt's Mill, The Bingley Five Rise Locks (an 18th Century lock which lifts the canal 60 ft), Keighley and Worth Valley railway, the setting of the Railway Children film, Haworth (home of the Brontes) which is particularly popular with Japanese tourists and Ilkley Moor which overlooks the Roman settlement and Victorian spa town.

Figure 7.14 The main attractions and visitor figures 1995

National Museum of Photography, Film and TV	737098
Bronte Parsonage Museum	101900
Haworth Village	over 1 million
The 1853 Gallery, Saltaire Village	500 000
Esholt (Emmerdale)	750 000
Ilkley – the Moor and Cow and Calf Rocks	555 000
Five Rise Locks	505 000
Bradford Cathedral	202 200

Figure 7.15 The origin of UK visitors to Bradford

Avon	7	Hampshire	26	Northern Ireland	5
Bedfordshire	8	Herefordshire	2	Northumberland	4
Berkshire	13	Hertfordshire	17	Nottinghamshire	27
Buckinghamshire	16	Humberside	26	Oxfordshire	11
Cambridge	16	Isle of Man	7	Scotland	59
Cheshire	21	Isle of Wight	1	Shropshire	9
Cleveland	9	Jersey	3	Somerset	8
Cornwall	6	Kent	34	Staffordshire	11
Cumbria	17	Lancashire	57	Suffolk	19
Devon	22	Leicestershire	14	Surrey	24
Derbyshire	10	Lincolnshire	19	Sussex	30
Dorset	13	London	33	Tyne and Wear	17
Durham	7	Merseyside	12	Warwickshire	8
Essex	22	Norfolk	25	West Midlands	15
Gloucestershire	13	Northamptonshire	9	Wiltshire	9
Guernsey	1			Worcestershire	4

Figure 7.16 The origin of overseas visitors

Australia	7
Austria	1
Algeria	2
Belgium	5
Canada	12
Denmark	1
France	17
Germany	23
Hungary	1
Iceland	1
Iran	1
Ireland	4
Israel	1
Italy	4
Japan	1
Malta	1
Netherlands	5
New Zealand	2
Poland	2
Portugal	1
Spain	7
Sweden	2
Switzerland	1
USA	1

Questions

4 Describe, and account for, the changes in Bradford's employment structure between the end of the nineteenth century and the end of the twentieth century.

5 On a map of the UK, plot the data given in **Figure 7.15**. Use density-shading (such as is used in **Figure 5.18**) to differentiate between counties which provide many tourists and those which do not. Comment on the results that you have drawn.

6 Use a flow diagram (with the width of the line proportional to the number of tourists) to show the origin of international visitors to Bradford. What conclusions can you draw from the pattern you have shown?

7

Services

The service industry includes a variety of types of jobs including banking, transport, tourism, health, education, retailing and entertainment. Some services are very poorly paid such as cleaning and catering whereas others are extremely well paid such as banking and accountancy. Some services are provided by the Government such as health care, while some services are paid for privately. Whereas jobs in manufacturing have traditionally been taken by men many jobs in the service industry are held by women. Some of these jobs are part time and poorly paid.

TYPES OF SERVICES

High order services include financial services, advertising, and market research – these are generally only found in the city centre and are concentrated in capital cities. Most of the highest order services in Britain, for instance, are found in London. Other services may be considered to be **lower order**, for example health care, retailing and education. Although retailing is found in most town centres and neighbourhood centres, educational services such as primary schools are generally found where the population is found, ie. in the suburbs. Post offices are also localised. Other services are found in special locations, notably tourism. Coastal areas, mountain resorts and scenic attractions have concentrations of jobs and facilities related to tourism – notably accommodation and catering.

Questions

7 Study **Figure 7.17** which shows the growth of services and the decline of manufacturing industry between 1970 and 1997.

a Which industries have declined most between 1970 and 1997?

b Which industries have increased the most between 1970 and 1997?

c Which parts of the service sector have shown the most growth between 1978 and 1998? Which, if any, sectors have declined?

d Which service sector is the only one to lose business since 1995? Suggest reasons why this sector may be at risk to changes in economic performance.

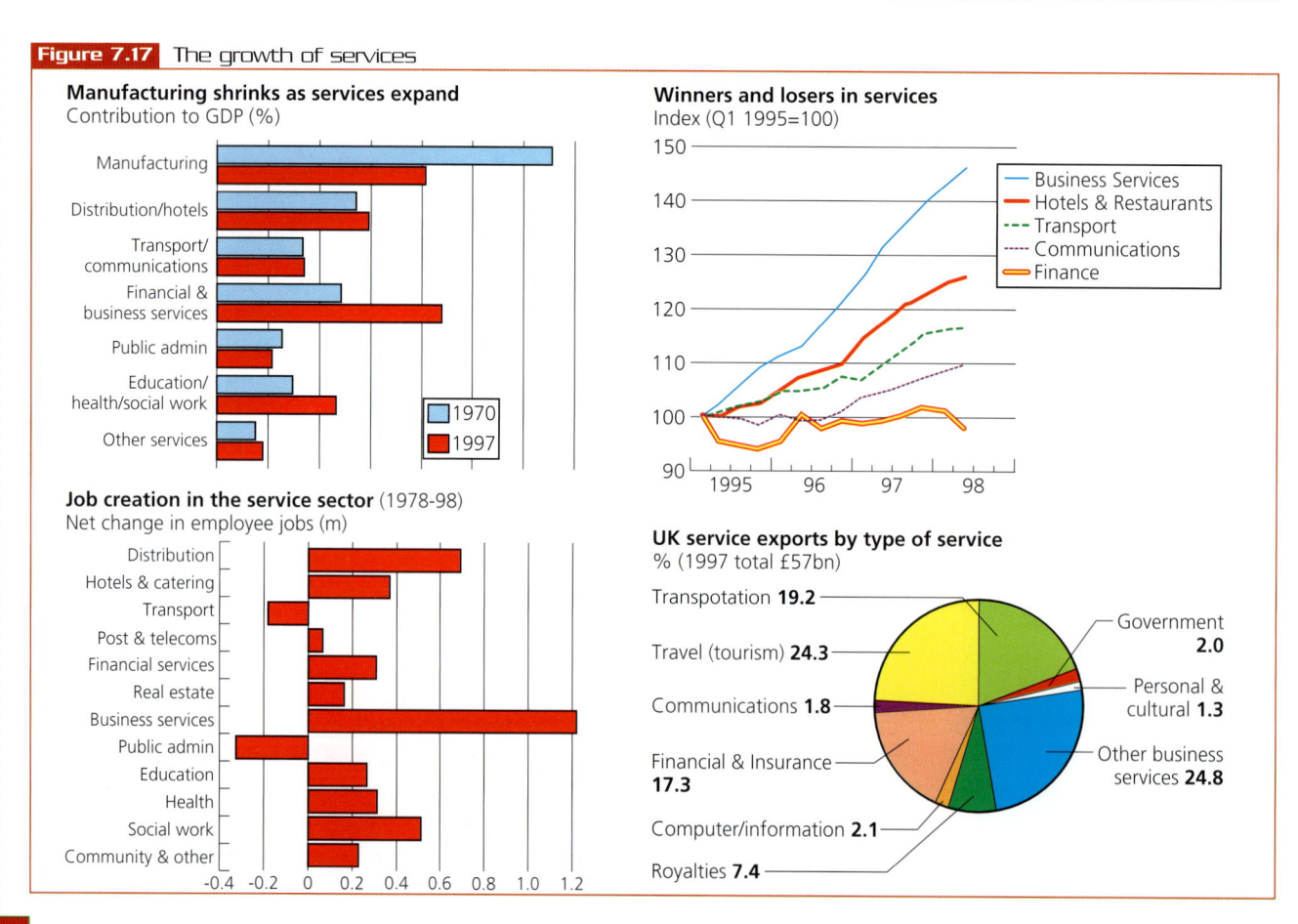

Figure 7.17 The growth of services

Manufacturing shrinks as services expand
Contribution to GDP (%)
(1970, 1997) – Manufacturing, Distribution/hotels, Transport/communications, Financial & business services, Public admin, Education/health/social work, Other services

Job creation in the service sector (1978-98)
Net change in employee jobs (m)
Distribution, Hotels & catering, Transport, Post & telecoms, Financial services, Real estate, Business services, Public admin, Education, Health, Social work, Community & other

Winners and losers in services
Index (Q1 1995=100)
Business Services, Hotels & Restaurants, Transport, Communications, Finance

UK service exports by type of service
% (1997 total £57bn)
- Transpotation 19.2
- Travel (tourism) 24.3
- Communications 1.8
- Financial & Insurance 17.3
- Computer/information 2.1
- Royalties 7.4
- Government 2.0
- Personal & cultural 1.3
- Other business services 24.8

THE LOCATION OF SERVICES IN A SMALL TOWN

In most small towns there is a clear separation of certain types of services. For example:

- financial services such as banks and solicitors are located close to the central business district because this is the most accessible area of a town or city;
- DIY and garden centres tend to be located on the outskirts of town where more land is available for large retail outlets and car parks – these stores are very accessible for people with cars;
- primary schools will be scattered around the urban area so that they are close to residential areas.

Figure 7.18 shows the distribution of services in a small town. For each of the services listed in column A suggest what type of service it is from the list in column B:

A	B
Banks	Welfare Service
Schools	Financial Service
Solicitors	Administrative Service
Estate Agents	(political service)
Town Councils	Recreational Service
Churches	Retail Service
Hospital	Educational Service
Health Centre	Religious Service

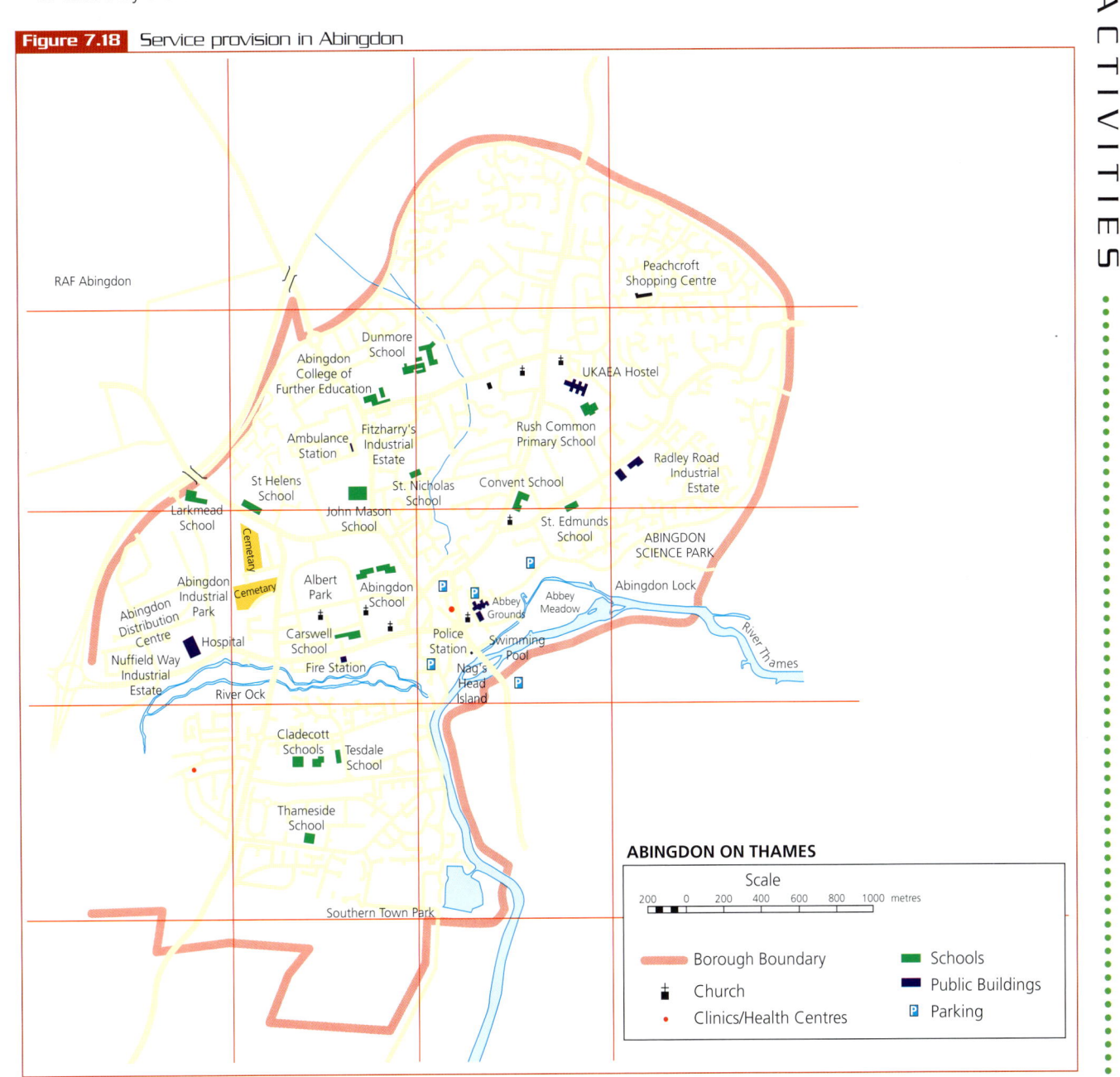

Figure 7.18 Service provision in Abingdon

ECONOMIC ACTIVITIES

89

RETAIL DEVELOPMENTS – THE CASE OF BLUEWATER

One of the latest out-of-town shopping centres to be built is the £1.2 billion Bluewater shopping and leisure centre at Dartford in Kent **(Figure 7.19)**. When it opened in 1999 it became the largest shopping centre in the UK, and indeed in Europe **(Figure 7.20)**. On a 110 ha site, it contains the largest winter garden built this century and the largest new park in Kent. It is also one of the last out-of-town centres to be built in Britain, following the government's decision to prevent further such developments.

Bluewater has about 10 million people living within an hour's drive. It is estimated that they spend some £5.5 billion annually. What makes Bluewater unusual, apart from its sheer scale, is the mix of retail outlets. As well as Marks and Spencer, John Lewis, House of Fraser and other High Street stores, it also contains specialty up-market shops. The centre has a range of restaurants from McDonalds to a five-star restaurant, and there are pubs with beer, TV and sport to attract reluctant male shoppers! The centre is open from 10 am to 9 pm with the restaurants open until 11 pm. It is possible to see a film in the evening and then dine in the restaurant afterwards.

The developers predicted that people would visit the centre on account of its architecture, its lakes, the gardens, its walks, as well as its shops **(Figure 7.21)**. The developers claim that Bluewater is not competing with town centres. Instead it is competing with the West End of London.

Figure 7.19 The location of Bluewater

Figure 7.20 Out of town retail centres in the UK

Name	Date of opening	Retail space sq m	Number of shops
Bluewater, Dartford	1999	155 669	320
MetroCentre, Gateshead	1986	144 928	323
Merry Hill, Dudley	1986	130 060	260
Lakeside, Thurrock	1990	121 000	309
Trafford Centre	1998	120 770	276
Meadow Hall, Sheffield	1990	106 125	285
Brent Cross, North London	1976	76 364	109
Cribbs Causeway, Bristol	1998	65 030	140
White Rose Centre, Leeds	1997	60 385	86

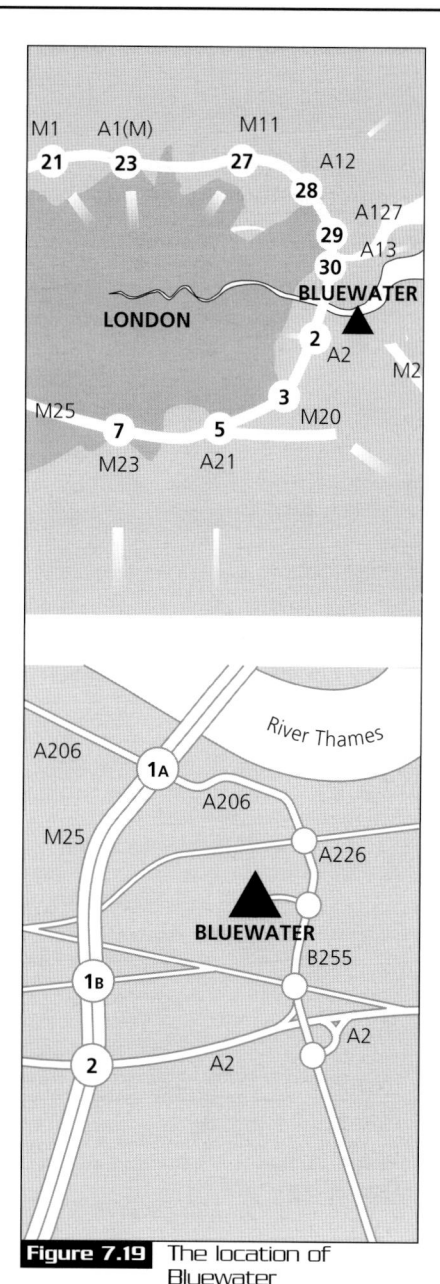

Figure 7.21 Bluewater

Figure 7.22 Recreational facilities at Bluewater

Figure 7.23 Guest services at Bluewater

Family and children
Baby care rooms
Baby changing facilities
Nappy vending
Bottle warming and mothers feeding area
Dining areas with high chairs and space for pushchairs
Creche facilities

Transport
Thirteen thousand free parking spaces
Extra width bays
Five taxi ranks
Bicycle parking
Over 60 buses per hour
Over 130 trains per day

Special Needs
Convenient parking spaces
Wheelchair accessibility
Shopmobility

Development

What is development?

The term 'development' is one that we are very familiar with but it has become difficult to pin down. In geography, development refers to a number of features such as population change, economic growth, increased use of resources, modernisation, increased use of technology and political freedom.

Many 'development reports' provide statistical 'evidence' of levels of development, such as as population growth, life expectancy, health, education, urbanisation, industrialisation and energy consumption **(Figure 8.1)**. Using these features, geographers and developers have produced maps which show levels of development in the world. In the 1950s every country was categorised as belonging to either the First, Second or Third Worlds:

Figure 8.1 Different types of poverty

- The **First World** contained Western Europe, North America, Australia, New Zealand and Japan;
- The **Second World** consisted of the state-controlled Communist countries such as the former-USSR;
- The **Third World** consisted of all the other less developed countries

In the 1960s and 1970s the terms **Less Developed Countries (LDCs)** and **Developed Countries (DCs)** were used to identify certain economic identities. However, this division was not very useful and in the early 1980s the **North-South** divide was identified by the Brandt Commission, an influential body of politicians who examined development issues in the **Developed World** (the **North**) and the **Less Developed World** (the **South**). However, many so-called LDCs were in fact quite advanced socially and politically, while there was much poverty in so-called developed countries **(Figure 8.2)**. In addition, the **oil rich countries** of the Middle East and the **Newly Industrialising Countries**, such as South Korea, did not fit into any category very well.

Countries are now classified as belonging to one of the following

More Economically Developed Countries (MEDC): such as the UK and the USA. These are the most 'developed' countries and have high standards of living.

Less Economically Developed Countries (LEDC): e.g. Namibia and India. These countries are at a lower stage of development and have a lower quality of life.

Centrally Planned Economies (CPEs): socialist countries (such as North Korea) strictly controlled by the government. Living standards are higher than in LEDCs although freedom of speech is limited.

Figure 8.2 A person sleeping rough in Oxford

Oil rich countries: Countries which are very rich in terms of **GNP (Gross National Product)** per head although it may not be distributed very evenly. Without oil many of these countries would be LEDCs (e.g. Saudi Arabia and Libya).

Newly Industrialising Countries (NICs): Countries which have experienced rapid industrial, social and economic growth since 1960 (e.g. South Korea and Taiwan).

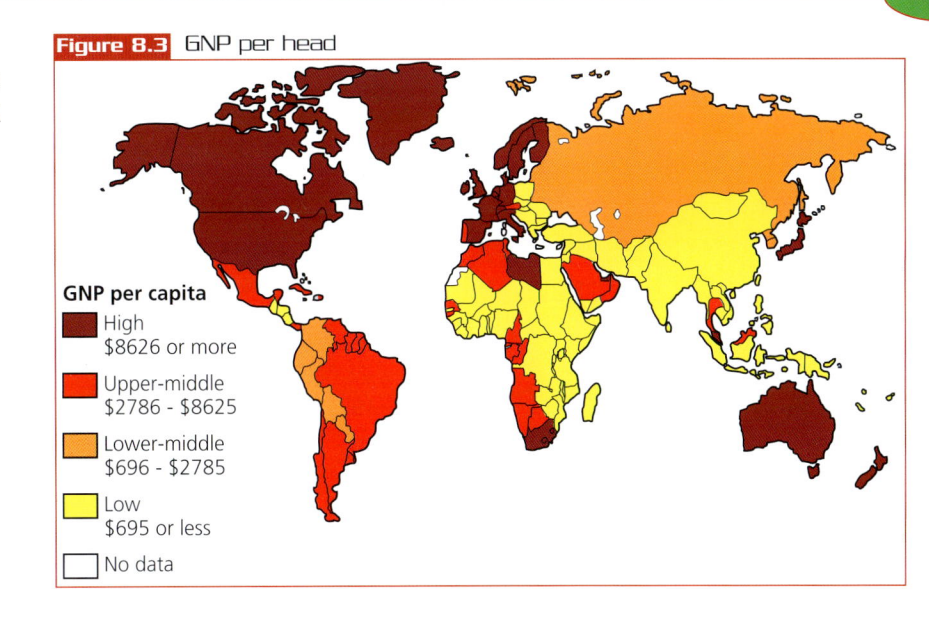

Figure 8.3 GNP per head

GNP per capita
- High $8626 or more
- Upper-middle $2786 - $8625
- Lower-middle $696 - $2785
- Low $695 or less
- No data

MEASURING DEVELOPMENT

The most common way of measuring development is by the use of GNP/head **(Figure 8.3)**. GNP/head is found by dividing a country's wealth by its population. The world map of GNP/head clearly shows that the countries of Western Europe, Japan, North America and Australia have a much higher value than the LEDCs such as India, Bangladesh, Nigeria and Zimbabwe. In fact, some countries including Rwanda, Burundi, Ethiopia, Tanzania and Mozambique even have a GNP/head of less than $200. However, average GNP/head has its shortcomings. It hides regional variations and fails to take into account local costs of living.

Since 1980 the UN has used the **Human Development Index (HDI)** to measure levels of development **(Figure 8.4)**. This, they believe, is a more reliable and accurate measure of development as it includes three indices of well-being:

- life expectancy;
- literacy and schooling;
- GNP (related to local purchasing power).

According to the 1999 figures Canada has the highest HDI, with a value of 0.932 (1.0 is the maximum value) closely followed by Switzerland. MEDCs dominate the higher levels of the HDI while LEDCs such as Afghanistan, Burkina Faso, and Sierra Leone, are at the bottom. As with GNP/head national HDIs can conceal widespread inequalities.

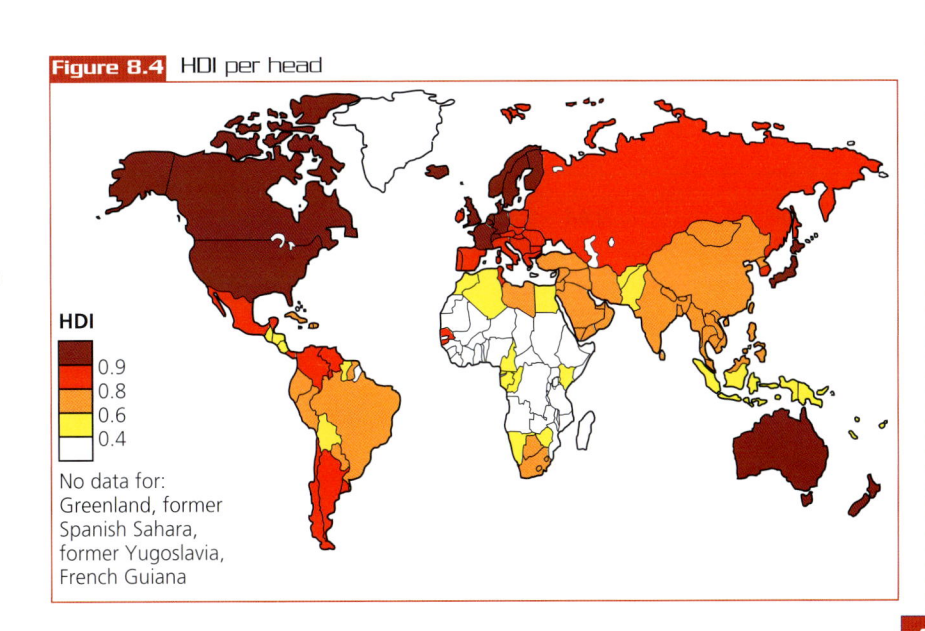

Figure 8.4 HDI per head

HDI
- 0.9
- 0.8
- 0.6
- 0.4

No data for: Greenland, former Spanish Sahara, former Yugoslavia, French Guiana

Figure 8.5 Selected statistics

	Brazil	Japan	South Africa	UK	USA
Population (m)	159.1	125.1	44.0	58.3	263.6
Area (000 km sq)	8,512	378	1221	244	9809
Population density	19/km sq	332/km sq	36/km sq	241/km sq	28/km sq
Population growth	2.1 p.a.	0.3% p.a.	3% p.a.	0.2% p.a.	1.1% p.a.
Birth rate (per 1000)	26	12	31	14	14
Death rate (per 1000)	8	8	9	12	9
Infant mortality rate (per 1000 live births)	57	5	62	8	8
Urban population (%)	76	77	50	89	76
Fertility rate (no. of children per woman)	3	2	4	2	2
Age structure					
0–14	35	18	37	19	21
15–59	58	64	57	61	62
≥ 60	7	17	6	21	17
Land use (%)					
Arable	7	11	10	27	19
Grass	22	2	67	46	25
Forest	58	67	4	10	30
Employment					
Agriculture	25	7	13	2	3
Industry	25	34	25	28	25
Services	50	59	62	70	72
Average income (GNP) ($US)	2920	31 450	2900	17 970	24 750
Energy use (tonnes/person/year)	0.44	4.74	2.49	5.4	10.74
Literacy (%)	81	99	81	99	99
Spending on education (as % of GNP)	3.7	5.0	3.8	5.3	7.0
Spending on military (as % of GNP)	1.2	1.0	3.0	4.0	5.3
Aid per person (US$)	1.2 received	90 given	4.9 received	50 given	38 given

(Source: Nagle, G., 1998, *South Africa*, Heinemann, p.60)

Questions

Study **Figure 8.5** which shows selected data on five countries.

1. Which country has
   a. the highest life expectancy
   b. the highest income levels
   c. the highest energy consumption?
2. a. Which country has the highest
      a. birth rate,
      b. death rate,
      c. infant mortality rate?
   b. Which of these statistics do you find most surprising? Why do you find it surprising? How do you explain this result?
   c. Which of the statistics in Figure 8.5 is **not** a measure of development. Give reasons for your answer.

Figure 8.6 Scatter graph

Rates per thousand / I.M.R. / G.N.P. ($)
- Burkina Faso
- Rwanda
- Egypt
- Peru
- Mexico
- Canada

Questions

3 A scatter graph is a type of graph which shows whether two pieces of data are related to each other or not. **Figure 8.6** is a scatter graph which shows the relationship between GNP and IMR. A number of countries have already been plotted.

  a Complete the graph by adding the data from Figure 8.5. Label the points clearly. Draw a line of best fit to pass as closely as possible to the points and show the main trend of the graph. (The line of best fit can be curved.)

  b Describe the graph that you have drawn. (A good description will use data – i.e. names and numbers – from the graph.) How do you explain this pattern?

Figure 8.7 Principles of sustainable development

- Respect and care for the community of life
- Improve the quality of human life
- Conserve the earth's vitality and diversity
- Minimise the depletion of non-renewable resources
- Keep within the earth's carrying capacity
- Change personal attitudes and practices
- Enable communities to care for their own environments
- Provide a national framework for integrating development and conservation
- Create a global alliance

(Source: Nagle, G., 1998, *Geography through Diagrams*, Oxford)

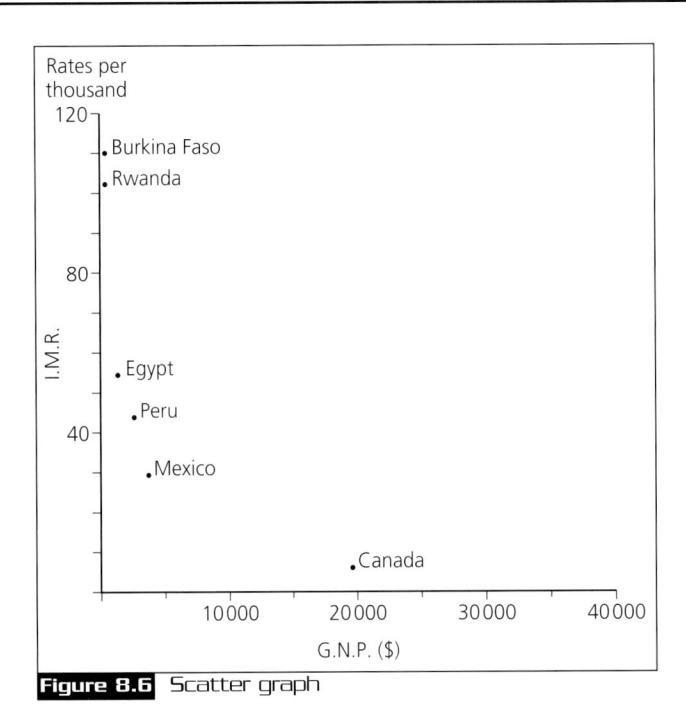

As a result of the Earth Summit national governments are obliged to formulate national plans or strategies for sustainable development – *Agenda 21*. It is **people** who do development, not governments, and therefore sustainable development is a local activity. Moreover, all people, however poor, however constrained, have some ability, of changing what they do, in small ways. Managing and preserving the environment has a number of advantages.

Local authorities are beginning to translate the global sustainability agenda – *Agenda 21* – into local action. Just as global sustainability cannot exist without national sustainable policies, national *Agenda 21* is incomplete without local *Agenda 21*.

Questions

4 Read the extract on Sustainable development **(Figure 8.7)** and answer the following questions:

  a What is sustainable development?

  b In what ways is it possible to use resources now but preserve them for the use of future generations?

5 In what ways does your school follow practices which could be said to be forms of sustainable development (energy conservation, recycling, renewable forms of energy, low flush toilets). In what ways could your school become more environmentally responsible?

Figure 8.9 Principles of sustainable development

Types of development

TOP-DOWN DEVELOPMENT

- This is usually large-scale.
- Carried out by governments, international organisations and 'experts'.
- It is done by people from outside the area.
- It is imposed upon the area or people by outside organisations.
- It is often well funded and can respond quickly to disasters.
- The local people are not involved in the decision making process.
- Emergency relief can also be considered top down.

BOTTOM-UP DEVELOPMENT

- This is small-scale.
- It involves local communities and local people.
- It is labour intensive.
- There is usually limited funding available.
- The local people are involved in the decision making process.
- It is run by the locals for the locals.
- Common projects include building earthen dams, creating cottage industries.

APPROPRIATE DEVELOPMENT

- Development which is culturally acceptable, technologically understandable and economically affordable.
- It is for the community, by the community with the community's own resources.
- It is a type of bottom-up or sustainable form of development.

SUSTAINABLE DEVELOPMENT

- This is a development which safeguards natural resources for future generations.
- It aims at increasing standards of living without destroying the environment.
- It aims to satisfy basic needs such as food supply and water rather than large-scale developments which may be inappropriate.
- It reduces waste.
- It increases efficiency and recycling.

NON-GOVERNMENT ORGANISATIONS

- They are mostly charities.
- They are not allied to any political party.
- NGOs normally work with local communities and small groups.
- They also help with emergency relief (short-term disaster relief).
- These include Oxfam, Save the Children, Cafod.

MULTI-PURPOSE SCHEMES

- These have a number of aims.
- A water scheme might include a mixture of water supply, flood relief, HEP, tourism, navigation, industrial development.

(Source: Nagle, G. 1998, Geography Through Diagrams, OUP)

Figure 8.8 Japanese fish market

Trade

Trade is the **import** (buying) and **export** (selling) of goods such as food, fuel, manufactured goods, raw materials, finance, and technology. The **balance of trade** is the difference in money terms between imports and exports. A **positive balance of trade** means that exports > imports while a **negative balance of trade** means that imports cost more than exports.

MEDCs and LEDCs have different export and import patterns. MEDCs mostly export machinery, transport equipment, chemicals, and services. Their range of imports is similar. By contrast, LEDCs have a much smaller range of exports – these are mostly agricultural products and raw materials. Their range of imports is similar to MEDCs but is likely to be cheaper and less sophisticated.

The pattern of **international trade** is very uneven:

- MEDCs account for the largest amount of world trade;
- LEDCs account for a decreasing amount of world trade;
- Socialist countries account for an increasing amount of world trade.

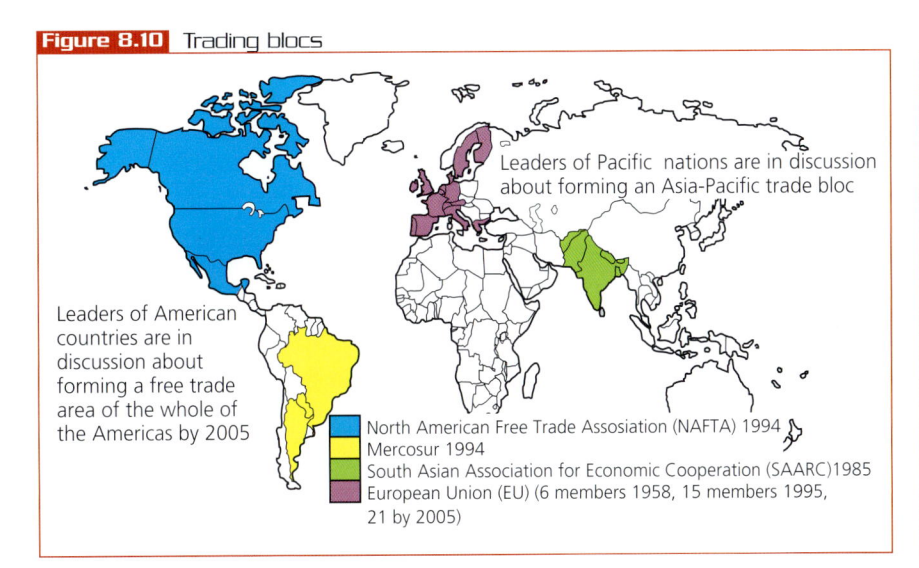

Figure 8.10 Trading blocs

Leaders of American countries are in discussion about forming a free trade area of the whole of the Americas by 2005

Leaders of Pacific nations are in discussion about forming an Asia-Pacific trade bloc

- North American Free Trade Assosiation (NAFTA) 1994
- Mercosur 1994
- South Asian Association for Economic Cooperation (SAARC) 1985
- European Union (EU) (6 members 1958, 15 members 1995, 21 by 2005)

Questions

6 Describe the main type of goods that
  a developed countries **export**
  b less developed countries export.

7 What are the main types of goods that
  a developed countries **import**
  b less developed countries import.

8 What are the geographical implications of the patterns you have described (think about poverty, debt and dependence for example).

TRADING BLOCS

A trading bloc is a group of countries which protect their industries and markets. They allow free trade within the trading bloc, and they place restrictions on the amount of imports from other countries. For members of the trading bloc there are two main advantages:

1 They have access to a large market, in the case of the European Union (EU) 370 million people;
2 They protect industries against foreign competitors.

Figure 8.11 Cargoes awaiting loading in Japan

Aid

Aid is any help or assistance given to improve the quality of life of the receiver. It includes money, equipment, goods, staff, and services. Most aid is from MEDCs to LEDCs but there is aid to the poorer regions in EMDCs. For example, Northern Ireland and Scotland receive much **regional aid** from the EU, and parts of Croatia and Bosnia receive aid from the United Nations.

Aid to LEDCs is often divided into:
- **short-term** aid or **emergency relief**;
- **long-term** aid.

There are three main forms of aid:

1 **Bilateral** aid – when one country gives to another country. Often the MEDC uses it to its own advantage, so that it can dictate the conditions of aid. There are political ties between the countries.

2 **Multilateral** – when more than one country gives aid to a number of countries. The amount of aid to each country may be quite low, and the interest rates are often very high.

3 **Charities** – such as Cafod, Save the Children and Oxfam. The monies involved are small by comparison to bilateral and multilateral aid but there are no political ties. Charities work independently from governments and they are called **non-government organisations**.

The amount of aid given varies between countries. The United Nations suggest that most countries donate up to 1% of GNP. However, only Norway and Sweden reach this target. The largest donors are the USA, France, Germany and the UK. The UK donates nearly £2 billion to over 150 countries.

Aid money is spent on a number of schemes such as:
- health care;
- education;
- water and sanitation;
- agricultural development.

What's wrong with aid

- small print
- political ties
- unsuitable aid
- inappropriate projects
- it creates debt
- interest payments are high
- it creates dependency
- it can go to the wrong people
- it undermines local producers

When aid is effective:	When aid is ineffective:
- It provides humanitarian relief. - It provides external resources for investment and finances projects that could not be undertaken with commercial capital. - Project assistance helps expand much needed infrastructure. - Aid contributes to personnel training and builds technical expertise. - Aid can support better economic and social policies.	- Aid might allow countries to postpone improving economic management and mobilisation of domestic resources. - Aid can replace domestic saving, direct foreign investment and commercial capital as the main sources of investment and technology development. - The provision of aid might promote dependency rather than self-reliance. - Some countries have allowed food aid to depress agricultural prices, resulting in greater poverty in rural areas and a dependency on food imports. It has also increased the risk of famine in the future. - Aid is sometimes turned on and off in response to the political and strategic agenda of the donor country, making funds unpredictable, which can result in interruptions in development programmes. - The provision of aid might result in the transfer of inappropriate technologies or the funding of environmentally unsound projects. - Emergency aid does not solve the long-term economic development problems of a country. - Too much aid is tied to the purchase of goods and services from the donor country, which might not be the best or the most economical. - A lot of aid does not reach those who need it, that is, the poorest people in the poorest countries

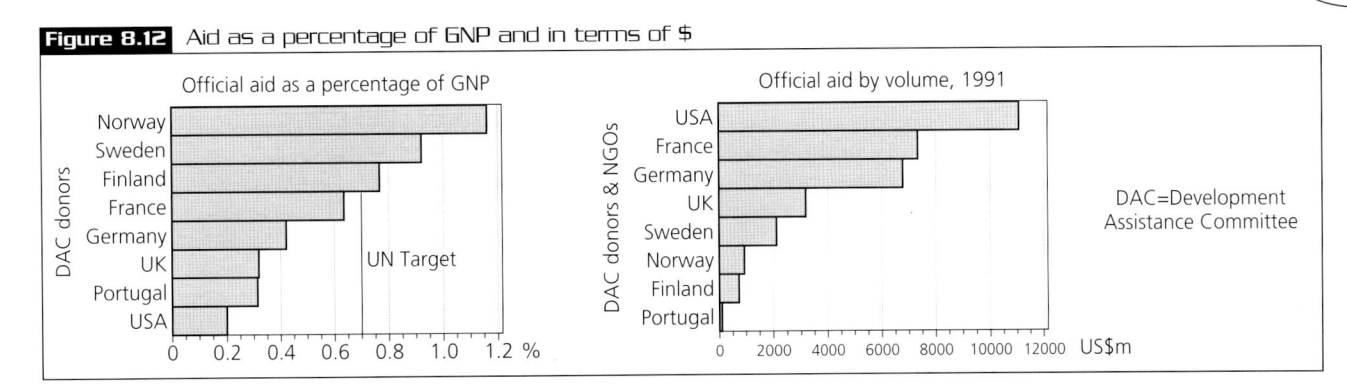

Figure 8.12 Aid as a percentage of GNP and in terms of $

Official aid as a percentage of GNP (DAC donors): Norway, Sweden, Finland, France, Germany, UK, Portugal, USA — scale 0 to 1.2%, with UN Target marked.

Official aid by volume, 1991 (DAC donors & NGOs): USA, France, Germany, UK, Sweden, Norway, Finland, Portugal — scale 0 to 12000 US$m.

DAC = Development Assistance Committee

Water development schemes

The Three Gorges Dam Flat over 2km long and 100m high – will be one of the biggest dams in the world. Like most other large-scale developments it has raised a number of issues.

THE ADVANTAGES

- It will generate up to 18,000 megawatts, eight times more than the Aswan Dam in Egypt and 50% more than the world's largest existing HEP dam.
- It will enable China to reduce its dependency on coal.
- It will supply Shanghai, population over 13m, one of the world's largest cities, and Chongqing, population 3m, an area earmarked for economic development.
- It will take between 15 and 20 years to build and could cost as much as $70 billion.

Questions

9. Which countries in **Figure 8.12** donate the most money in US$?
10. Which countries shown in **Figure 8.12** reach the UN suggested % level of GNP?
11. Describe briefly **three** problems associated with trade.

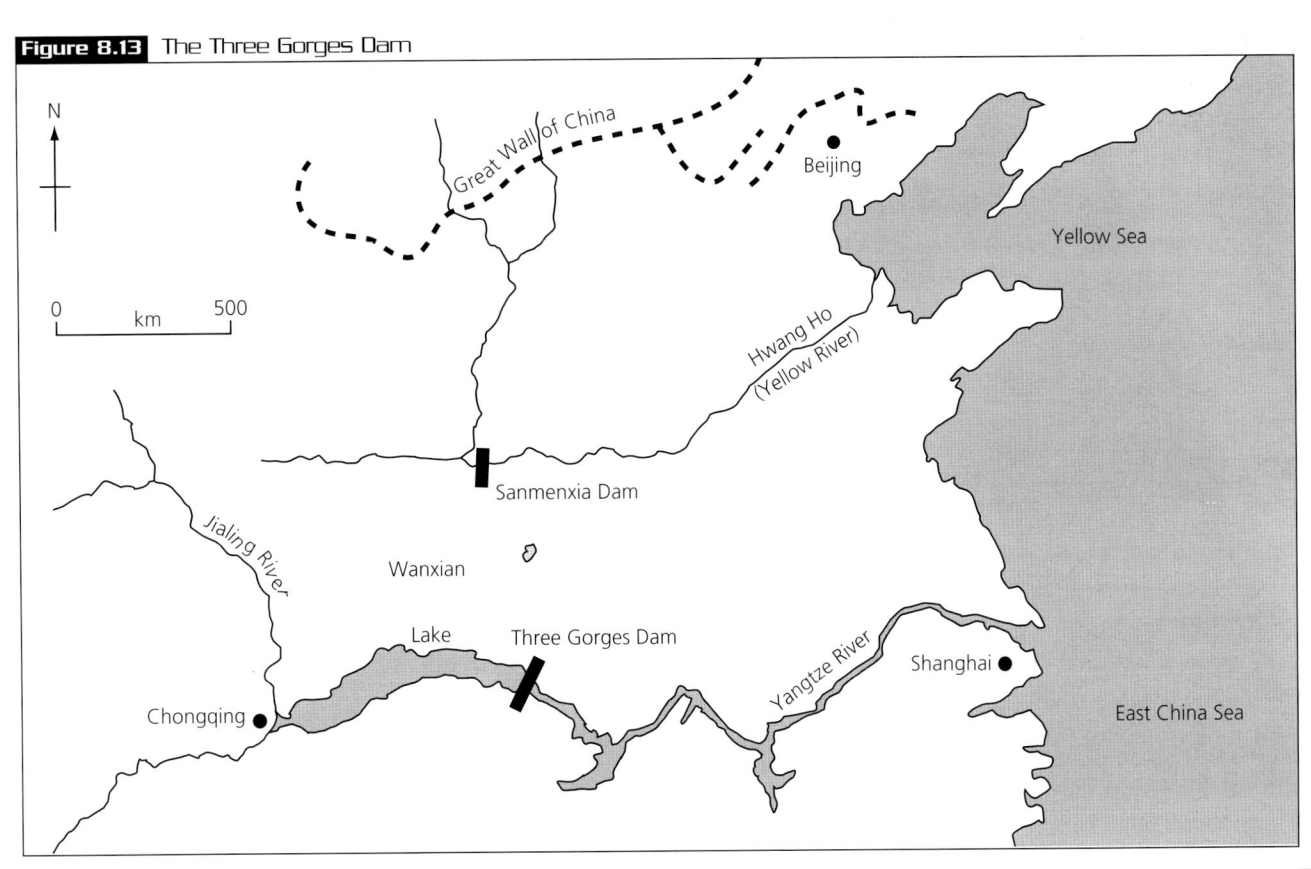

Figure 8.13 The Three Gorges Dam

Map showing: Great Wall of China, Beijing, Yellow Sea, Hwang Ho (Yellow River), Sanmenxia Dam, Jialing River, Wanxian, Lake, Three Gorges Dam, Chongqing, Yangtze River, Shanghai, East China Sea. Scale 0–500 km.

- It will protect 10 million people from flooding (over 300 000 people in China have died as a result of flooding this century).
- It will allow shipping above the Three Gorges: the dams will raise water levels by 90m, and turns the rapids in the gorge into a lake.
- The Yangtze provides 66% of China's rice and contains 400m people.
- The Yangtze drains 1.8m km^2 and discharges 700 cubic kilometres of water annually.

THE DISADVANTAGES

- Most floods in recent years have come from rivers which join the Yangtze below the Three Gorges Dam.
- The region is seismically active and landslides are frequent.
- The port at the head of the lake may become silted up as a result of increased deposition (Figure 8.15) and the development of a delta at the head of the lake.
- Up to 1.2 million people will have to be moved to make way for the dam and the lake.
- Much of the land available for resettlement is over 800m above sea level, and is colder with infertile thin soils and on relatively steep slopes.
- Dozens of towns, for example Wanxian and Fuling with 140,000 and 80,000 people respectively will be flooded.
- Up to 530 million tonnes of silt are carried through the Gorge annually: the first dam on the river lost its capacity within seven years and one on the Yellow River filled with silt within four years.
- To reduce the silt load afforestation is needed but resettlement of people will cause greater pressure on the slopes above the dam.
- The dam will interfere with aquatic life – the Siberian Crane and the White Flag Dolphin are threatened with extinction.
- Archaeological treasures will be drowned, including the Zhang Fei temple (Figure 8.14).

Figure 8.14 The archaeological treasures that the Three Gorges Dam will bury

Questions

12 Briefly explain how the Three Gorges Dam could lead to a reduction in the Greenhouse Effect.
13 Imagine that you are a farmer forced to move as a result of the dam. How would you feel about being moved out of the area into a new place? Explain your reasons.
14 Should the Three Gorges Dam be built? Support your answer with reasons.

Figure 8.15 The effect of a dam upon erosion and deposition

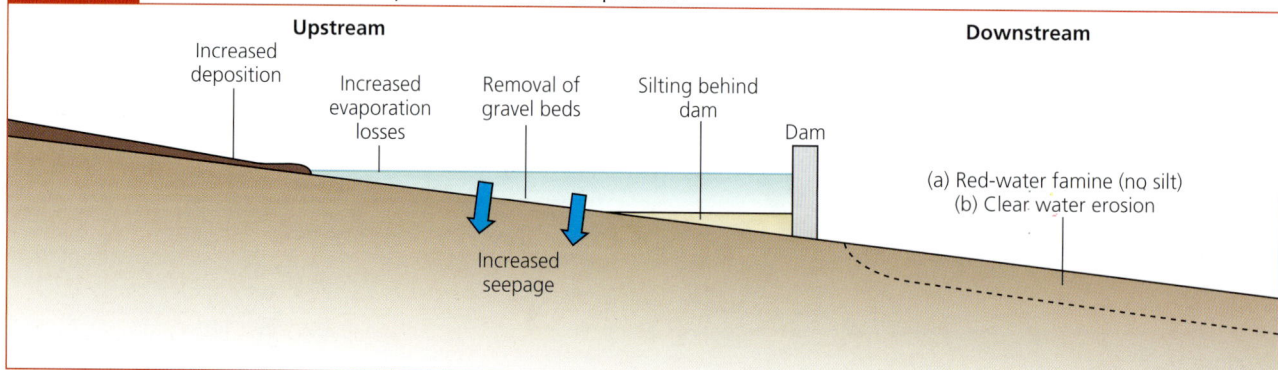

Upstream — Increased deposition, Increased evaporation losses, Removal of gravel beds, Silting behind dam, Increased seepage

Downstream — Dam — (a) Red-water famine (no silt) (b) Clear water erosion

Development and pollution

Pollution is defined as the contamination of the earth, water and atmosphere to such an extent that normal environmental processes are badly affected **(Figure 8.16)**. It includes a wide range of solids, liquids and gases which are toxic, harmful and ugly. Pollution can be natural, such as from volcanic eruptions, as well as human in origin **(Figure 8.17)**. It can be deliberate or it may be accidental. It includes the release of substances which harm the sustainable quality of air, water and soil, and which reduces human quality of life. It is difficult to define the levels which constitute 'pollution'. Much depends on the nature of the environment.

Pollution normally increases with population growth and with economic growth **(Figure 8.18)**. There are certainly more records of pollution in developed countries, but there are increasing levels of pollution in *NICs* and in developing countries. Many are related to the activities of *multinational companies* such as the Bhopal disaster in India (1984) and the impacts of maquiladora developments in Mexico. Pollution has often been regarded as *'the price of progress'* or as the result of developments to improve the quality of life.

The atmosphere has long been regarded as a dumping ground for gaseous and particulate waste. In 1306 a Royal Proclamation banned people from using sea coal in London furnaces because of the impact it had on human health. However, it was not until the industrial revolution in the nineteenth century that air pollution intensified in dramatic fashion. Over the last century or so, land and water surfaces have been used on an increasing and unsustainable scale.

In the twentieth century, however, air pollution continued to increase for a number of reasons:

- population expansion;
- industrial and technological growth;
- increased standards of living;
- greater manufacturing and energy consumption;
- urbanisation, concentrating people and manufacturing in close proximity.

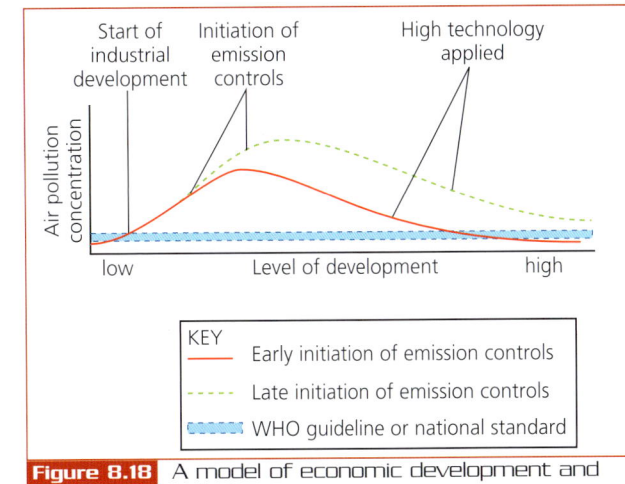

Figure 8.16 Urban dereliction

Figure 8.17 Air pollution in Mexico City

Figure 8.18 A model of economic development and pollution

KEY
— Early initiation of emission controls
--- Late initiation of emission controls
≈≈≈ WHO guideline or national standard

8 DEVELOPMENT

Atmospheric pollution has been an important local issue for at least 2000 years, but has come to the fore as a global issue since the 1970s. It is especially bad in large cities (Figure 8.19). Much is related to the increase in manufacturing, energy production, and the increase in vehicle ownership. Air pollution has proved difficult to control, given the wide variety of sources and emissions.

The main sources of air pollution include industries, vehicles and homes. Much suspended particulate matter (SPM – smoke) is burnt in inefficient domestic burners and fires, while up to 90% of sulphur dioxide comes from industrial and power stations.

Motor vehicles account for about 35% of total UK emissions (and about 60% of US emissions). The main pollutants from vehicles include carbon monoxide (CO) (92% of the total emitted), hydrocarbons (4.5%) nitrous oxides (NOx) (3%) and sulphur oxides (SO) (0.5%).

Sulphur is the major pollutant from the burning of coal and oil, and more than two-thirds of sulphur dioxide emissions occur in the northern hemisphere.

Figure 8.19 Air pollution in the world's largest cities

Columns: SO_2, SPM, Pb, CO, NO_2, O_3

Cities listed: Bangkok, Beijing, Bombay, Buenos Aires, Cairo, Calcutta, Delhi, Jakarta, Karachi, London, Los Angeles, Manila, Mexico City, Moscow, New York, Rio de Janeiro, São Paulo, Seoul, Shanghai, Tokyo

Legend:
- Serious problem, WHO guidelines exceeded by more than a factor of two
- Moderate to heavy pollution, WHO guidelines exceed by up to a factor of two (short-term guidelines exceeded on a regular basis at certain locations)
- Low pollution, WHO guidelines are normally met (short-term guidelines may be exceeded occasionally)
- No data available or insufficient data for assessment

THE DEBATE

There are a number of views and issues. First, is pollution a necessary effect of growth and is it the price of progress? Are economic development and environmental management two opposing themes? Are they merely a battle between short-term profits and long-term costs?

Pollution is associated with development, in particular capitalist development. But pollution is not restricted to capitalist countries. The communist countries of the former-Eastern Bloc seem to have large-scale pollution problems. In particular, the former East Germany has the highest sulphur dioxide emission rates per person in the world. There is evidence that many multinationals are exporting (or developing) pollution to many NICs and developing countries.

Questions

15 Study **Figure 8.19**.
   a Find out what the following terms stand for: SO_2, SPM, Pb, CO, NO_2, O_3.
   b Which is the most common pollutant in all of the cities mentioned?
   c Which city is the most polluted?
16 'Pollution is the price of progress.' Discuss, using examples to support your answer.

Development and hazards: tropical cyclones

Hurricanes are violent storms that affect a very large part of the earth's surface (Figure 8.20). They are intense hazards which bring heavy rainfall, strong winds, high waves and cause flooding and mudslides. Hurricanes are also characterised by enormous quantities of water. This is due to their origin over moist tropical seas. High intensity rainfall totals up to 500 mm in 24 hours, invariably causing flooding. Their path is erratic, hence it is not always possible to give more than twelve hours notice. This is insufficient for proper evacuation measures.

Hurricanes begin life as small-scale tropical *depressions*, which cause thunderstorms, and may develop into *tropical storms*, which have greater wind speeds of up to 117 kmph (73 mph). However, only about 10% of tropical depressions ever become *hurricanes*, storms with wind speeds above 118 kmph (above 74 mph).

Hurricanes only develop when sea temperatures are over 27°C (warm water gives off large quantities of heat when it is condensed – this is the heat which drives the hurricane). Once the rising air has become established the hurricane matures. The rising air releases large quantities of heat during condensation. The eye of the hurricane refers to the calm area at the centre of the hurricane. Hurricane winds can cause 15 metre waves in the open ocean. Peak heights on land can be as high as 6 metres.

It is very costly to evacuate an area. It is estimated that the cost of evacuating a 500 km stretch of the US coastline is about US$ 50 million. This is due to losses in business, tourism, and protection measures taken. The hurricane hazard is greatest on islands and coastal areas. Once a hurricane is deprived of its source of heat and moisture it begins to decay.

Hurricanes create a major threat to human life, property and economic activities. They are a seasonal hazard, peaking between June and November in the Northern Hemisphere. Because of their impact, and the cost of their destruction, they are monitored intensely by satellite, and hurricane paths are predicted by complex computer programmes.

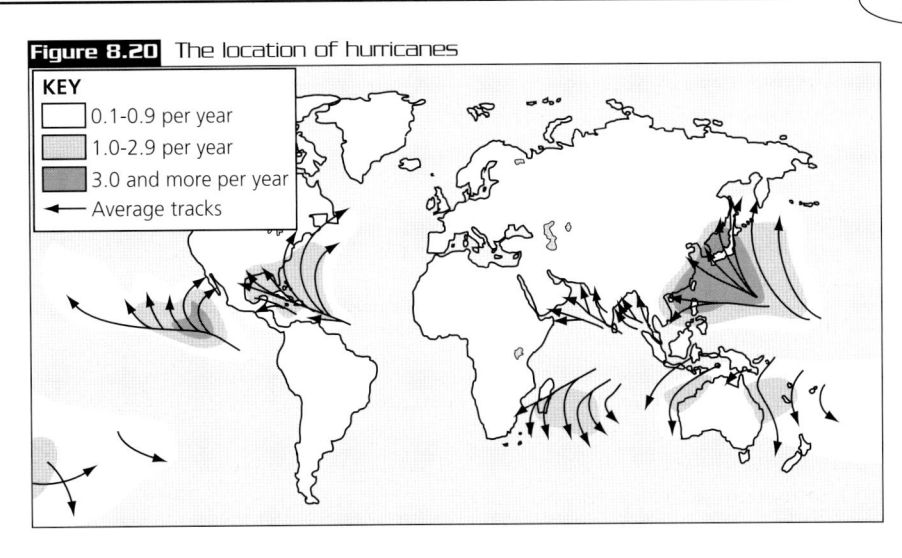

Figure 8.20 The location of hurricanes

KEY
- 0.1-0.9 per year
- 1.0-2.9 per year
- 3.0 and more per year
- Average tracks

HURRICANE MITCH

The death toll from the worst storm to hit Central America for over a century was over 7000. The floods and landslides caused by tropical storm Mitch in 1998 may have cost as many as 5000 lives in Honduras alone, but the true total will never be known.

The floods and landslides completely destroyed many villages and households as well as whole neighbourhoods of cities. In Nicaragua between 1000 and 1500 people were killed at the Casita volcano and 600 others died elsewhere.

Swollen by torrential rains caused by Mitch, the crater lake at the volcano's summit overflowed causing a mudslide that wiped out four communities. The mud was 30m high and tore down trees and the houses. The place became a desert. The mud, in places over 6m thick, covered an area of about 75 sq km. Most of the inhabitants were buried by the mud. There were very few survivors.

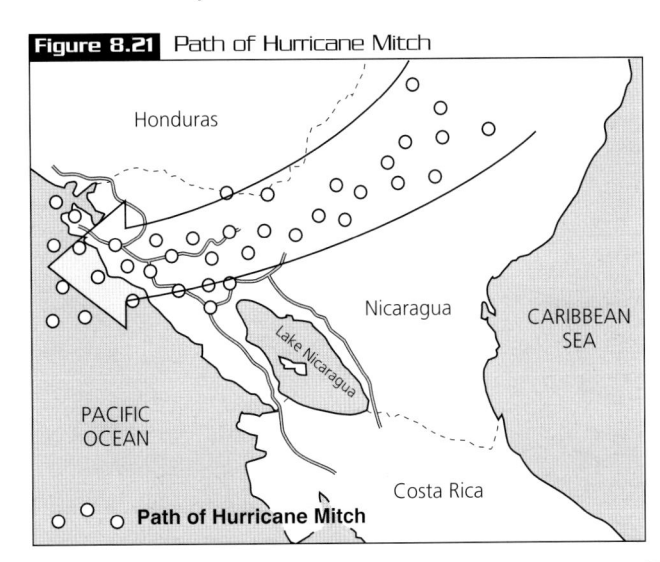

Figure 8.21 Path of Hurricane Mitch

In Guatemala, the swollen Rio Choluteca turned the city centre of Tegucigalpa into a vast lake, and the hillsides were strewn with the wreckage of shanty homes. In all, 800 000 of the country's 5 million inhabitants were made homeless.

A dam across the Rio Choluteca, caused by a landslide, threatened to burst and cause devastation in the city. Following the disaster, looting became commonplace. Over 200 people were arrested, and many businesses had to be protected by armed guards.

Up to 50 bridges on main highways, along with many minor bridges, were destroyed. These included all those on main roads in and out of the Nicaraguan capital Managua. Hundreds of small villages were cut off entirely, and food shortages occurred rapidly. In Managua food prices shot up rapidly.

With hundreds of bodies rotting in the open air, and water supplies and other utilities disrupted, another fear was of epidemics, including malaria and cholera.

Figure 8.22 Satellite image of Hurricane Mitch

Questions

17 What were the natural causes of the mudslides throughout Central America?
18 Why might the true number of casualties never be known?
19 Briefly describe some of the economic losses caused by the hurricane.
20 Briefly explain two potential hazards to threaten the Honduran capital, Tegucigalpa.
21 Why do you think looting became a problem following the disaster?
22 What other hazards were expected following the mudslides?
23 Why did food prices rise so much?

Figure 8.23 Devastation caused by Hurricane Mitch

Resources and Environmental issues

9

Acid rain

Acid rain – or acid deposition – is the increased acidity of rainfall and dry deposition, due to human activity (Figure 9.1). Rainfall is naturally acidic with a pH of about 5.6. This is because it picks up carbon dioxide from the atmosphere. However, acid rain can be a low as 3.0. The main causes of acid rain are sulphur dioxide (SO_2) and NOx (oxides of nitrogen) which are given off in the burning of fossil fuels, such as coal and oil, and from vehicle exhausts. Sulphur dioxide and nitrogen oxides are released into the atmosphere where they can be absorbed by the moisture and become weak sulphuric and nitric acids, sometimes with a pH of around 3.

The pH scale is used as a measure of a substance's acidity or alkalinity. 7 is neutral, less than 7 is acidic and more than 7, alkaline. The pH scale is **logarithmic**, so a decrease of one pH unit represents a tenfold increase in acidity. Thus pH 4 is ten times more acidic than pH 5.

Power stations that burn coal are the major producers of **sulphur dioxide**, although all processes that burn coal and oil contribute. Vehicles, especially cars, are responsible for most of the **nitrogen oxides** in the atmosphere. Some come from the vehicle exhaust itself, but others form when the exhaust gases react with the air. Exhaust gases also react with strong sunlight to produce poisonous ozone gas which damages plant growth and in some cases, human health.

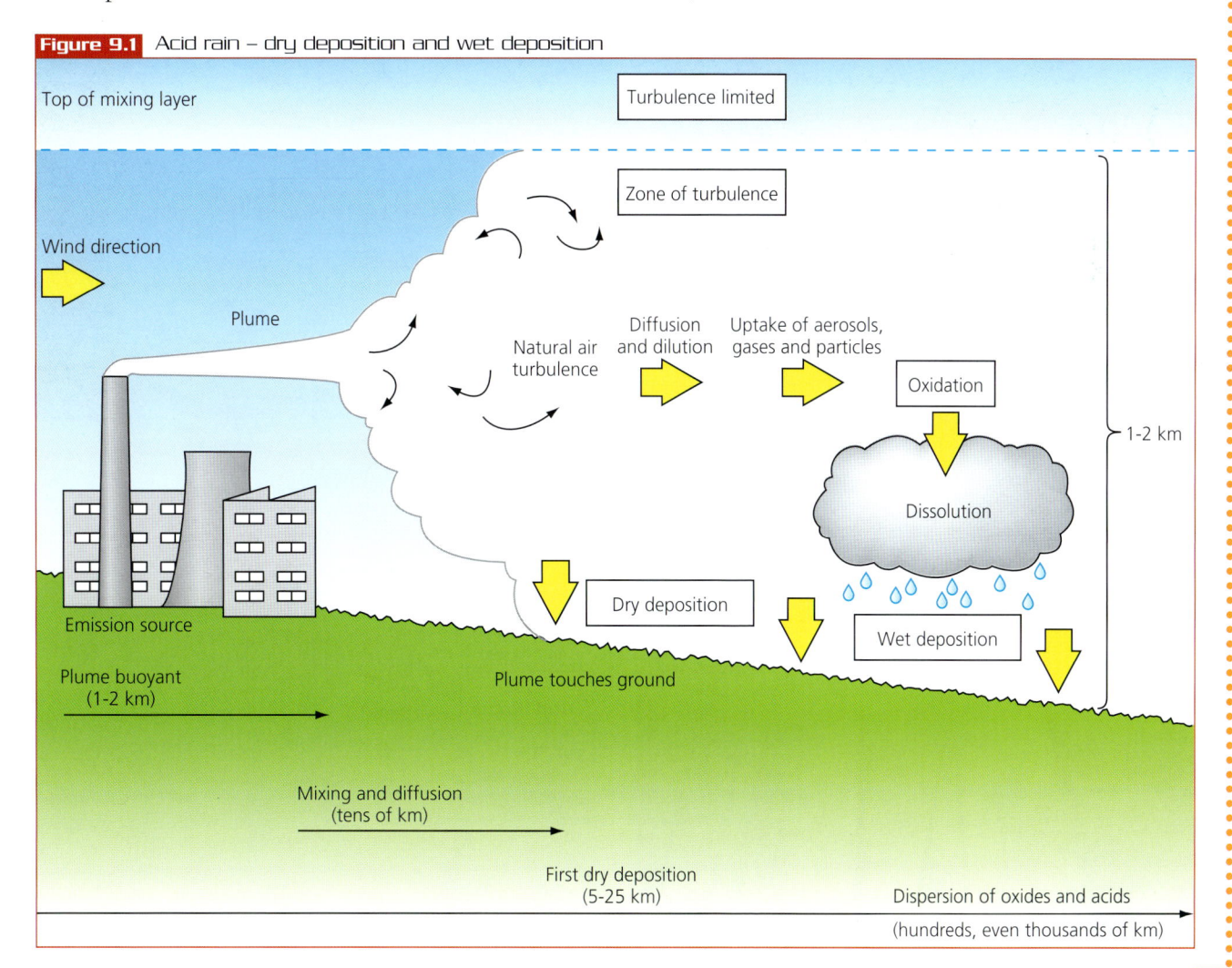

Figure 9.1 Acid rain – dry deposition and wet deposition

Dry deposition typically occurs close to the source of emission and causes damage to buildings and structures. **Wet deposition**, by contrast, occurs when the acids are dissolved in precipitation, and may fall at great distances from the sources. Wet deposition has been called a 'transfrontier' pollution, as it crosses international boundaries.

Although emissions of SO_2 are declining, those of NOx are increasing – partly as a result of increased car ownership. Acidification has a number of effects:

- buildings are weathered **(Figure 9.2)**;
- metals, especially iron and aluminium, are carried by acidic water, and flushed into streams and lakes;
- aluminium damages fish gills;
- forest growth is severely affected;
- soil acidity increases;
- mental illness in humans increases.

The effects of acid deposition are greatest in those areas which have high levels of precipitation (causing more acidity to be transferred to the ground) and those which have base acidic rocks,

Figure 9.2 The increased weathering of buildings

Figure 9.3 Acid rain damage to trees

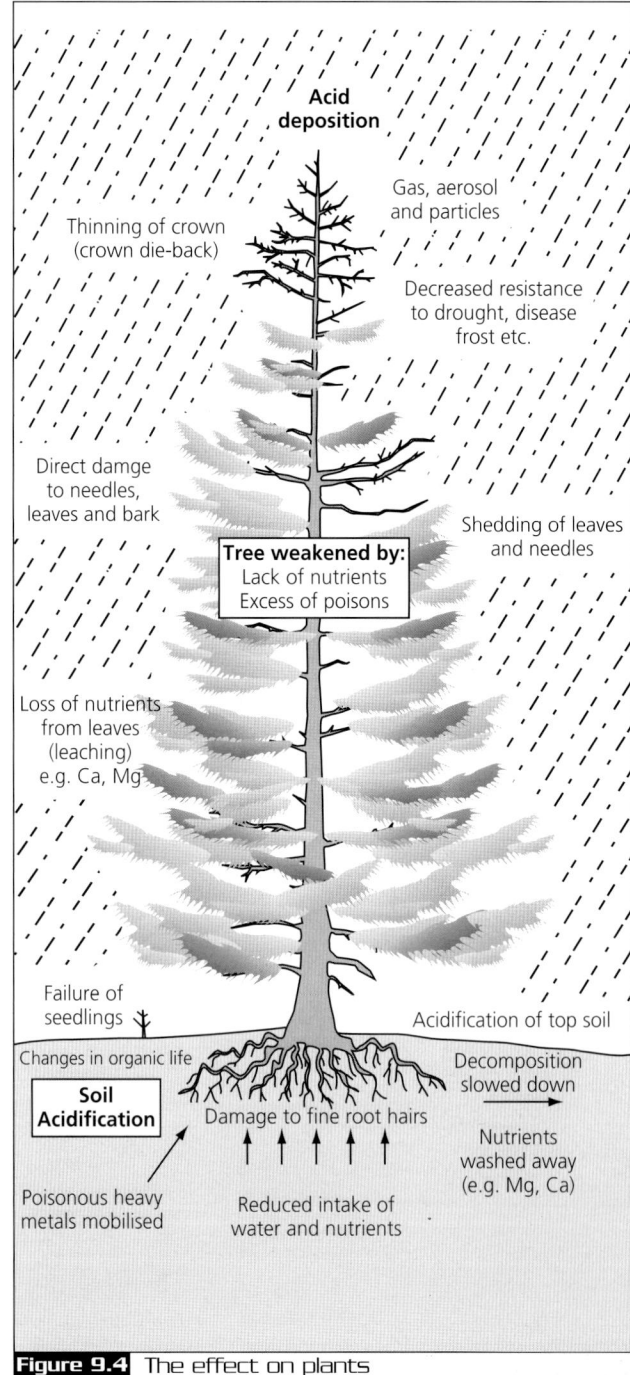

Figure 9.4 The effect on plants

such as granite or gravel, which cannot neutralise the deposited acidity. By contrast, limestone and chalk, which are alkali, are able to neutralise the increased acidity. (Traditionally, farmers placed lime on acids soils to make them more fertile – now governments are having to put lime into acidified lakes and soils.)

THE SOLUTIONS

Various methods are used to try to reduce the damaging effects of acid deposition. One of these is to add powdered limestone to lakes to increase their pH values. However, the only really effective and practical long-term treatment is to reduce the emissions of the offending gases. This can be achieved in a variety of ways:

- by reducing the amount of fossil fuel burnt;
- by using coal with little sulphur;
- by using alternative energy sources such as hydroelectric power or nuclear power;
- by removing the pollutants with filters before they reach the atmosphere.

However, while victims and environmentalists stress the risks of acidification, industrialists stress the uncertainties. For example:

Questions

1. Study Figure 9.1. Define the terms *dry deposition* and *wet deposition*. How do dry deposition and wet deposition vary in terms of distance from the source of pollution?
2. What are the impacts of acid rain on
   a water
   b buildings?
3. What can be done to reduce the impacts of acid rain?
4. Suggest ways in which the causes of acid rain have changed over the last fifty years. Think about types of industry, heating in the home and transport to suggest changes.

- rainfall is naturally acidic;
- no single industry/country is the sole source of SO_2/NOx;
- car owners with catalytic convertors are now environmentally friendly;
- different types of coal have variable sulphur content.

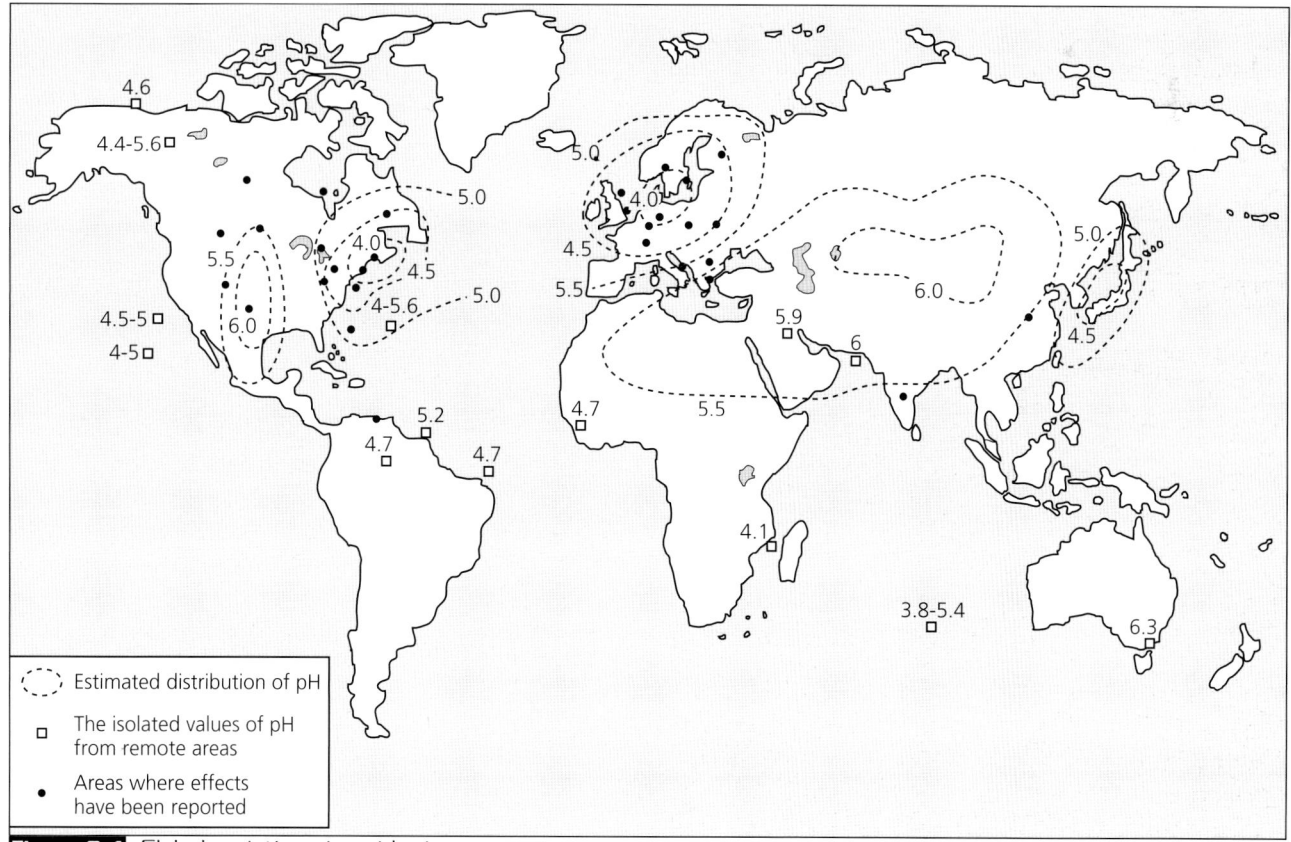

Figure 9.4 Global variations in acid rain

9 Global warming

The greenhouse effect is the term given to global warming. The earth's atmosphere acts like a greenhouse. It allows short-wave ultra-violet radiation in but it stops long wave infrared radiation from escaping. So, over time, the atmosphere heats up.

Greenhouse gases include:
- carbon dioxide released by the burning of fossil fuels;
- methane produced by livestock;
- CFCs from aerosols.

The **Greenhouse Effect** refers to the increase in the level of carbon dioxide (CO_2) in the atmosphere. CO_2 allows incoming short-wave radiation to pass through but blocks out-going long-wave radiation (**Figure 9.5**). This traps heat which would otherwise escape from the lower atmosphere. Since 1850 the CO_2 level in the atmosphere has increased from 220 ppm to 360 ppm. Sea level is rising at a rate of 6 mm per year. Flooding of low lying areas will be accompanied by an increase in the frequency and intensity of storms.

If nothing happens, global CO_2 emissions will be twice as much as they were in 1996, although the Developed Countries will have stabilised their emissions i.e. most emissions will be from Developing Countries. Saying all that, of course, not every country wants to cut CO_2 levels – NICs are unhappy to reduce growth as their economies accelerate. Oil producers, which depend upon the export of fossil fuels for their GNP, do not want to see a reduction in the demand for oil and gas, as carbon-based fuels account for 90% of the world's energy.

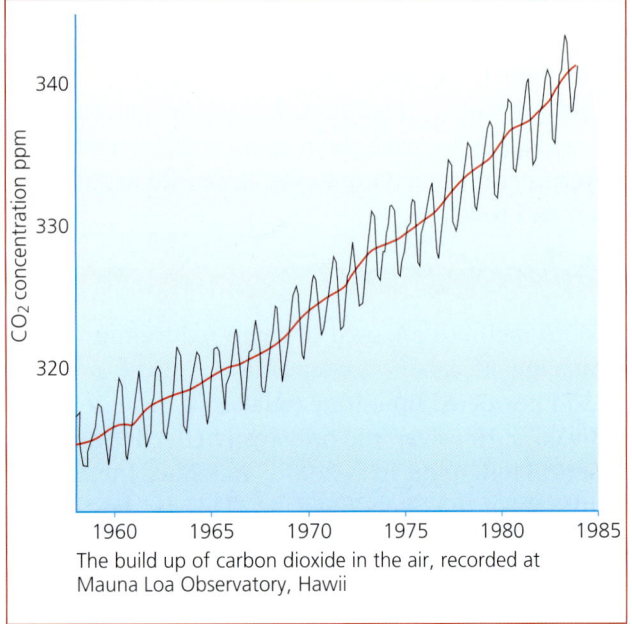

Figure 9.5 The greenhouse effect and global warming

The build up of carbon dioxide in the air, recorded at Mauna Loa Observatory, Hawaii

Source	Share	Production of CO_2
Oil	41%	Moderate
Coal	24%	High
Gas	17%	Low
Biomass	15%	High
Nuclear	2%	None
HEP	2%	None

Figure 9.6 Global energy sources

Figure 9.7 Islands at risk of global warming

- Members of the Alliance of Small Island States
- Cities in danger of flooding

Questions

5 Illustrate the data above by means of a pie-chart. What proportion of the world's energy come from fossil fuels? What impact are renewable forms of energy likely to have on most nation's energy mix? Explain your answer.

6 Study **Figure 9.7** which shows the risks associated with global warming on low lying areas. Describe the hazards that will affect low lying islands. Why will islanders be forced to leave the islands before the islands are flooded?

The ozone hole

Ozone (O_3) is a type of oxygen that absorbs damaging ultraviolet radiation from the sun. It is continuously being created and destroyed in the atmosphere as part of a natural process. Oxygen (O_2) is broken down into individual atoms by ultraviolet radiation. Some of these atoms form with oxygen to form ozone. Ozone is later broken down by ultraviolet radiation – so there is a natural cycle of growth and decay.

Ozone is important as it filters out harmful ultraviolet radiation. Increased levels of ultraviolet radiation are associated with increased levels of skin cancer and reduced crop yields. For every 1% decrease in ozone, skin cancer will rise by 5%.

However, increasing use of chlorofluorocarbons (CFCs) are destroying the ozone layer. CFCs are chemicals used in foams, aerosols, refrigerators, and air-conditioning units. The link is very strong (Figure 9.8). When they are broken down in the atmosphere they release chlorine, which destroys ozone. As this destruction of ozone is faster than its natural regeneration – the amount of ozone is decreasing (Figure 9.9).

The ozone 'hole' is a large area over Antarctica (and to a lesser extent over the Arctic) where there are very low levels of O_3 – less than half normal levels (Figure 9.10).

The effects of reduced O_3 include:
- increased risk of skin cancer;
- more eye diseases such as cataracts;
- crop yields to decline by 25% (if O_3 declines by 25%);
- decline of oceanic plankton – disrupting marine ecosystems.

The Montreal Protocol (1987) requires cuts of CFCs by 1999. However, many developing countries did not sign – as it would affect their attempts to develop. It means that alternatives need to be found to CFCs.

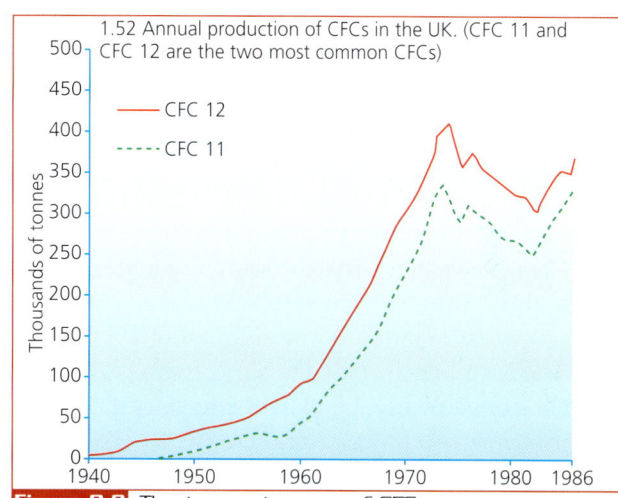

Figure 9.9 The increasing use of CFCs

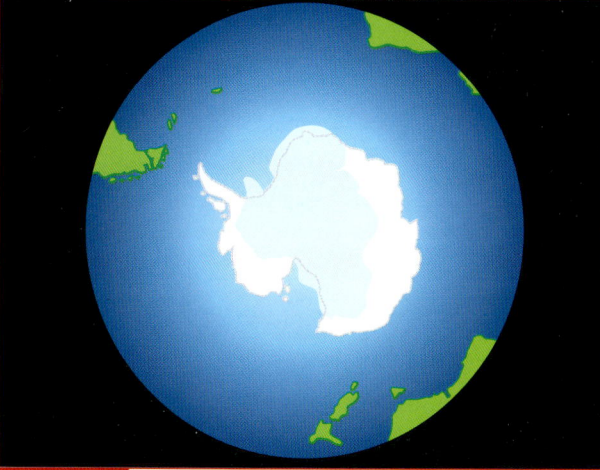

Figure 9.10 The ozone hole over Antarctica

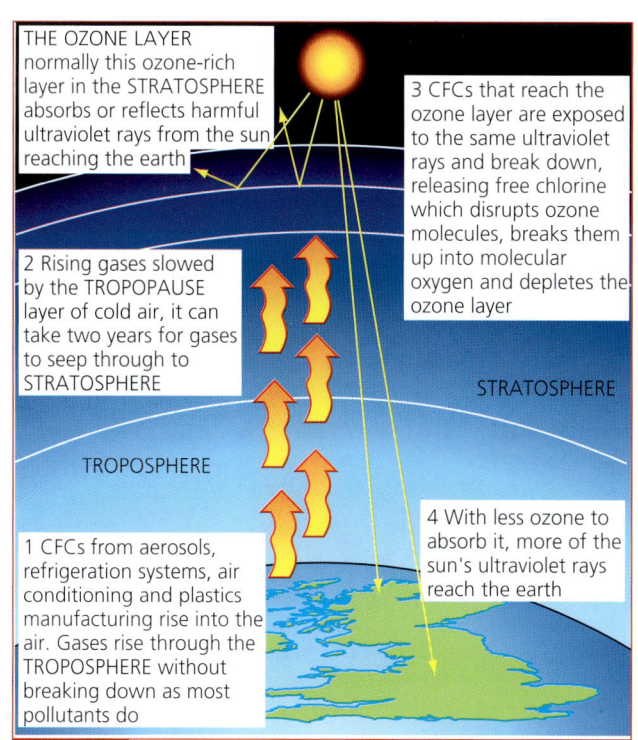

Figure 9.8 The link between CFCs and ozone depletion

THE OZONE LAYER normally this ozone-rich layer in the STRATOSPHERE absorbs or reflects harmful ultraviolet rays from the sun reaching the earth

2 Rising gases slowed by the TROPOPAUSE layer of cold air, it can take two years for gases to seep through to STRATOSPHERE

3 CFCs that reach the ozone layer are exposed to the same ultraviolet rays and break down, releasing free chlorine which disrupts ozone molecules, breaks them up into molecular oxygen and depletes the ozone layer

1 CFCs from aerosols, refrigeration systems, air conditioning and plastics manufacturing rise into the air. Gases rise through the TROPOSPHERE without breaking down as most pollutants do

4 With less ozone to absorb it, more of the sun's ultraviolet rays reach the earth

Questions

7 Why is ozone important?

8 Make a survey in your class. What are CFCs? Where are they found? Which ones do people use?

9 Why are many developing countries unwilling to reduce their production of CFCs?

9

The El Niño effect

El Niño, (which means the Christ Child) is an irregular appearance of warm surface water, usually around Christmas time, in the Pacific off the coast of South America **(Figure 9.11 and 9.12)** that affects global wind and rainfall patterns. El Niño occurs at intervals between 2 and 10 years, and lasting for up to two years. Originally, El Niño referred to a warm current that appeared off the coast of Peru, but it is now realised that this current is part of a much larger system.

In July 1997 the sea surface temperature in the eastern tropical Pacific was 2.0 – 2.5°C above normal, breaking all previous climate records. The El Niño's peak continued into early 1998 before weather conditions returned to normal.

The unusual weather events of 1997, such as the flooding in central Europe and the drought in Korea and China have been linked to an early and strong appearance of the El Niño weather system. The El Niño event that started in the summer of 1997 could be even more catastrophic than the 1982-3 El Niño which claimed nearly 2,000 lives and caused over $13 billion damage to property and crops!

Figure 9.11 Normal circulation and El Niño circulation

NORMAL CONDITIONS

Normally the trade winds push warm surface water across the Pacific to an area from the Philippines to north-east Australia.

The sea in the western Pacific becomes several degrees warmer and builds up to over a metre higher than it is in the east.

Upwelling cold water replaces warmer surface water. Nutrients encourage the growth of plankton and fish stocks thrive.

'EL NIÑO' CONDITIONS

Every few years the trade winds drop. Warm water surges back across the southern Pacific, stopping the upwelling of cold water. This affects the marine cycle causing a loss of fish. Torrrential rain and drought occur.

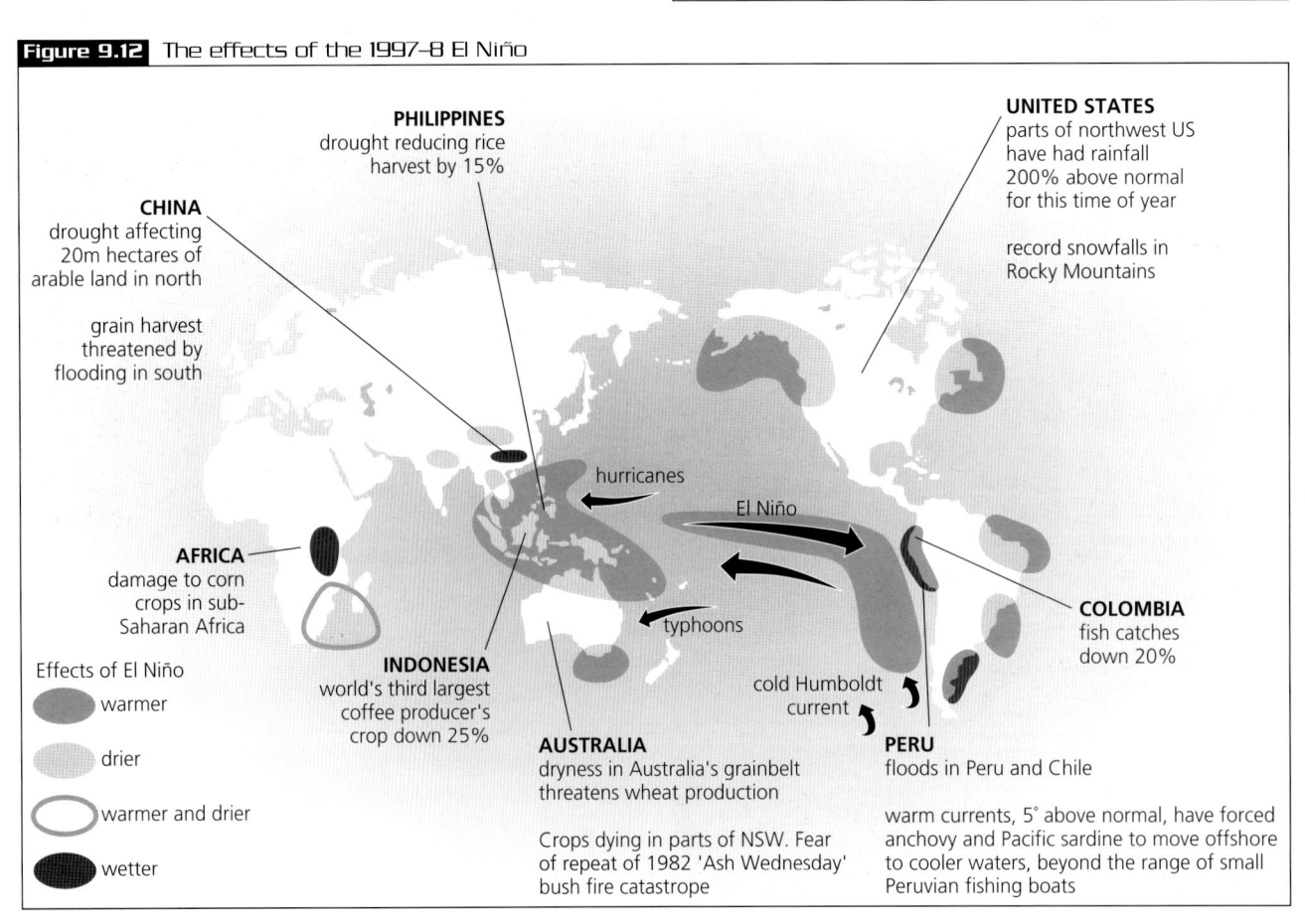

Figure 9.12 The effects of the 1997–8 El Niño

PHILIPPINES drought reducing rice harvest by 15%

UNITED STATES parts of northwest US have had rainfall 200% above normal for this time of year

record snowfalls in Rocky Mountains

CHINA drought affecting 20m hectares of arable land in north

grain harvest threatened by flooding in south

AFRICA damage to corn crops in sub-Saharan Africa

INDONESIA world's third largest coffee producer's crop down 25%

AUSTRALIA dryness in Australia's grainbelt threatens wheat production

Crops dying in parts of NSW. Fear of repeat of 1982 'Ash Wednesday' bush fire catastrope

COLOMBIA fish catches down 20%

cold Humboldt current

PERU floods in Peru and Chile

warm currents, 5° above normal, have forced anchovy and Pacific sardine to move offshore to cooler waters, beyond the range of small Peruvian fishing boats

Effects of El Niño
- warmer
- drier
- warmer and drier
- wetter

110

Among the effects of the 1997-8 El Niño were:

- a stormy winter in California (the 1982-3 event took 160 lives and caused $2 billion damage in floods and mudslides);
- above average rainfall in the south of the USA;
- worsening drought in Australia, Indonesia, the Philippines, southern Africa and north east Brazil;
- increased risk of malaria in South America;
- lower rainfall in northern Europe;
- higher rainfall in southern Europe.

Scientists still do not know what causes the appearance or strength of El Niño. However, it appears to be increasing in frequency and strength, raising suspicions that it may be related in some way to global warming.

The impact of El Niño is great. For example, the huge tropical island of Papua New Guinea (PNG) experienced a six month drought in 1997 which lead to the death of hundreds of indigenous people. Over 400 people died in the western half of the island from malnutrition. Mountain streams and deep 10-metre wells dried up and there were severe frosts – the worst in living memory. Of the 3.5 million people living there up to 85% are subsistence farmers. Many depend upon the sweet potato. Drought and frosts can destroy the crop. Hence, many farmers were forced to forage from the forest in order to survive – but the forest was badly affected by the drought too.

Questions

10 What is meant by the term 'El Niño'? Why is it called this?

11 a What was the damage caused by the 1982-3 El Niño?

b What were the effects of the 1997-8 El Niño season.

Figure 9.13 Drought in Papua New Guinea

Figure 9.14 Eroded Californian Coastline, February 1983

Drought, desertification and soil erosion

Drought is a deficit of water due to high evaporation rates and low rates of rainfall. Areas prone to drought cover about one-third of the world's surface. It has a greater impact in drier areas because it generally lasts longer and there are less reserves. Drought in the 1980s saw the cattle population decline 55% while maize yields dropped by 80% in the 1990s.

Desertification is the spread of desert conditions. It is a long-term process in which desert processes and features gradually creep into an area. Natural causes of desertification include climatic change such as reduced rainfall and increased seasonality. This causes vegetation to die. With less vegetation, the soil is increasingly exposed to erosion by wind and water. Man made causes are varied and are linked to increased population pressure i.e. more people and livestock using the land. Population growth and resettlement in the early 1990s increased demand for scarce resources such as fuelwood for cooking, shelter, heating and fencing.

Some geographers question whether desertification is actually taking place. Desert climates are at best unpredictable. Reduced vegetation cover may, they claim, be just a short term trend, and studies using satellites have failed to pick out significant changes in the spread of sand dunes and other desert features. They suggest that changes in vegetation cover are linked to changes in the annual rainfall amounts.

Figure 9.15 Drought and desertification in the Sahel

Figure 9.16 The causes of desertification

Figure 9.17 Desertification may occur as a result of overgrazing

Figure 9.18 Soil erosion and vegetation cover

	erosion (mm/yr)
Forest	0.08
Pasture	0.03
Scrub forest	0.1
Barren abandoned land	24.4
Crops (contour ploughing)	10.6
Crops (downslope ploughing)	29.8

Figure 9.19 Soil erosion rates

	(tonnes/ha/yr)
South Downs	250
Norfolk	160
West Sussex	150
Shropshire	120
China (Loess)	250
Nepal	70
Ethiopia	42
Burkina Faso	35

Figure 9.20 Controlled and uncontrolled grazing

Questions

12. **Figure 9.20** shows the effects of controlled and uncontrolled grazing on a hillside. Which slope has been affected by uncontrolled grazing? Give reasons for your answer. Explain how overgrazing may lead to desertification.

13. **Figure 9.21** shows a diguette. How can diguettes prevent desertification? What evidence is there that the advantages of having a diguette are already happening?

14. Study **Figure 9.18** which shows rates of soil erosion and vegetation cover. What is the relationship between vegetation cover and soil erosion. Which vegetation cover is associated with the highest rate of soil erosion? Which vegetation cover is associated with the lowest amount of soil erosion. Briefly suggest reasons to explain the patterns you have noted.

15. **Figure 9.19** shows rates of soil erosion in developing countries, such as China and Nepal, which are often thought to have some of the highest rates of soil erosion in the world. It also shows rates of soil erosion in the UK. What evidence is there to suggest that the risk of soil erosion in the UK is serious. How might it change as a result of global warming?

16. 'Soil is a valuable resource that is used without thought.' Discuss.

Figure 9.21 Diguettes – one way of solving desertification

9

RESOURCES AND ENVIRONMENTAL ISSUES

Managing flooding and tourism in Venice

St Mark's Square in Venice could be flooded every day by 2050. Flooding of the Square has increased from seven per year at the start of the twentieth century to between 40 and 60 annually at the end of the twentieth century, and will become a daily occurrence by the middle of the twenty-first century because of world-wide rises in sea levels. Rising sea levels brought about by man-made global warming are likely to equal the 30 cm of extra tide height it takes at present to send water pouring into the Doge's palace and St Mark's Cathedral. In addition to sea-level rise, Venice's position at the top of the Adriatic makes it particularly vulnerable to storm surges.

The Italian government's preferred solution to Venice's threat from the sea is a £3.6 billion system of concrete flap gates fixed on the sea bed at three entrances to the Venetian lagoon. These can be raised to counter high tides and lowered again to let ships pass (rather like the Thames Barrier). However, the likely savings in flood damage will in no way justify the cost of the system and with the sea level rise expected by 2050, the gates will probably have to be closed every day, thus in effect sealing off the lagoon from the sea. Environmentalists claim that it would be better to seal off the lagoon by natural means, while tackling the pollution problems caused by industrial and agricultural wastes, and build a series of small scale local flood defence works.

The Italian government had recently postponed the long-awaited decision to proceed with its system of massive sea gates to control tidal surges into the city, which was first proposed in 1973. Over thirty years years on from the devastating tidal flood of November 1966 nothing has yet been created and Venice is still as vulnerable.

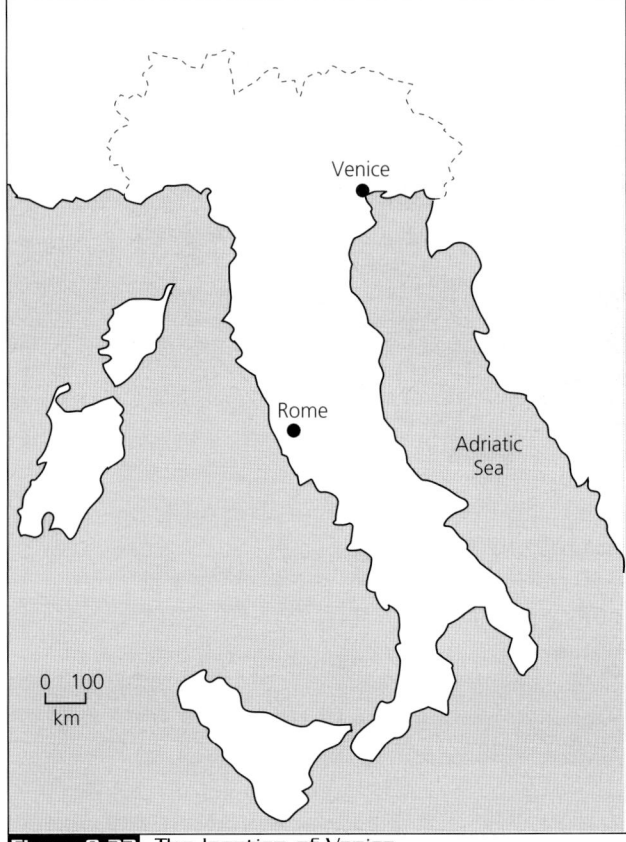

Figure 9.22 The location of Venice

TOURISM IN VENICE

The term **carrying-capacity** refers to the number of people that an environment can support without causing any long-term damage. Given the size of Venice (the historic centre of Venice comprises 700 ha with buildings protected from alterations by government legislation), and the conflict of interests between those employed in the tourist industry (and who seek to increase the number of tourists) and those not

Figure 9.23 Flooding is an increasing threat to Venice

Figure 9.24 Venice as an important tourist centre

Questions

17 What do the terms
   a carrying capacity mean
   b vicious circle mean?
18 What are the environmental implications of tourism in Venice. How might these effect Venice's other environmental problems?
19 Why is Venice at risk of flooding? Use an atlas to help you.

employed in the tourist industry (and who wish to keep visitor numbers down) it has been calculated that the optimum carrying capacity for Venice is 9780 tourists who use hotel accommodation, 1460 tourists staying in non-hotel accommodation and 10 857 day trippers on a daily basis. This gives an annual total of over 8 million people. This is 25% greater than the number of tourists actually arriving in Venice. However, the pattern of tourism is not even. There are clear seasonal variations with an increase in visitor numbers in Summer and at weekends. Research has estimated that an average of 37 500 day trippers a day visit Venice in August. A ceiling of 25 000 visitors a day has been suggested as the maximum carrying capacity for Venice.

The large volume of visitors which travel to Venice create a range of social and economic problems for planners **(Figure 9.24)**. Over-population causes congestion and competition for scarce resources. Day tripping is becoming increasingly important. while residential tourism is becoming less important. Thus the local benefits of tourism are declining.

Thus, Venice is a small historic city at risk from a late twentieth century invasion by tourists and day-trippers. The excessive numbers of day trippers have also led to a deterioration in the quality of the tourist experience. But it takes political will to solve the pressures posed by tourism in Venice. Managing the threat of rising sea levels, with the conservation of tourist attractions will not be easy.

Figure 9.25 Venice is a unique combination of water and culture

RESOURCES AND ENVIRONMENTAL ISSUES

9 Resources

A resource is anything that is useful such as oil, coal, water, vegetation, soil, people, education and technology. It is sometimes said that 'resources are not, they become . . .'. This means that something becomes a resource when it has a purpose or is useful to people. For example, in the Middle Ages oil was used for a medicine whereas now it is used as a fuel and as a basis for the chemicals industry. The value of a resource may increase as it becomes scarcer.

ENERGY RESOURCES

There are two main types of energy resources:
- non-renewable energy or fossil fuels
- renewable or alternative energy.

Non-renewable resources such as coal, oil, gas, and nuclear power can be used only once. By contrast, renewable energy can be used over and over again. Renewable energy includes hydroelectric power, wind, solar, tidal and geothermal. Renewable energy is often thought to be much better for the environment because it does not use up or destroy as many resources as non-renewable energy. However, renewable energy is expensive, unreliable, inconsistent and cannot be used everywhere.

The energy mix and energy consumption of a country

The **energy mix** of a country is the variety of energy sources that a country uses to make up its total energy needs. For example, some oil-rich countries, such as Saudi Arabia, depend almost entirely on oil, whereas others, such as Japan, depend upon hydroelectric power and nuclear power. Others may use a much greater mix including coal, oil, solar, nuclear, hydroelectric and so on.

The consumption of energy in a country is the amount of energy per head that a country uses. In general, as a country develops there is a greater use of energy, although much of this is due to industrial and commercial use.

The factors explaining how much energy is used are shown in (Figure 9.26).

Figure 9.26 Factors affecting the amount of energy used in a country

1. Availability and reliability of supply
2. Climate factors
3. Costs of production, distribution and use
4. Type of market
5. Political factors
6. Demand for energy
7. Population growth
8. Economic growth
9. Stage of development

EXPLANATION

A Less developed countries (LDCs) use a smaller amount of energy and more basic energy, such as fuelwood, whereas developed countries (DCs) use more energy and more expensive forms such as nuclear and oil.
B The UK used to have coal, now it has oil, but it has limited potential for solar or geothermal energy.
C In 1973 OPEC (the Organisation of Petroleum Exporting Countries) raised the price of oil, causing other countries to develop their own cheaper resources.
D Certain climates allow certain types of energy such as solar or wind power; colder climates require more heating.
E Industrial agricultural or residential.
F Rapid economic growth leads to more energy being used.
G Rapid population growth leads to more energy being used.
H This depends on population size and their wealth.
I Developing countries are limited in their choice of energy source.

Questions

20 Define the following terms: renewable energy; non-renewable energy; resource.
21 Suggest ways in which resources change over time.
22 What forms of energy do you use in your home? How might this differ if you lived in somewhere such as the Amazon rainforest? Give reasons for your answer.

Figure 9.27 The energy mix of the UK, 1937 and 1990

	Coal	Oil	Gas	Others
1937	74	26	—	—
1990	33	34	23	10

Energy flow in a developed country

Figure 9.28 shows the energy flow through a developed country. Electricity generated by nuclear power stations and hydroelectric sources (and other renewable sources) is included as primary electricity or energy.

Oil

Oil is a fossil fuel (non-renewable resource). It is the fuel of the twentieth century as well as being the source of the petrochemicals industry.

The advantages of oil:

- easy to transport by tanker or pipeline or locally by lorry
- a versatile fuel/raw material
- it is cheap
- there is a large supply of it
- it is a relatively clean fuel

The disadvantages of oil:

- it causes pollution e.g. oil spills at Milford Haven, South Wales (1996) and Shetland, Scotland (1993)
- the burning of oil releases greenhouse gases and leads to global warming
- there is potential for terrorist attack (especially with the conflicts in the Middle East) e.g. the burning of Kuwait's oil fields in the Gulf War
- countries may be over-dependent on oil
- the price of oil is very sensitive to political manipulation (**Figure 9.31**)
- oil can be used as a political lever to hold countries to ransom e.g. Serbia in 1999 and Iraq, where sanctions and food for oil have been in place since the early 1990s
- oil producers often exploit LDC producers such as the exploitation of the Ogoni people in Nigeria.

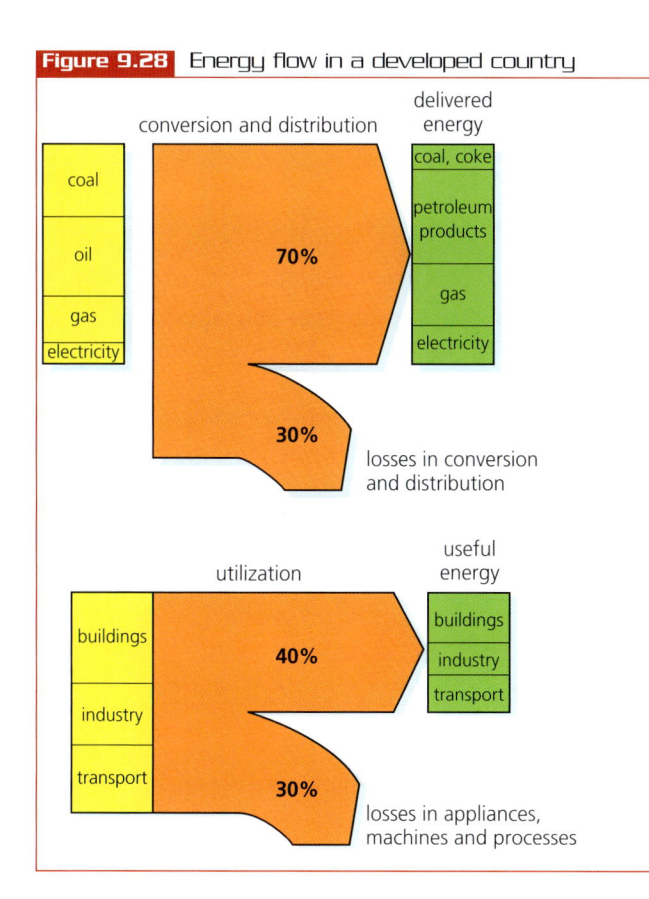

Figure 9.28 Energy flow in a developed country

Questions

23 Match the factors affecting energy consumption (as shown in **Figure 9.26**) with the explanations A to I.

24 Draw two pie charts to show the energy mix of the UK in 1937 and 1990. Compare the energy mix of the UK in 1937 with its energy mix in 1990.

25 What are the sources of Britain's energy as shown in **Figure 9.28**? Give approximate percentages for each of the four categories.

26 How much energy is lost in the conversion and distribution of energy sources into usable forms of energy such as electricity, gas and petroleum products?

27 In what ways is energy delivered to the consumer? Who are the main consumers of energy in the UK? Give percentages using **Figure 9.28**.

28 How much of the original energy source actually makes it to the consumer?

RESOURCES AND ENVIRONMENTAL ISSUES

Figure 9.29 The location of the world's main oil fields

• Oil

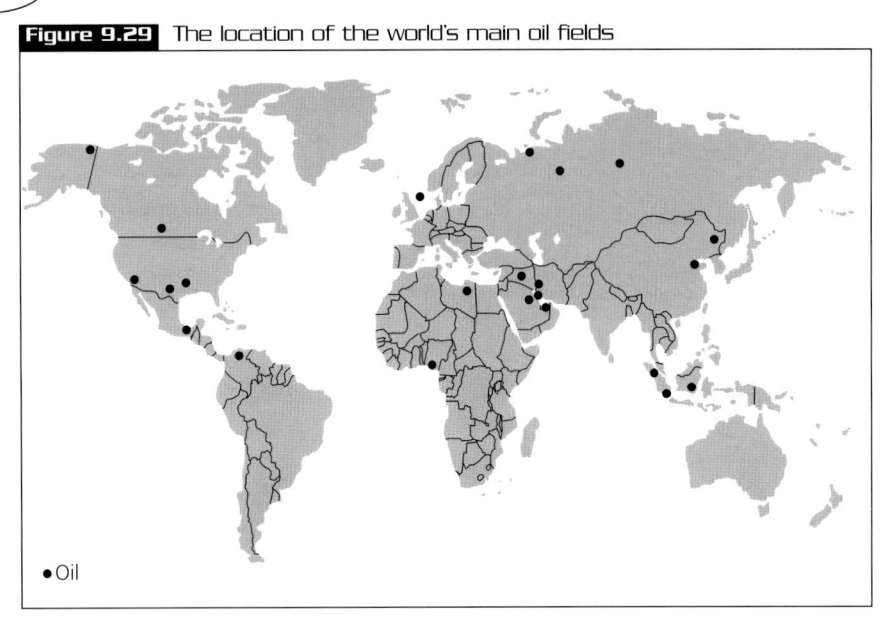

Figure 9.30 The world's main oil routes

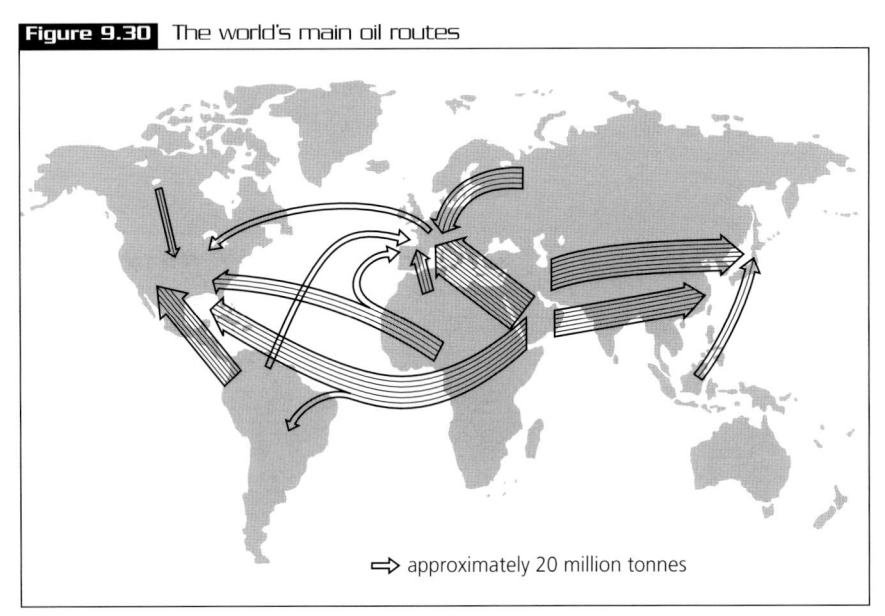

⇒ approximately 20 million tonnes

Questions

29 Where are the world's main oil fields as shown in **Figure 9.29**?

30 Where does most oil come from as shown in **Figure 9.30**?

31 Where does it go to?

32 Figure **9.31** shows changes in the price of oil between 1900 and 1990. All prices have been converted to the price they would have been in 1989, and so can be directly compared.

 a) What was the price of oil in 1900?

 b) Suggest why the price of oil rose between 1915 and 1919.

 c) Why did it fall between 1920 and 1925?

 d) Why did it continue to fall into the 1930s?

 e) Describe the trend in oil prices up until 1973.

 f) What was the price of oil at the start of 1973?

 g) What was it at the end of 1973?

 h) When was the peak in oil prices, and how much was the price of oil?

 i) How and why did the price of oil change in the 1980s?

 j) Suggest reasons why the strength of the British economy varies with price of oil.

118

Figure 9.31 Changes in the price of oil

Events marked on chart: Discovery of Spindletop, Texas; Growth of Venezuelan production; Fears of shortage in USA; East Texas field discovered; Post-war reconstruction; Loss of Iranian supplies; Suez crisis; Yom Kippur war; Iranian revolution; Iraq invaded Kuwait; OPEC introduce netback pricing and, later, production quotas.

— $ 1989   — $ money of the day
1900-44 average   1945-85 Arabian Light posted at Ras Tanura   1986-89 Brent spot

Oil tanker spills

Figure 9.32 Oil tanker spills

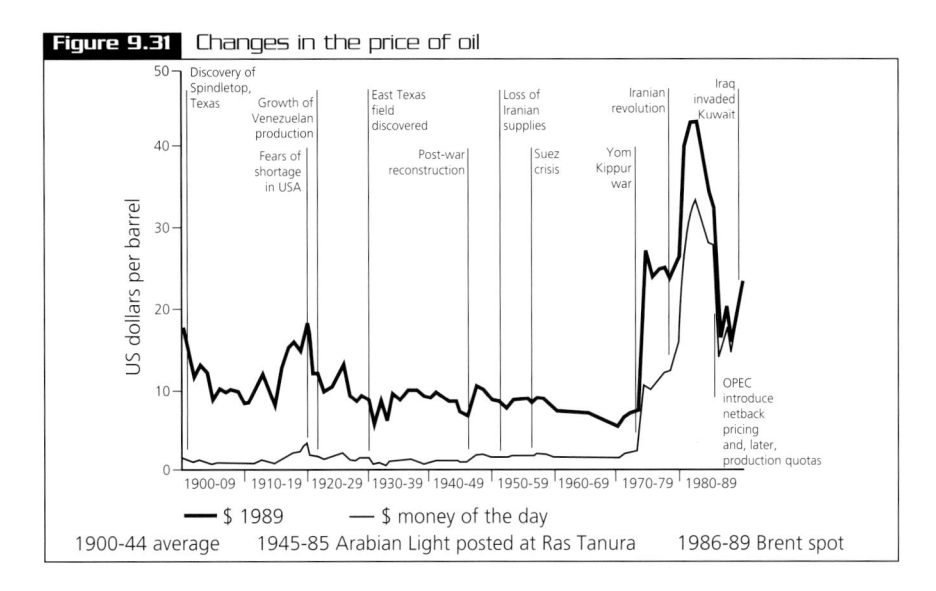

Country affected	Oil spilled ('000 tonnes)	Name	Flag	Year
Trinidad and Tobago	276	Atlantic Express	Greece	1979
South Africa	256	Castello de Belvar	Spain	1983
France	228	Amoco Cadiz	Liberia	1978
Canada	140	Odyssey	Liberia	1988
UK	121	Torrey Canyon	Liberia	1967
Oman	120	Sea Star	South Korea	1972
Greece	102	Irenes Serenade	Greece	1980
USA	99	Hawaiian Patriot	Liberia	1977
Turkey	95	Interdependenta	Romania	1979
UK	85	Braer	Liberia	1993

Figure 9.33 World map for oil spills

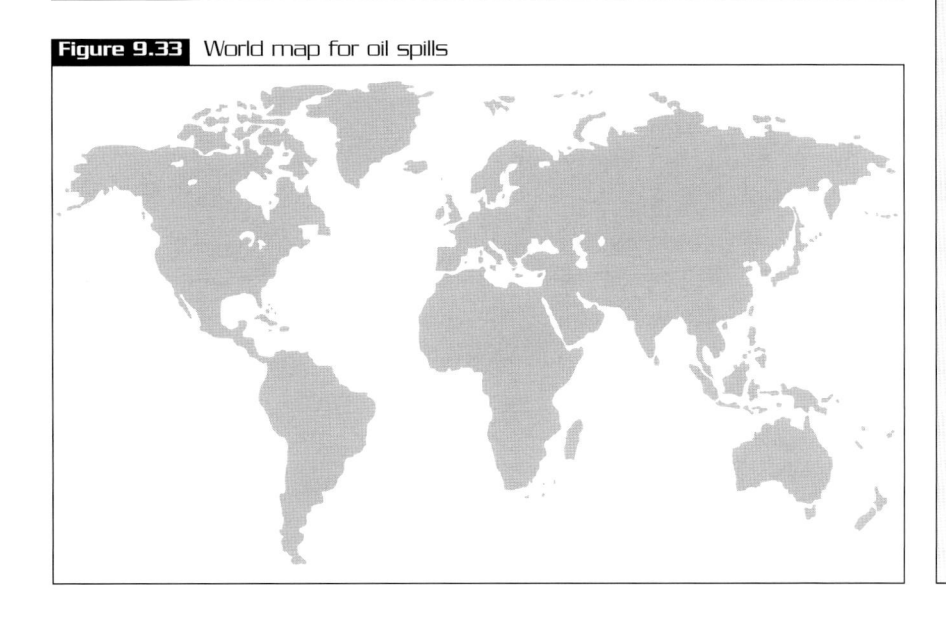

Questions

33 On the world map (**Figure 9.33**) plot the distribution of oil spills as shown by the data in **Figure 9.32**. Is there any pattern to the distribution you have shown?

34 What does the term 'flag' mean, as used in **Figure 9.32**?

35 In which country were most of the vessels that crashed registered in?

36 What does this suggest about safety regulations in this country?

37 When did most of the oil spills occur?

38 What does this suggest about the ways in which regulations have changed since then?

39 Suggest some natural reasons and some human reasons why oil spills may occur.

The UK – an MEDC   10

Managing the Yorkshire Dales National Park

The Yorkshire Dales are well known for their bleak hills and their fertile vales **(Figure 10.1)**. The Yorkshire Dales was the seventh of ten National Parks in England and Wales to be designated. It included an area of about 1740 sq km. In 1972 a Local Government Act required National Parks to prepare a National Park Plan 'formulating their policy for the management of the Park'. In response, the Yorkshire Dales National Park Committee adopted a number of principles **(Figure 10.2)**.

Figure 10.1 The Yorkshire Dales National Park

KEY
- Tourist Information Centre
- National Park Centre
- Notable Church
- Car Park
- Nature Trail
- Museum
- Dales Barn or Bunkhouse
- Summit Height (in metres)
- Youth Hostel
- Passenger Station
- Dales Rail Station
- Yorkshire Dales National Park

In a survey of Park visitors a number of key results emerged:

- over 6 million people visit the Dales each year;
- August is the peak month with almost 20% of visitors;
- the peak day is the August Bank holiday with over 80 000 people visiting the park;
- the largest attraction is Wharfedale [Figure 10.3] with over 493 000 visitors;
- 86% of visitors used cars for their visit to the Dales;
- the majority of visitors were day visitors.

The most popular activity was sightseeing, followed by picnicking and exploring villages. Of the active activities walking was by far the most popular. Up to 50% of visitors had a walk – 27% of all visitors over 8 km and 23% between 3 and 8 km. By and large, a high proportion of visitors kept to the villages or their cars!

Visitors to the Yorkshire Dales National Park bring many benefits. These include jobs, income spent in the area and the support of facilities available to local communities, and increased choice of shops in the area. Total visitor spending in the Yorkshire Dales National Park is estimated at about £46 million. A further £14 million is spent by visitors staying outside the park who visit for the day. Spending by visitors to the Park supports a total of 1505 jobs within the park, and a further 355 in the areas surrounding the Dales. Many of these are part-time and seasonal however, and it is estimated that the number of equivalent full-time jobs are 989 within the Park and 256 outside it.

Visitors also bring problems: physical damage, disturbance to farm livestock and wildlife, congestion, development pressure on the landscape and social pressures on local communities. These pressures include:

Figure 10.2 Principles for managing the Yorkshire Dales

1 **Landscape change:** to ensure that as change takes place in the Dales, the landscape evolves without losing its special character, its high standard of scenery or its special features of cultural and scientific interest.
2 **Landscape enhancement:** to enhance the landscape of the Dales by the enrichment of its natural beauty, and by the removal and mitigation of disfigurements.
3 **Social and economic needs:** to give every possible consideration to the social and economic needs of the area, and so to regulate the recreational uses and the provision of facilities for public enjoyment of the National Park that farming and the social and economic life of the resident population are not dislocated or impaired.
4 **Public understanding:** to promote a better understanding between town and country by giving the townsman a deeper comprehension of the significance of nature, an appreciation of country lore and an insight into the essential processes of primary production in which the countryman is engaged, and to associate local people with the purposes of the National Park and to enlist their goodwill.
5 **Access and accommodation:** to enable visitors to the Dales to enjoy the qualities on natural beauty by ensuring the existence of appropriate access and accommodation
6 **Recreational activities:** to ensure that recreational activities in the Dales are compatible, and that each is practised in such manner and by such means as will leave natural beauty unimpaired for this and future generations.

Figure 10.3 Attractions of the YDNP

- **honeypot sites** – increasing numbers of visitors destroy the sites they come to see;
- **landowners** – do not like people roaming over their land;
- **visitors want car parks**, visitor centres and so on;
- **crops** get trampled on, gates are left open;
- **congestion** leads to noise and air pollution;
- **second homes** causes an increase in local house prices, and a decline in housing for local people;
- **agricultural developments** remove dry stone walls, heathlands, hedgerows, meadows and woodlands;
- **excessive commercialisation**.

AGRICULTURE

Farming has helped shaped the Dales landscape and remains an important source of employment and income for many people. A difficult climate and topography combine to make farming mostly based on grass. However, there are a number of changes in agricultural practises that are effecting the landscape of the Dales. For example, increasing use of chemical fertilisers and herbicides has made lowland grasslands more fertile and more productive, but less valuable for wildlife compared with fields managed in a traditional way. In the traditional hay meadow and pasture there were more habitats for wildlife, and a greater variety of grasses and flowering plants. Manuring by grazing stock helped raise soil fertility. By contrast, chemical fertilisers favour perennial grasses.

QUARRYING

Mining is a traditional activity in the Dales. There are a number of important mines such as the ones at Giggleswick (limestone), Horton-in-Ribblesdale, and Kilnsey and Threshfield, and Wharfedale (all limestone), and gritstone is mined at Helwith Bridge and Ingleton.

Existing quarries cause varying degrees of visual intrusion, especially in Ribblesdale and Wharfedale **(Figure 10.4)**. They also affect cave systems, archaeological remains, SSSIs, and agricultural activities.

Figure 10.4 Quarrying in the YDNP (Ribblesdale)

Questions

1. **a** What are the attractions of the Yorkshire Dales National Park?
   b How many youth hostels are there in the Yorkshire Dales National Park?
   c Which settlement has a railway station and a youth hostel?
   d What is the highest peak in the Yorkshire Dales National Park?
2. Using an atlas, find out which large urban areas are within 80 km of the Yorkshire Dales National Park.
3. Explain why traffic congestion is a major problem in the Dales.
4. Explain how changing agricultural practises are affecting the landscape of the Dales.
5. Briefly outline the problems in balancing development and management in the Yorkshire Dales National Park.

Ethnicity in the UK

A **racial minority** is a population group that is discriminated against on account of their colour. An **ethnic** minority is a group discriminated against on account of nationality, religion, language (i.e. not colour). However, both terms are often used to refer to groups discriminated against for any reason.

A **ghetto** is an area of low quality slum housing normally occupied by racial minorities.

ETHNICITY

Over 4 million British residents were born outside Britain. Of these:

- 245 000 were from Northern Ireland;
- 590 000 from the Republic of Ireland;
- 1.7 million from the New Commonwealth and Pakistan (NCWP);
- nearly 700 000 from Europe.

Up to 22% of London's population was born overseas, whereas elsewhere the proportion is less than 7%, and in the North it is only 2.4%. There is a strong regional variation in the location of Britain's ethnic and racial minorities. All are found to some degree in London and the South East. However, the Irish are relatively abundant in the West Midlands, North West and Strathclyde, whereas the NCWP are in the Midlands, North West and Yorkshire. By contrast 'others' are found in a variety of places for a variety of reasons such as Grampian (oil), London/Edinburgh (finance), Oxford, Cambridge, London (education), and Oxfordshire/Suffolk (military).

Figure 10.5 Ethnic groups by age and population 1991

Ethnic group	Population 000s	0–15	16–29	30–44	45–59	60+
West Indian/Guyanese	456	24	30	19	19	9
Indian	793	29	25	25	14	6
Pakistani	486	44	23	20	11	3
Bangladeshi	127	46	26	15	11	3
Chinese	137	25	28	29	13	5
All ethnic minority groups	2,682	34	26	22	13	5
White	51,805	19	21	21	17	21
TOTAL	54,983	20	22	21	17	20

Age breakdown of ethnic groups (%)

Non-whites make up a higher proportion of Britain's 0-15 year olds (9%) than the total population (5.5%). The location of ethnic minorities is explained largely by the location of employment opportunities. Early migrants were attracted to the textile and heavy industries of London, Midlands and Yorkshire. Since the collapse of Britain's industry most new migrants have tended to go to London and the South East where there are more jobs in service industries.

Indians form the largest single non-white group, followed by the Afro-Caribbeans and Pakistanis. Racial minorities are geographically concentrated in the UK. Over half of Britain's non-whites are found in the South East. London accounts for nearly half of Britain's non-whites. It accounts for over 60% of Afro-Caribbeans, 53% of Bangladeshis, over 40% of Indians but less than 20% of Pakistanis. In 1991 45% of the population of Brent belonged to an ethnic minority, 42% in Newham and 37% in Tower Hamlets. The highest proportion outside London were Slough and Leicester.

Figure 10.6 Ethnic minorities in the UK

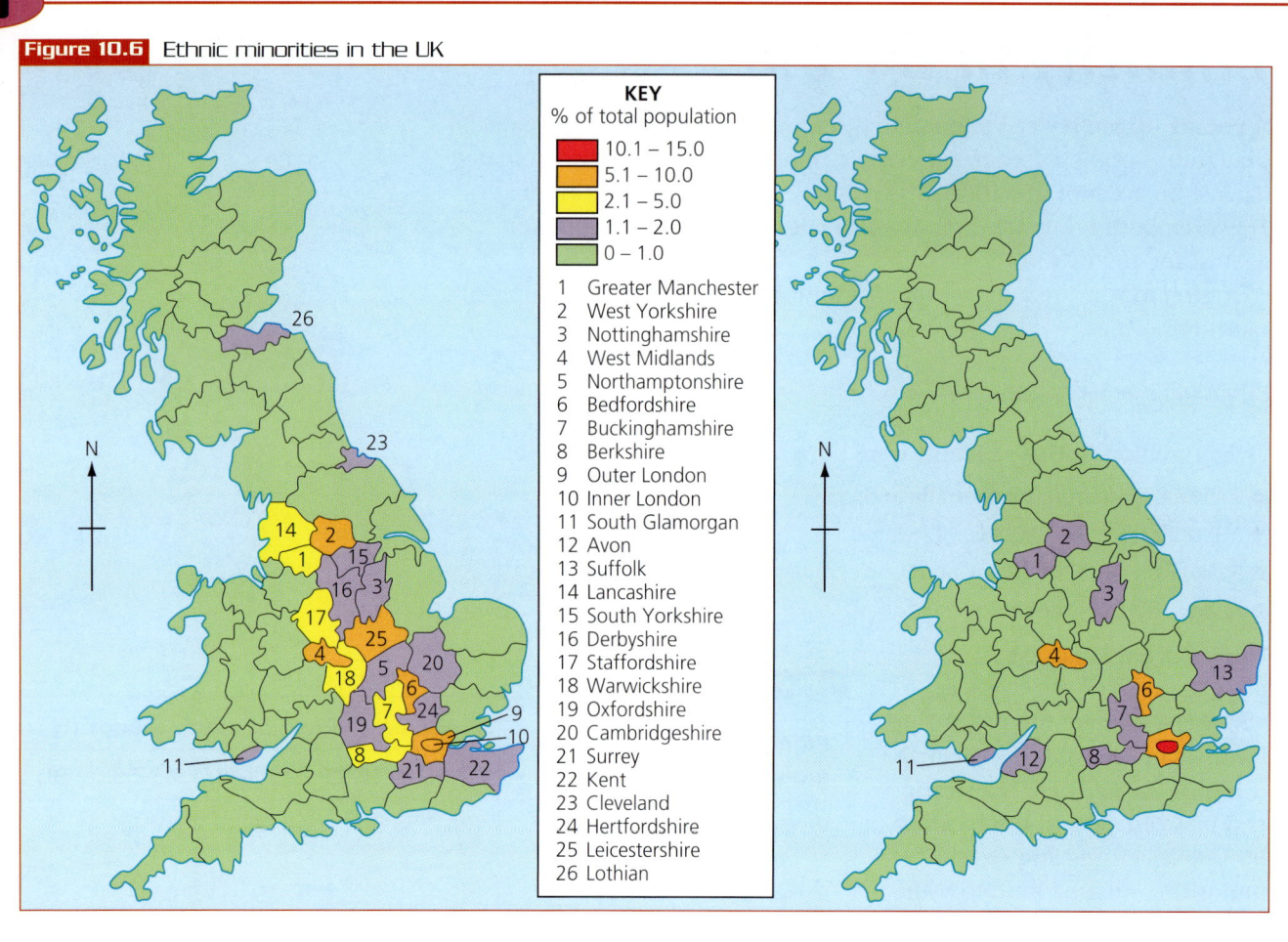

KEY
% of total population
- 10.1 – 15.0
- 5.1 – 10.0
- 2.1 – 5.0
- 1.1 – 2.0
- 0 – 1.0

1. Greater Manchester
2. West Yorkshire
3. Nottinghamshire
4. West Midlands
5. Northamptonshire
6. Bedfordshire
7. Buckinghamshire
8. Berkshire
9. Outer London
10. Inner London
11. South Glamorgan
12. Avon
13. Suffolk
14. Lancashire
15. South Yorkshire
16. Derbyshire
17. Staffordshire
18. Warwickshire
19. Oxfordshire
20. Cambridgeshire
21. Surrey
22. Kent
23. Cleveland
24. Hertfordshire
25. Leicestershire
26. Lothian

Racial minorities account for about 5% of the UK population. However, their distribution around the UK is not even **(Figure 10.6)**. They are concentrated in the main urban and industrial areas. For example, the Asian population is concentrated in Greater London (200 000), West Midlands (130 000), West Yorkshire (70 000) and Manchester (50 000). These are the large conurbations which have much employment in services (low paid menial jobs such as in transport and in health services) as well as industrial towns such as Bradford, Leeds and Huddersfield. These are associated with the textile industry and engineering.

The segregation of Asians is Leicester has been well recorded **(Figure 10.7)**. Out of a population of 300 000, there were 40 000 Asians, or about 14% of the population. These were largely concentrated in places such as Highfields, Evington and Belgrave. These are inner city areas, mostly on the eastern side of the city and also along radial transport routes. The housing is generally quite poor in these areas and is sub-standard in terms of density, central heating, modern amenities. Housing density is among the highest in Leicester. Much of the industry that originally attracted the Asians, in the 1950s, 1960s and early 1970s was concentrated in and around the CBD/inner city notably textiles, light engineering and services. The pattern is much less clear cut now.

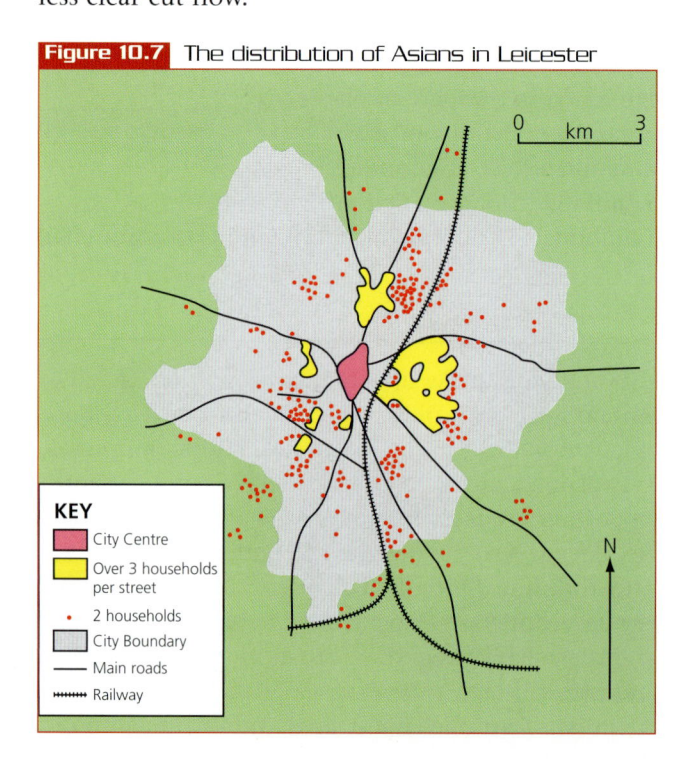

Figure 10.7 The distribution of Asians in Leicester

KEY
- City Centre
- Over 3 households per street
- 2 households
- City Boundary
- Main roads
- Railway

The level of racial prejudice and discrimination is increasing over time rather than decreasing **(Figure 10.8)**, and ethnic minorities are not being integrated in the sense of co-existing harmoniously alongside the majority white population. In 1994 there were up to 130 000 racial incidents in Britain, and the Anti-Racist Alliance estimates that fourteen people died as a result of racially motivated attacks in 1992–93. For example, in Greater Manchester the level of reported racially motivated attacks, threats and vandalism rose 20-fold between 1988 and 1993.

People from an ethnic background are more likely to be in lower status, lower paid, less skilled jobs than whites. However, it varies among ethnic groups. Up to two-thirds of Indians are in non-manual jobs (managerial, professional and technical) compared with only a half of whites. Young Indians are more likely to have higher educational qualifications than white – but Pakistani/Bangladeshi have much less. Unemployment rates for ethnics is twice that of whites.

There is still segregation of ethnic minorities, although Britain does not have any ghettos. Although there are more people from an ethnic background in and around London, they are more segregated in the North and Midlands.

In addition:

- 2 out of 3 Pakistanis and Bangladeshi households are the traditional family unit of husband, wife and children, but only 1 in 4 white households are traditional;
- unemployment among coloureds is higher (1 in 4);
- white families are twice as likely to live in houses with two or more bedrooms;
- 6% of males are coloured but they make up 17% of prisoners over 21.

Questions

6. What is an ethnic minority?
7. What is the largest ethnic minority in the UK?
8. Describe the location of the Bangladeshi population as shown on **Figure 10.6**.

Figure 10.8 Graffiti in Tower Hamlets

10 Industrial change in Scotland

The manufacturing sector contributed a third of Scottish GDP in 1966 but less than one-fifth by the 1990s, while the share of services rose from a half to two-thirds. The most important industries include the oil and chemicals processing industries; electronics and high technology engineering industries, which have been the fastest growing manufacturing industries since 1981; whisky, which continues to be a major manufacturing earner, and high quality textiles, which is a key manufacturing industry in many rural areas.

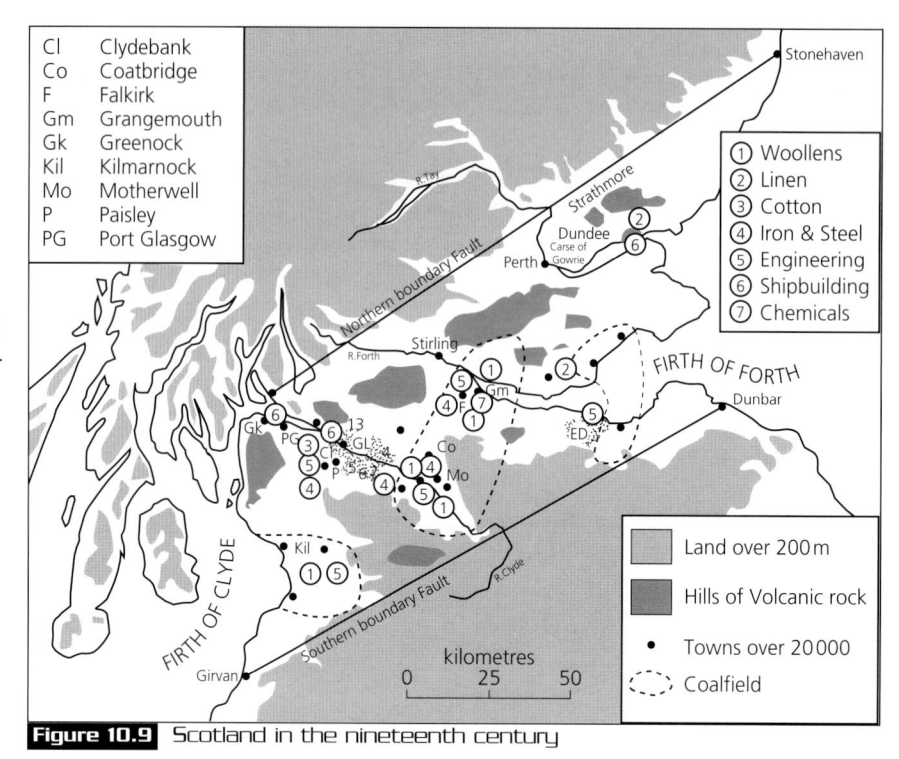

Cl	Clydebank
Co	Coatbridge
F	Falkirk
Gm	Grangemouth
Gk	Greenock
Kil	Kilmarnock
Mo	Motherwell
P	Paisley
PG	Port Glasgow

① Woollens
② Linen
③ Cotton
④ Iron & Steel
⑤ Engineering
⑥ Shipbuilding
⑦ Chemicals

Figure 10.9 Scotland in the nineteenth century

CENTRAL BELT

The Scottish metal, engineering and shipbuilding industries all reached their peak early in the twentieth century and have declined ever since. The economic transformation since 1945, especially in and around Glasgow, has led to periods of high unemployment and high outmigration. The cities of Glasgow, Dundee and Edinburgh and the depressed urban areas of Lanarkshire account for almost 60% of Scotland's unemployed and male unemployment rates of 25% are not uncommon.

Strathclyde is by far the most populous region and contains the main concentration of heavy industries. From the early 1960s, it experienced **deindustrialisation**, (the decline of manufacturing industry) more rapid and severe than elsewhere in Scotland.

Inward investment (investment by foreign companies) now accounts for the predominant part of Scotland's electronics industry and a very important part of the North Sea oil related activity.

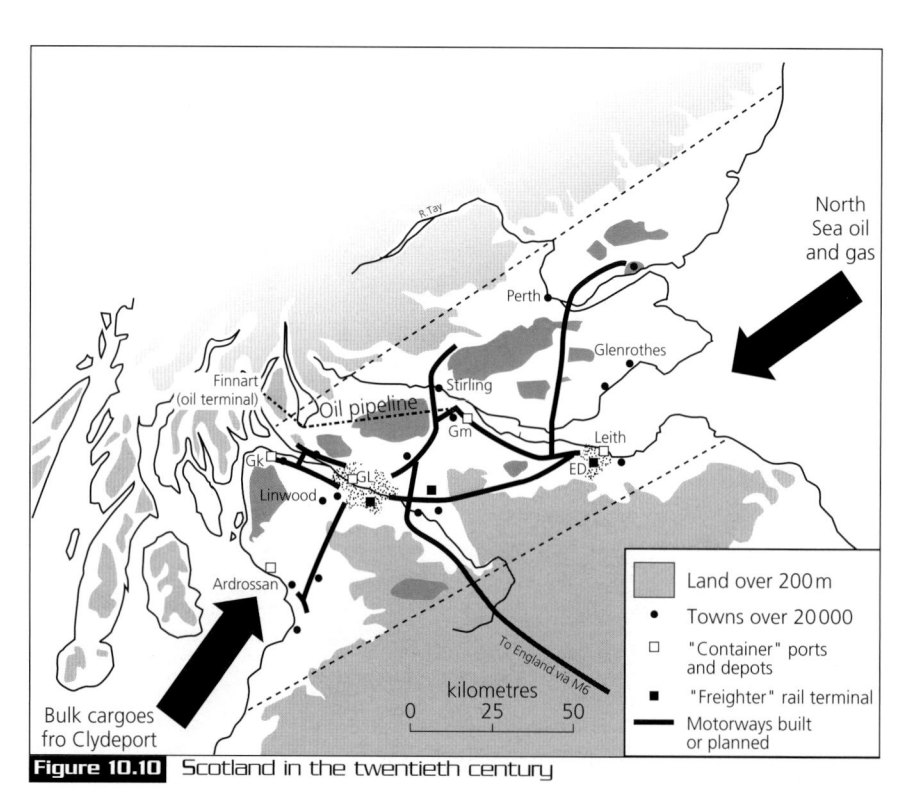

Figure 10.10 Scotland in the twentieth century

INWARD INVESTMENT, ELECTRONICS AND SILICON GLEN

In 1995–6 almost £1000 million worth of inward investment was committed to Scotland. Three-quarters of this was in electronics. Scotland now produces about 35% of all branded personal computers made in Europe, partly due to the presence of International Business Machines (IBM) and Compaq. **Silicon Glen**, as the Scottish electronics industry is known, employs 55 000 people, and in 1994 accounted for 30% of all Scottish manufacturing output.

The electronics industry in Scotland is quite recent. Much of it consists of assembly plants. The multinational spend very little on research and development in Scotland. Less than 20% of their spending on research and development goes to companies based in Scotland.

Inward investment into Scotland reached a record high between 1996 and 1997. The electronics sector remains the biggest area for new investment. Lite-On, a Taiwanese company announced that it would create over 1000 jobs assembling computer monitors in Lanarkshire. Oki Electric, the Japanese electronics company, is basing the manufacture of a new generation of fax machines in Scotland. Oki's factory in Cumbernauld, near Glasgow, is one of Britain's biggest production sites for office equipment, with output worth £350 million a year and nearly 1000 workers.

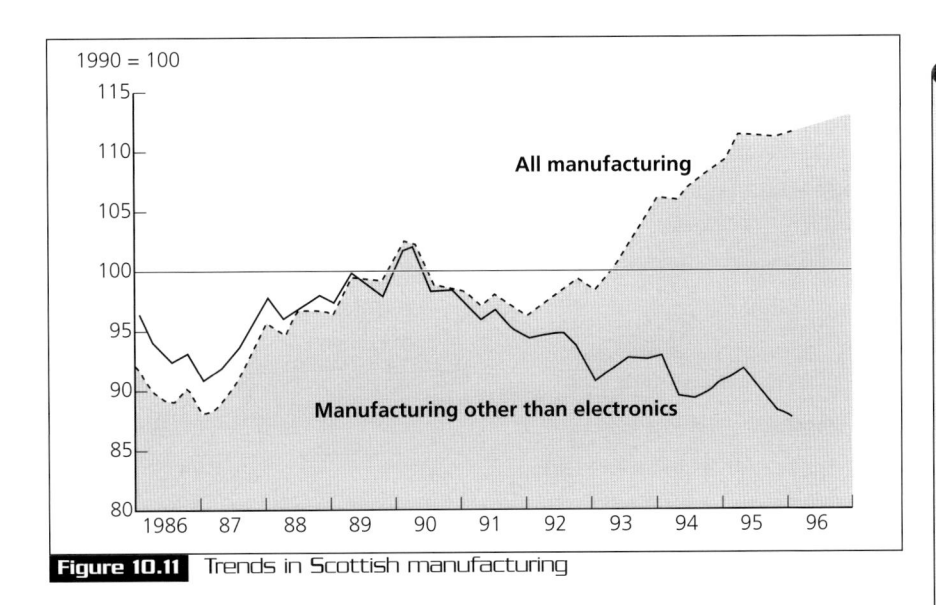

Figure 10.11 Trends in Scottish manufacturing

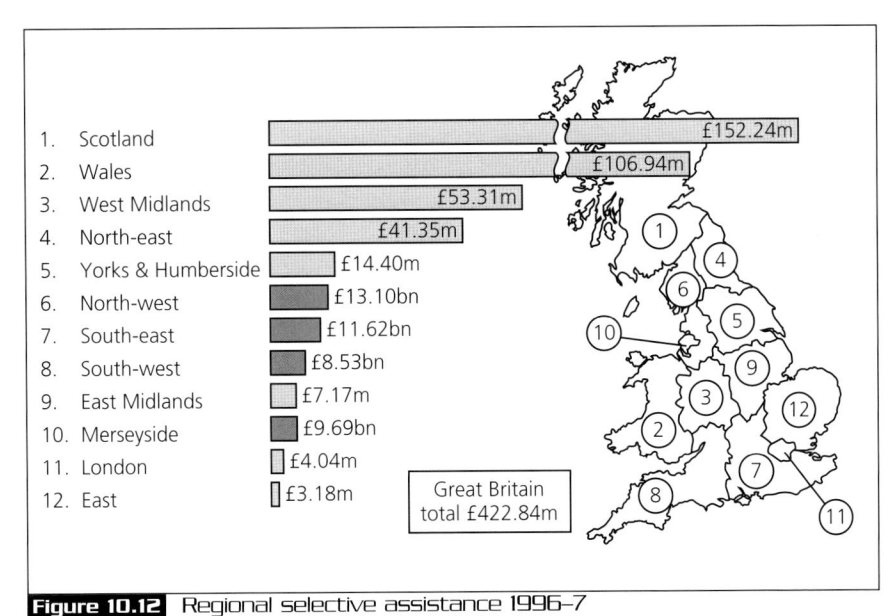

Figure 10.12 Regional selective assistance 1996–7

1. Scotland — £152.24m
2. Wales — £106.94m
3. West Midlands — £53.31m
4. North-east — £41.35m
5. Yorks & Humberside — £14.40m
6. North-west — £13.10bn
7. South-east — £11.62bn
8. South-west — £8.53bn
9. East Midlands — £7.17m
10. Merseyside — £9.69bn
11. London — £4.04m
12. East — £3.18m

Great Britain total £422.84m

Questions

9. Study **Figure 10.9** which shows Central Scotland in the nineteenth century. What were the physical factors that led to the growth of manufacturing industry in this region?

10. Study **Figure 10.11** which shows trends in manufacturing in Scotland.
    a. Compare the trends in all manufacturing (which includes the electronics sector) with that of manufacturing other than electronics. What conclusions do you reach?
    b. How do you explain these trends?

11. **Figure 10.12** shows regional selective assistance to the regions of Britain. Describe the pattern of investment as shown in Figure 10.12 Choose an alternative way of showing the data in Figure 10.12

China – an LEDC

11

The Hwang He (Yellow River)

The Hwang He (Yellow River) is one of the world's greatest rivers. The river drains an area of over 750 000 km sq, in which a population of 84 million people live, farming 13 million hectares of land **(Figure 11.1)**. It is called the Yellow river because of the large amount of yellow wind blown sediment (loess) that it erodes and deposits. The combination of this easily eroded material and the seasonal flow of the Yellow River cause great problems for the people who live in the lower parts of the catchment.

The Hwang He varies greatly on its course down from its source, a very cold plateau at an altitude of 5000m. It produces a stream which is clear, and a valley that is narrow and shallow. As it flows over solid rock (bedrock) it carves a meandering channel, sometimes with deep gorges.

In its middle stages the river flows across yellow wind-blown **loess** deposits rather than solid rock. In some places the loess deposits are over 300 m thick. The combination of the seasonal flow of the Hwang He and

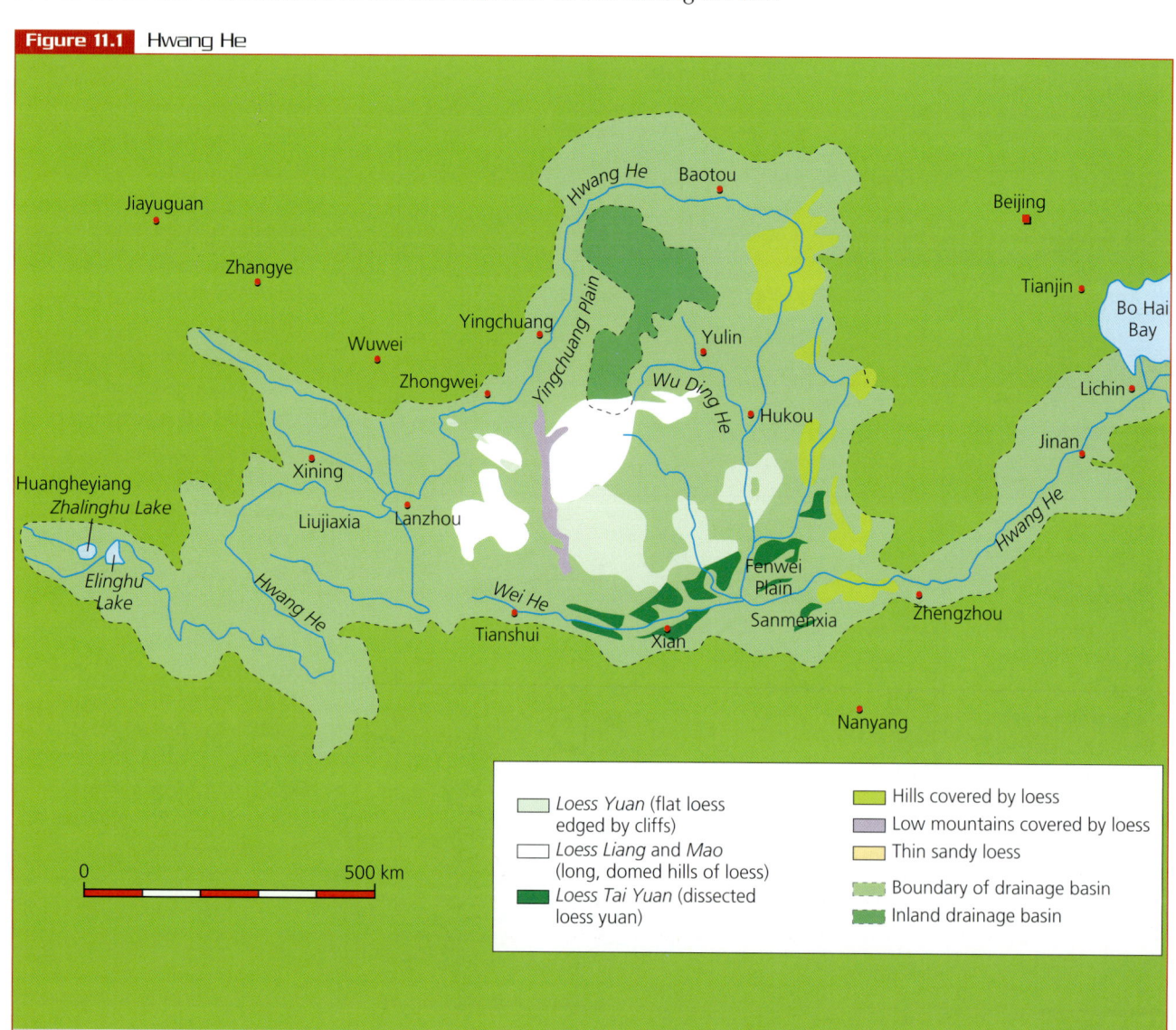

Figure 11.1 Hwang He

Legend:
- Loess Yuan (flat loess edged by cliffs)
- Loess Liang and Mao (long, domed hills of loess)
- Loess Tai Yuan (dissected loess yuan)
- Hills covered by loess
- Low mountains covered by loess
- Thin sandy loess
- Boundary of drainage basin
- Inland drainage basin

the highly erodable nature of the loess give rise to the extremely high rates of erosion and transport by the river. As the river flows through the loess plateau rates of erosion increase dramatically **(Figure 11.2)**.

The Hwang He then flows north through desert. As a result discharge and rates of erosion decrease. Here the river is said to be **braided** and consists of very wide channels separated by islands in the river.

As the river flows south into a wetter region it flows across thick beds of loess again. Rates of erosion increase dramatically. In some parts, such as near Yulin close to the Great Wall of China, up to 25 000 tonnes of loess are eroded per sq km!

The sediment that the river carries has its advantages. First, much of it is fertile soil and can be used for farming. Second, where the deposits have been dropped on the coastal plains they have formed a large alluvial fan, with a delta at the sea. The area houses over 10 million people, with population density of over 500 per km sq. It also contains a dense network of communications systems and many towns, forming the industrial base of northern China.

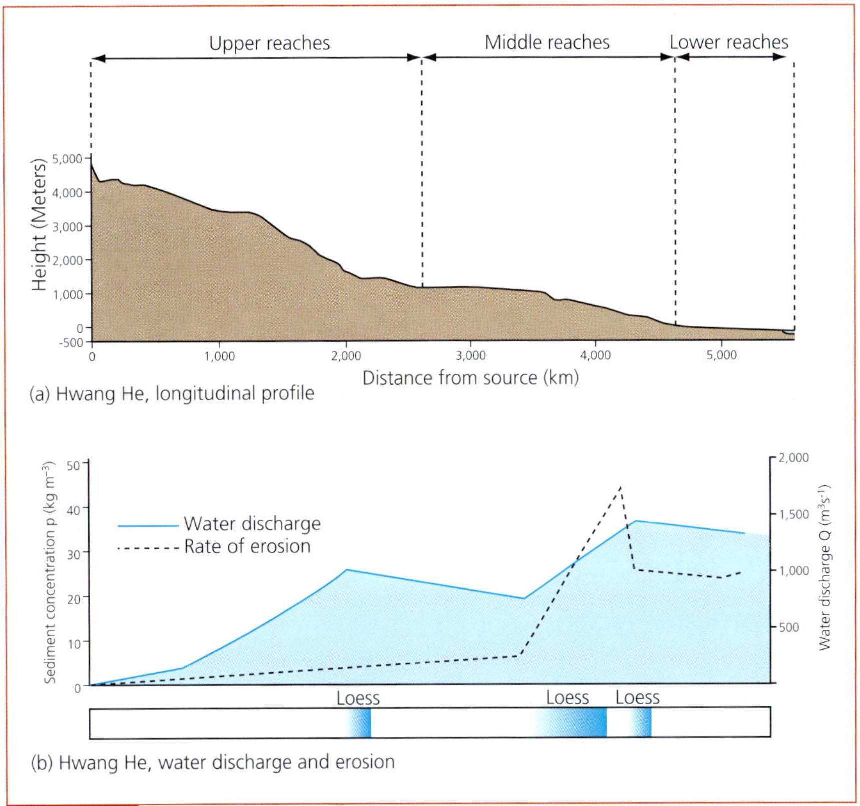

Figure 11.2 Geology and erosion on the Hwang He

FLOODS IN CHINA

Floods are a natural feature of all rivers. For most of the time a river is contained in its channel but at other times it may burst its bank and a flood occurs. Floods bring advantages such as water and fertile **alluvium** (river deposits or silt) which allow farmers to grow crops. But the problem is that they may bring too much water and too much silt. The results can be devastating as the experience of China shows.

The Hwang He river is said to have killed more people than any other natural feature and for this reason it is called the 'river of sorrow'. The worst flood occurred in 1332 – over 7 million people drowned and a further 10 million died as a result of the famine that followed.

Attempts to control the river go back at least as far as 2356 BC and there have been levees on the river for at least 2500 years! Despite this long history of engineering the Hwang He has shifted its course on at least ten occasions. When the river shifts its course it can change where it enters the sea by as much as 1100 km.

In 1887 the Hwang He overtopped its bank and flooded an area of 22 000 km sq 8 m deep! Over 1 million people were killed by the floods

Questions

12 Why is the Hwang He important? Give reasons to support your answer.
13 Study **Figure 11.2** which shows rates of erosion. How do rates of erosion vary with
   i geology
   ii the amount of water in the river?

CHINA – AN LEDC

Figure 11.3 Floods on the Hwang He

Figure 11.4 Flood defence methods on the Hwang He

Questions

14 Why do people live in floodplains if they are so dangerous?

15 Why is the Hwang He known as the 'river of sorrow'?

and the famine that happened afterwards. It is ironic that famine should follow floods but the silt carried by the river destroys the crops that it is dumped on. During normal flow conditions the river contains a large amount of silt. In fact, 40% of the river flow is sediment. An 8m flood might be expected to dump over 3m of material on the ground.

Now the river is 20m higher than the floodplain and the risk of flooding is great. As China's population continues to grow more and more people are living on the fertile floodplains. This makes the risk of a disaster even greater. To prevent flooding the Chinese authorities have built levees to contain the water. How long these will last is a very real problem for the people living in the floodplain.

WATER IN CHINA

Millions of Chinese do not have access to clean water. In particular, China's northern regions are suffering a severe water shortage **(Figure 11.5)**. Action is required but it will cost millions of pounds. The scale of the problem is immense: more than half of China's large- and medium-sized cities faced shortages in 1996 and over 100 cities were severely deprived of water. Water pollution adds to the problem.

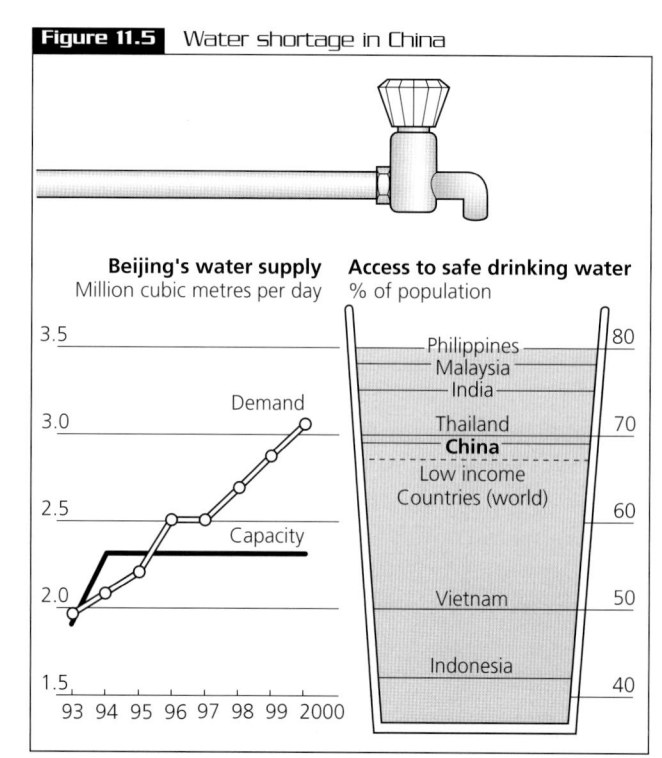

Figure 11.5 Water shortage in China

Beijing's water supply — Million cubic metres per day (Demand rising to 3.0 by 2000; Capacity ~2.2)

Access to safe drinking water — % of population: Philippines, Malaysia, India, Thailand, China (~70), Low income Countries (world), Vietnam (~50), Indonesia (~40)

130

Worst affected cities include Taiyuan, capital of Shanxi province south-west of Beijing, and Datong, also in Shanxi **[Figure 11.6]**. Water is available there only at certain times of the day. In the rural areas it is not much better. 70 million farmers and 60 million livestock lack sufficient water. Since 1990 26 million hectares of China's 110 million hectares of arable land have been affected by **drought**. In addition, grain outputs have decreased as a result.

China has a total water resource of 2.8 billion cubic metres. This gives an average per capita availability of 2300 cubic metres. However, in the nine northern provinces it is just 500 cubic metres. In Beijing it is less than 400 cubic metres. This is less than 14% of China's average, and just 3% of the world average. Local reservoirs cannot meet Beijing's demand. Consequently, Beijing is tapping nearly 3 billion cubic metres of **groundwater** each year. This has caused the **water table** to drop by 50 metres and **subsidence** is now an increasing problem. In Tianjin, a city of over 10 million people, and one of China's busiest ports, the situation is even worse! Water availability is the lowest in China.

The water problem in China is so intense largely as a result of its population size. The situation is not made worse by a series of problems:

- 25% of China's urban water supply is lost through leakages;
- an even greater share is lost in manufacturing;
- leaking pipes cost China over £230 million worth of water annually;
- in rural areas porous canals lose 50% of their water;
- efficient forms of irrigation, such as drip irrigation and sprinklers are rarely used, because of their cost.

Questions

16 Using an atlas explain which areas of China are most likely to have a water shortage.

17 Explain the human factors which intensify China's water problem.

18 What are the links between water shortages and ground subsidence (sinking). Why has the problem of subsidence increased in the China since the 1980s?

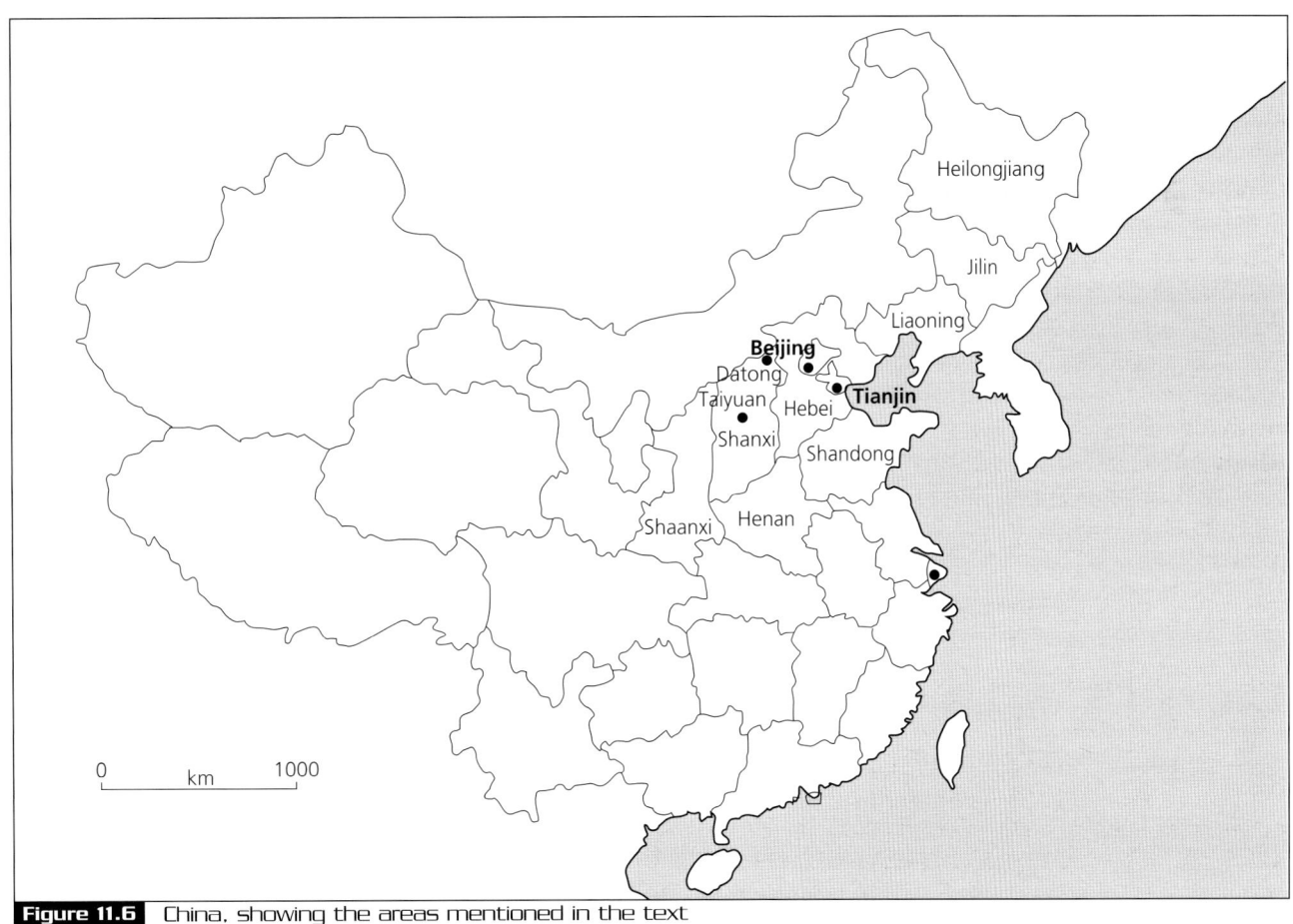

Figure 11.6 China, showing the areas mentioned in the text

11

CHINA'S CHANGING AGRICULTURE

In China there is a broad distinction between the drier pastoral lands dominating the north west and the moister cultivated lands in the south east. In the cooler north-east wheat and millet are grown whereas in the warm and moist south-east rice is grown. Given China's vast size and its range of climates it is not surprising that there is a great variation in its agriculture.

China's farming is changing for a number of reasons. These include:

- improvements in technology, such as irrigation, tractors and the use of fertilisers;
- changes in demand for food products;
- a decline in soil and water resources;
- environmental problems such as the Chicken flu in Hong Kong in 1998.

Figure 11.7 Agricultural population (%)

	1930–44	1945–64	1970	1980	1993
World	—	—	55	51	45
China	—	—	78	74	65
Egypt	71	57	52	46	39
Japan	48	27	20	1	6
South Africa	64	30	33	17	13
Thailand	89	82	80	71	62
UK	6	5	3	3	2
USA	—	7	4	4	2

Changes in dietary patterns in China are having an negative effect on global food supplies. As the Chinese population change from a rice-based diet to a grain-based one, supplies of rice will decline. China's import of grain is likely to rise from 16 million tonnes in 1995 to 43 million tonnes in 2010, thereby reducing global stocks. In addition, as more of the urban-based population consume more meat, there will be further falls in food production. This is because 1 ha of land can produce large amounts of cereals, but it takes a large amount of cereal or grass to feed every cow or pig. Farmland can provide far more in terms of crops than it ever can in terms of livestock.

Figure 11.8 Agricultural land use

I	Land area ('000 km sq.)	V	Forest
II	Arable land (%)	VI	Other land
III	Permanent crops (%)	VII	Irrigated area ('000 km sq.)
IV	Permanent grassland (%)	VIII	Population (million)

	I	II	III	IV	V	VI	VII	VIII
World	131 163	10.3	0.7	26.1	29.6	33.3	2 496	5 718
China	9 326	10.0	0.3	42.9	14.0	32.8	490.3	1 226
Egypt	995	2.2	0.4	0.0	0.0	97.4	26.5	64
Japan	377	10.8	1.2	1.7	67.0	19.3	28.0	125
South Africa	1 221	10.1	0.7	66.6	3.7	18.9	11.4	44
Thailand	511	33.3	6.1	1.6	26.4	32.6	44.0	58
UK	242	27.1	0.2	46.0	10.0	16.7	1.1	58
USA	9 573	19.4	0.2	25.0	29.9	25.5	203.0	263

Questions

19 Choose an appropriate method, such as a series of bar graphs, to illustrate the data shown in **Figure 11.7**. Classify the countries into those which have
   i a small proportion engaged in agriculture
   ii a large proportion engaged in agriculture.

20 Which countries in **Figure 11.7** have shown the greatest change
   i since 1930–44
   ii since 1980?
   How do you explain these changes and differences?

21 Choose an appropriate method to show variations in land use among the countries shown in **Figure 11.8**. Describe the variations you have shown. What are the implications of this for food production.

Figure 11.9 Regional inequalities in China

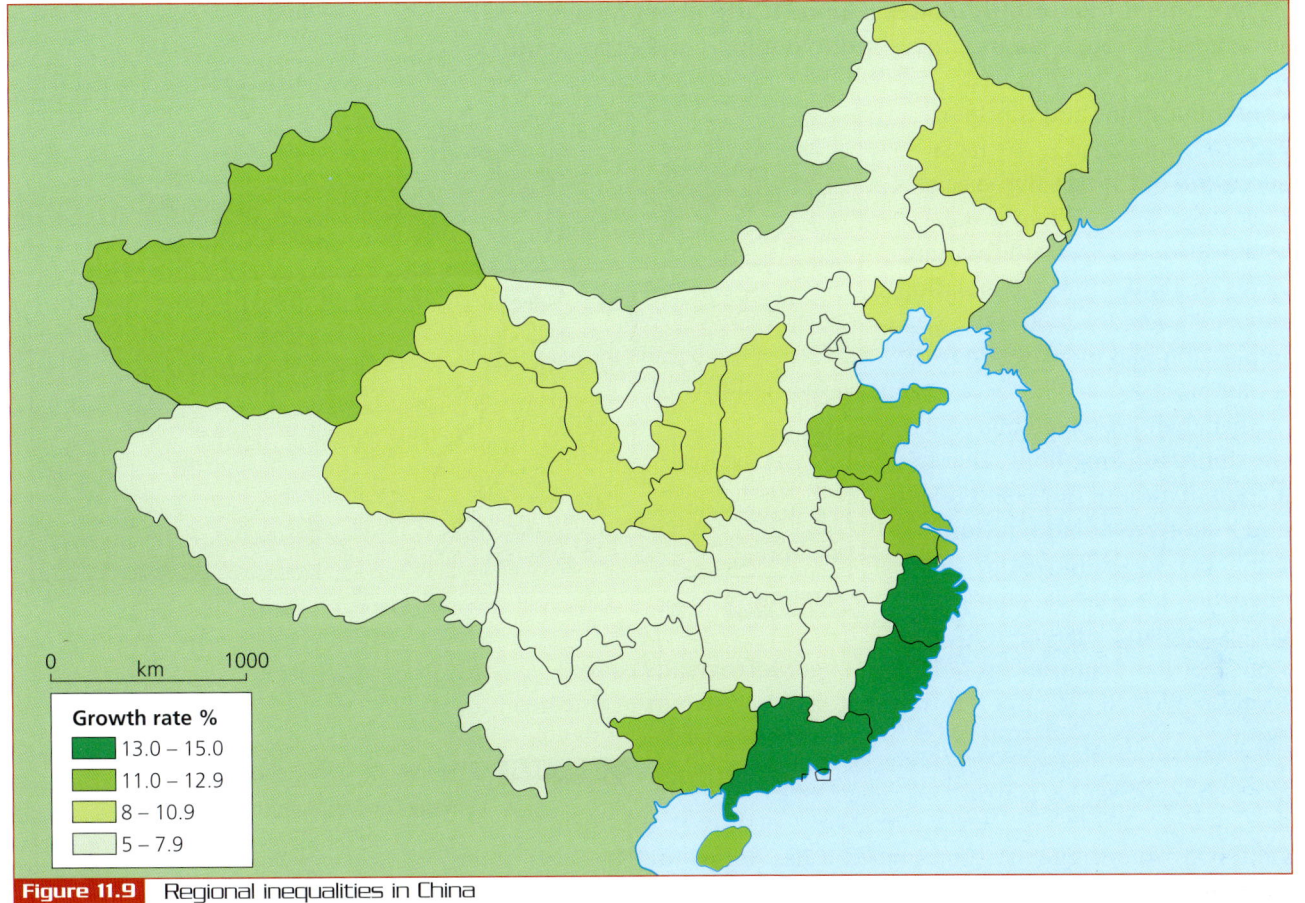

REGIONAL INEQUALITIES IN CHINA

Regional inequalities are very important in China. There are major differences in physical geography, quality of life, and employment opportunities. In the west of China the rugged Tibetan plateau dominates the landscape, reaching over 3500m in height. By contrast, the east of China is much lower with fertile river valleys and deltas. Rainfall increases towards the east. The far west is very dry while the east receives summer rain.

These physical differences have led to important social and economic inequalities. The western plateau regions remain underdeveloped and isolated whereas the eastern coastal regions are more developed. They form China's economic core. China's coastal locations are especially important. For example, they account for about 66% of industrial production, 80% of export earnings, and 90% of foreign capital **(Figure 11.9)**.

11

The Special Economic Zones (Figure 11.10) attract foreign investment through tax incentives, reduced import and export tariffs, cheap labour, and improved communications and transport facilities. Shenzhen is the most successful of China's five special Economic Zones. When it was established as a Special Economic Zone, in 1980, it has a population of just 30 000. By 2000 its population had increased to over 3 million.

Shenzhen prospered due to its proximity to Hong Kong. Due to a combination of high land prices and a shortage of land in Hong Kong, developers looked to Shenzhen for a needy supply of cheap land and labour – both were less than half the cost of Hong Kong. Moreover, its coastal location allowed the import of raw materials and export of finished goods.

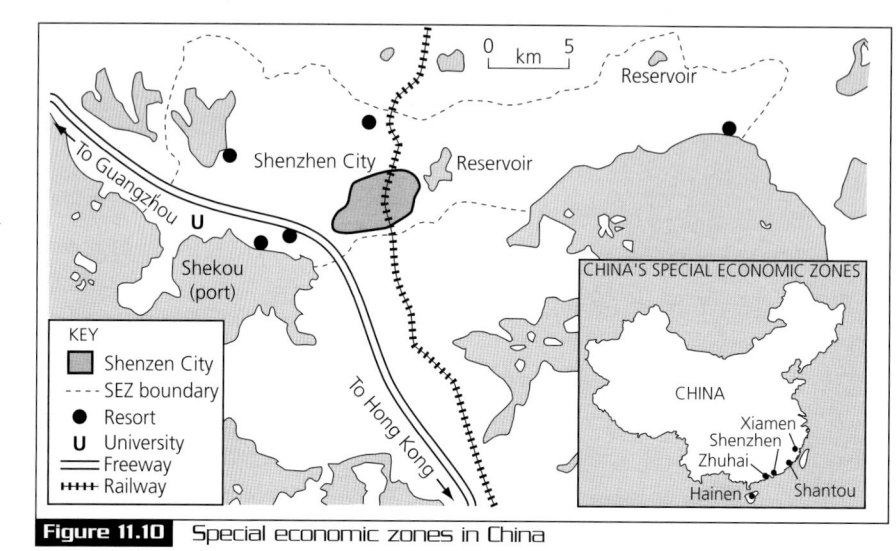

Figure 11.10 Special economic zones in China

ENERGY IN CHINA

China has an energy crisis looming – if it has not already got one. With the economy increasing rapidly there is a huge demand for more energy to fuel China's development. China attempted to increase its energy resources by 50% between 1996 and 2000. However, power shortages continue to slow economic growth and the Chinese authorities are keen to make energy a reliable resource.

Although China is among the world's top three users of energy (in terms of total energy used) it is only 80th in terms of use of energy per person. Most of China's energy comes from coal **(Figure 11.11)**.

Figure 11.11 The use of coal in China

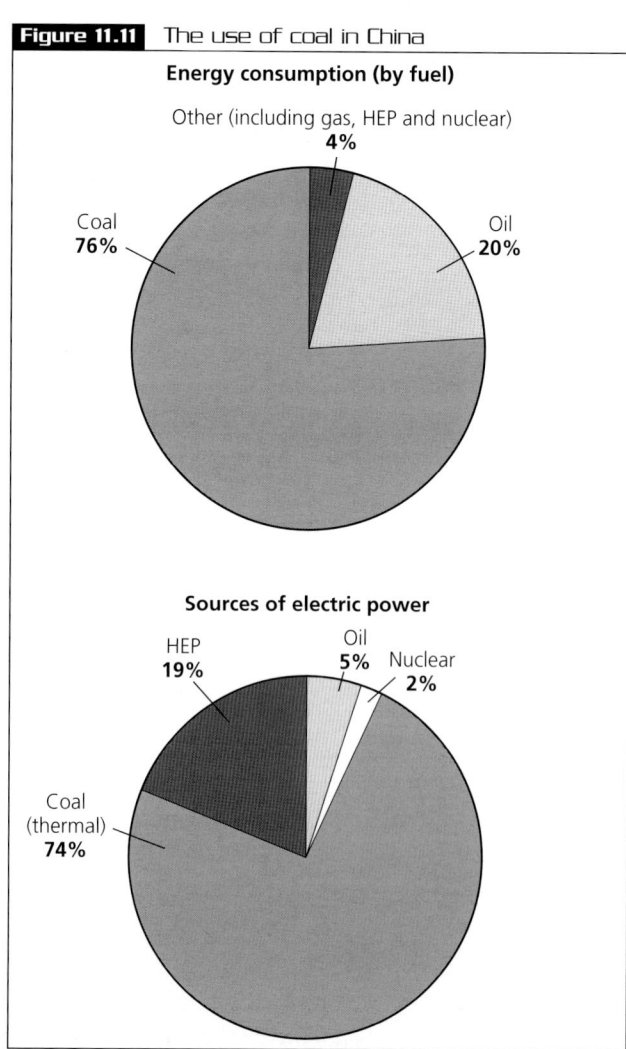

Energy consumption (by fuel)
- Coal 76%
- Oil 20%
- Other (including gas, HEP and nuclear) 4%

Sources of electric power
- Coal (thermal) 74%
- HEP 19%
- Oil 5%
- Nuclear 2%

Questions

22 a State **two** physical factors which cause regional inequalities in China.

b State **two** human factors which cause regional inequalities in China.

23 Which of the factors that you have mentioned do you think are the most important. Give reasons to support your answer.

24 Draw a spider diagram to show some of the effects of regional inequalities.

134

It is unlikely that China's consumption of energy will decrease. This is for two main reasons. First, China is one of the world's largest economies. As the economy expands and modernises more energy will be needed. Second, the use of energy in homes is low. As people's standards of living increase more energy will be used. At present this means that more coal will be burnt. China is the last great coal economy. Production is immense, 1.2 billion tonnes in 1995 and forecast for 1.4 billion tonnes in 2000. The workforce exceeds 5 million people. Internal demand is massive, hence there is little left for export. Coal accounts for 75% of China's energy consumption. China is faced with major problems. First, there are difficulties in moving coal from the mines to the consumers. China's coal is mainly in the north [**Figure 11.12**]. Shanxi province alone accounts for 25% of the country's output. But the bulk of the demand is in the south and south west. Second, it will need to develop further coalfields to meet future demand. Shenmu in the north west is the only big coalfield likely to make a lasting impact over the next decade.

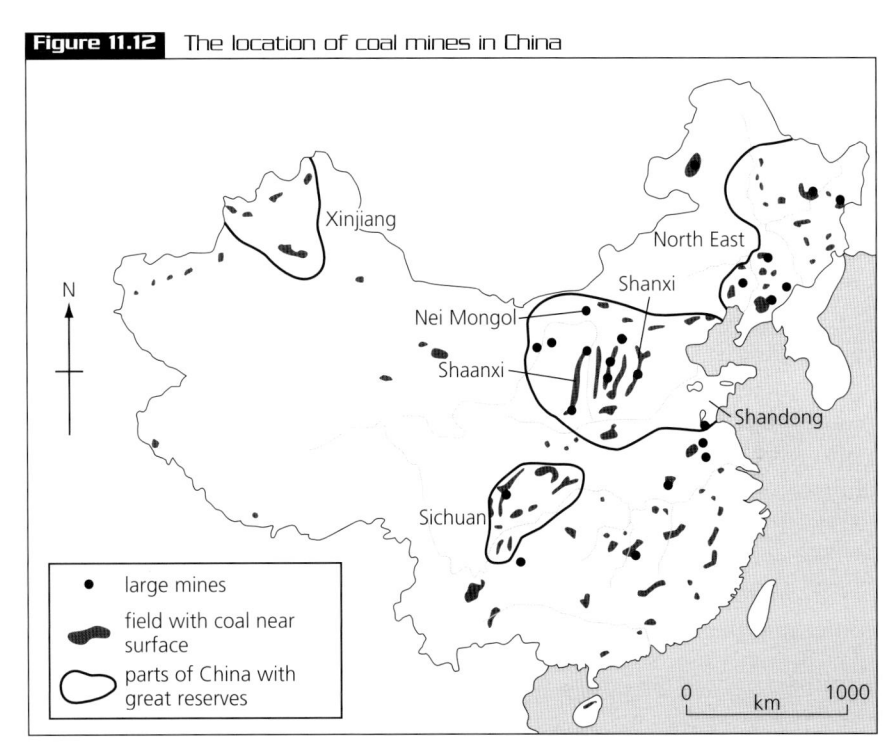

Figure 11.12 The location of coal mines in China

MIGRATION IN CHINA

Migration in China accounts for some of the largest and most important rural to urban migrations in the world. The main pattern is from less developed parts of the country to the more prosperous cities, especially in the South East and, in particular, Beijing.

When the Communist Party came to power in 1949 China's urban population was about 70 million or 12.5% of the total population (575 million). From 1949 when the People' Republic of China was founded, to 1970 most population migration in China took place in rural areas, i.e. most migrants moved from densely populated rural areas to sparsely populated frontiers. Some also migrated to work in construction and on the mines. However, the overwhelming purpose was the population of, exploitation of, and consolidation of China's frontiers.

One of the first main surveys of migration in China analysed data for the years 1982-7. It reached three main conclusions. First, population migration increased between 1982 and 1987 compared with earlier estimates. Between 1982 and 1987, 'official' migrants accounted for nearly 3% of the population (over 30 million people!). Second, the direction of migration changed. Most migrants moved from rural areas to cities. During the same period urban areas grew at the expense of rural areas by some 13 million people. Third, most people migrated from inland provinces to coastal areas. A smaller proportion migrated to

Questions

25 Describe the location of coal in China, as shown in **Figure 11.12**.

26 State **three** reasons why coal is important to China.

factories and mines in inland areas. Of the 30 million migrants 79% stayed within their own province, whereas the other 21% were involved in inter-provincial migration.

Provinces which gained migrants included Shanghai, Beijing, Hebei, Shandong, Jiangsu, Guangdong, Tianjin, Liaoning, Hubei and Ningxia [Figure 11.13]. By contrast, Heilongjiang, Inner Mongolia, Xinjiang and Gansu, which used to attract migrants, lost people during that period. The most popular location is Beijing. Within the city certain regions attract migrants from different parts of the country. The suburb of Dahongemen contains over 400 000 people from Zhejaing province in south-east China and is referred to as Zhejiang village. Another is Xinjiang village, containing Muslim Chinese from the west of China.

The 1990 census revealed that these trends were continuing. Between 1985 and 1990 the population officially moving to other cities, provinces or overseas was 3%. The vast majority of migrations were internal, and 81% involved moves within or to urban areas. Less than 18% were moves to rural areas, and of these only 5% were new residents to rural areas, the others were moving from one rural area to another.

Figure 11.13 Migration in China

Region	Map	Moving from other areas	Moving to other areas	Net removal population into the region
Beijing	22	6.13	1.13	5.00
Tianjin	23	3.54	0.98	2.56
Hebei	24	0.78	1.10	−0.32
Shanxi	25	0.96	0.80	0.16
Inner Mongolia	26	1.13	1.32	−0.19
Liaoning	27	1.29	0.68	0.61
Jilin	28	1.01	1.38	−0.37
Heilongjiang	29	0.96	1.71	−0.75
Shanghai	15	4.87	1.11	3.76
Jiangsu	16	1.23	0.86	0.37
Zhejiang	17	0.79	1.53	−0.74
Anhui	18	0.61	0.96	−0.35
Fujian	19	0.97	0.74	0.23
Jiangxi	20	0.59	0.72	−0.13
Shandong	21	0.73	0.63	0.10
Henan	10	0.57	0.67	−0.10
Hubei	11	0.75	0.64	0.11
Hunan	12	0.41	0.40	1.44
Guangdong	14	1.84	0.40	1.44
Guangxi	13	0.37	1.74	0.34
Hainan	30	2.08	1.74	0.34
Sichuan	1	0.42	1.21	−0.79
Guizhou	2	0.61	0.95	−0.34
Yunnan	3	0.64	0.74	−0.10
Shaanxi	5	0.94	1.02	−0.08
Gansu	6	0.70	1.17	−0.47
Qinghai	7	2.36	2.22	0.14
Ningxia	8	1.67	1.19	0.48
Xinjiang	9	2.19	1.78	0.41

Since 1979 over 100 million people have left rural areas for urban areas. The implications are great:

- an ageing population in rural areas;
- the selective removal of the younger, more able population to urban areas;
- over-population in urban areas causing a strain on housing, education, health and services such as water and electricity.

Most of the migrants are young and they move in search of employment in the construction industry, factories, textile sweatshops, and in service occupations. However, working conditions are often poor, and wages are low. Many migrants send a large part of their wages home as remittances, in order to support their family in the rural area.

Figure 11.14 China's regions

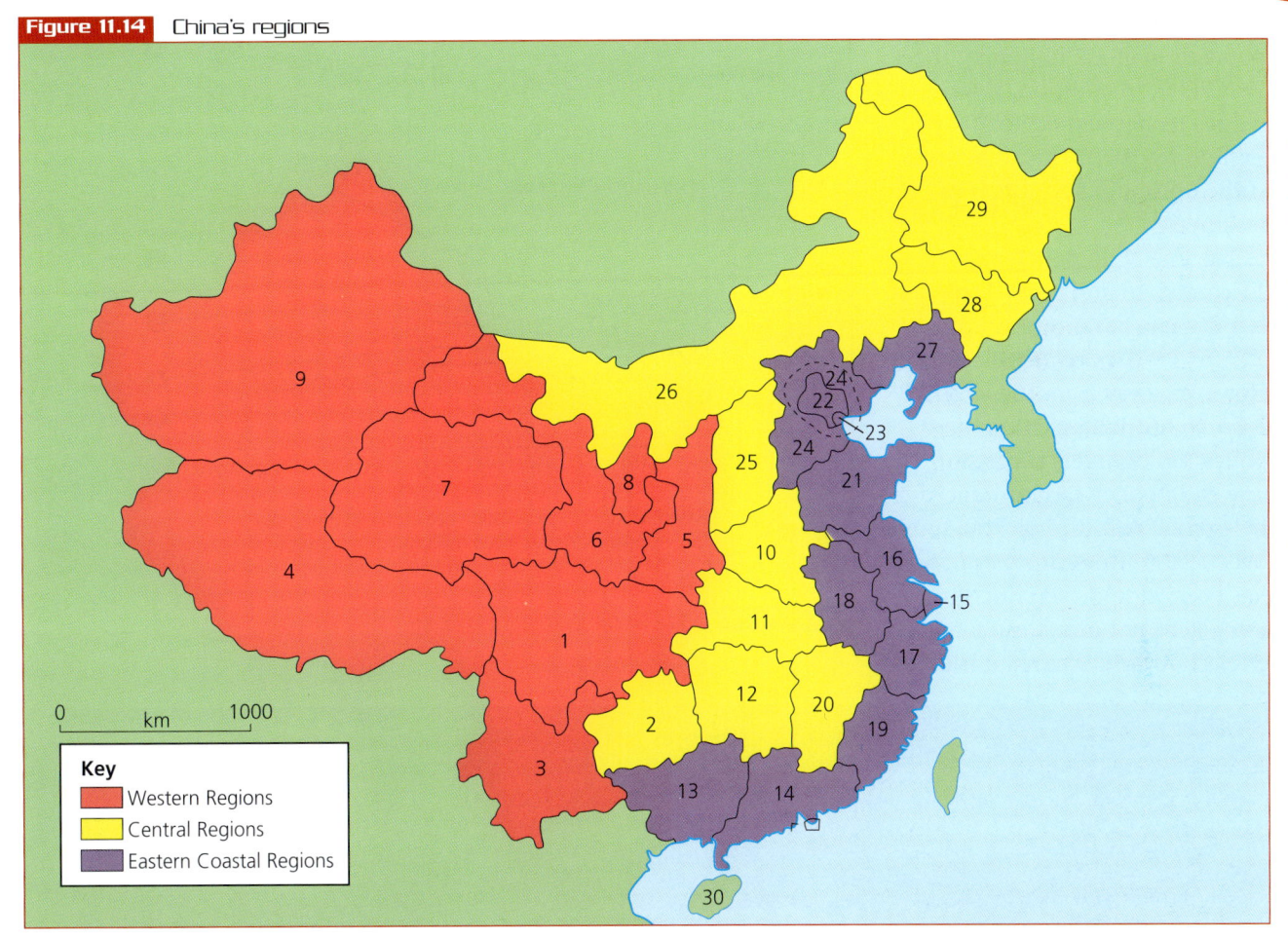

Key
- Western Regions
- Central Regions
- Eastern Coastal Regions

Family planning in China

Family planning refers to attempts to limit family size. Family planning methods include contraceptives such as the pill and condoms, as well as drastic methods such as forced sterilisations (for example the removal of a women's womb or the cutting of male reproductive tubes), abortion, and infanticide (the killing of children).

China operated the world's most severe, and controversial family planning programme. China's family planning drive started in the early 1970s but it was in 1979 that the 'one child' policy was imposed. The impact was drastic. A 1970 birth rate of 33 per 1000 fell to 17 in 1979.

Most Chinese families in urban areas have only one child (Figure 11.16), and the growing middle classes do not discriminate against daughters as much. However the countryside remains very traditionally focused on male heirs. But the policy was relaxed. In most provincial rural areas, couples could have two children without penalties. Increasingly, rich farmers were able and willing to pay fines or bribes in order to get permission to have more children; poor families simply take the view that they have nothing much to lose.

The sex ratio at birth in China is around 118 boys to 100 girls, compared with the natural rate of 106:100. Selective abortion is a major cause, but many baby girls are probably not registered.

Questions

27 On a copy of **Figure 11.14** draw a map to show the rates of migration into and out of China's regions (the final column in **Figure 11.13**). Use two colours – one for regions in which there has been an increase and a different one for regions in which there has been a decrease. Use no more than four groups such as +/– 0.0 –0.99; +/– 1.00 – 1.99; +/– 2.00 – 2.99; +/– 4.00.

Describe the results you have shown? What do they suggest about regional inequalities in China?

CHINA – AN LEDC

China wanted to stabilise its population at 1.2 billion by the year 2000. In addition, it wants to reduce its population to 700 million by 2010. This, it believes, is the optimum size, given its resources.

The one-child policy has succeeded, to an extent. The fertility rate has dropped from 2.25 to 1.9 **(Figure 11.15)**. However, away from the larger, more industrialised cities, the policy has been less successful. The one-child policy has introduced a new problem to China – the spoilt, overweight 'little emperors'. There has been widespread criticism of the policy, not only from foreign critics but from internal dissidents.

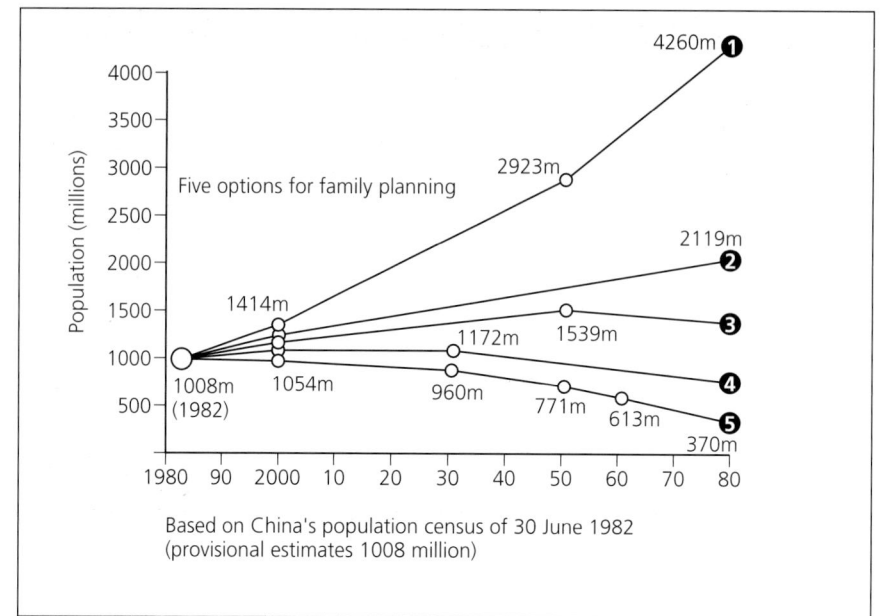

Figure 11.15 Population growth in China

Based on China's population census of 30 June 1982 (provisional estimates 1008 million)

Figure 11.16 Advertisement for China's one-child policy

Questions

28 Describe the changes in China's birth rate as shown in **Figure 11.15**.

29 How far do you agree that China should have a one-child policy. Give reasons for your answer.

China's toy industry

The toy industry is one of the most important manufacturing industries in China (Figure 11.17). China (including Hong Kong) accounts for about 60% of the world's $31 billion toy trade. Early Light Industrial is one of the largest toy makers in China, employing over 20 000 people. Despite its strength China's toy trade remains largely invisible. Coverage in the western press is almost exclusively about inhuman working conditions or unfair trade.

In the 1960s and 1970s Hong Kong produced vast quantities of cheap plastic toys, which, for a while, were Hong Kong's main export. They stimulated growth in a number of linked industries. For example, there was growth in model making industries, mould makers, suppliers of fake fur, child proof pigments and so on. However, as the toy industry in Hong Kong prospered, salaries and land prices escalated. By the 1980s Shenzhen, just across the border from Hong Kong in China's Guangdong province, had become a **Special Economic Zone**, tariff-free and open to foreign investment. Labour costs were less than a tenth of that in Hong Kong and there were plenty of sites for factories. Hong Kong's toy factories began to leave Hong Kong and most relocated across the border in Shenzhen (Figure 11.18).

The companies that now operate in Shenzhen are largely large-scale operations. While many small factories close, consolidation in the toy industry has left fewer but larger companies. Large companies are better able to weather bad years than small companies. For example, 1998 was a bad year for toy companies, with Toys 'R' Us closing 90 stores. Small toy companies were hardest hit. Large companies are also able to to provide the working conditions that the companies in the West now want. The 'codes of conduct' insisted on by the retailers and consumer associations are also changing China's toy industry. Complying with such codes is something that only the large companies can afford, and this favours consolidation.

Figure 11.17 Toy manufacturing in China

Figure 11.18 Shenzhen – a key player in China's toy industry

Questions

30. Make a class survey – what toys are manufactured in China?
31. Why is the toy industry so important in China?
32. Why is China so important for the manufacturing of toys.

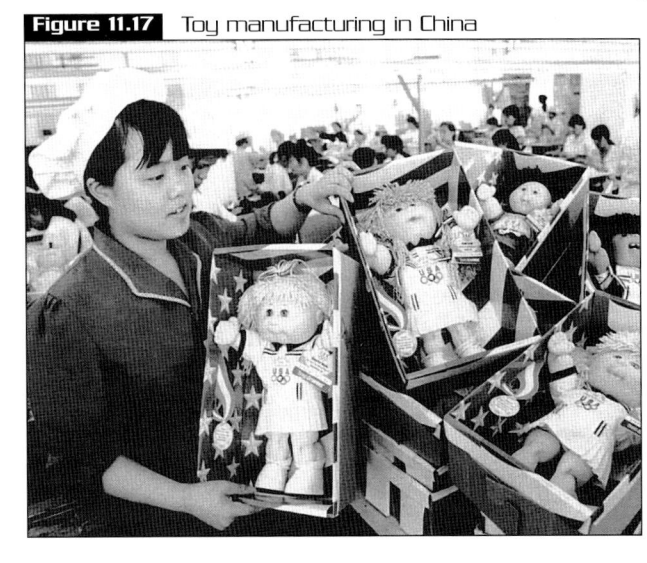

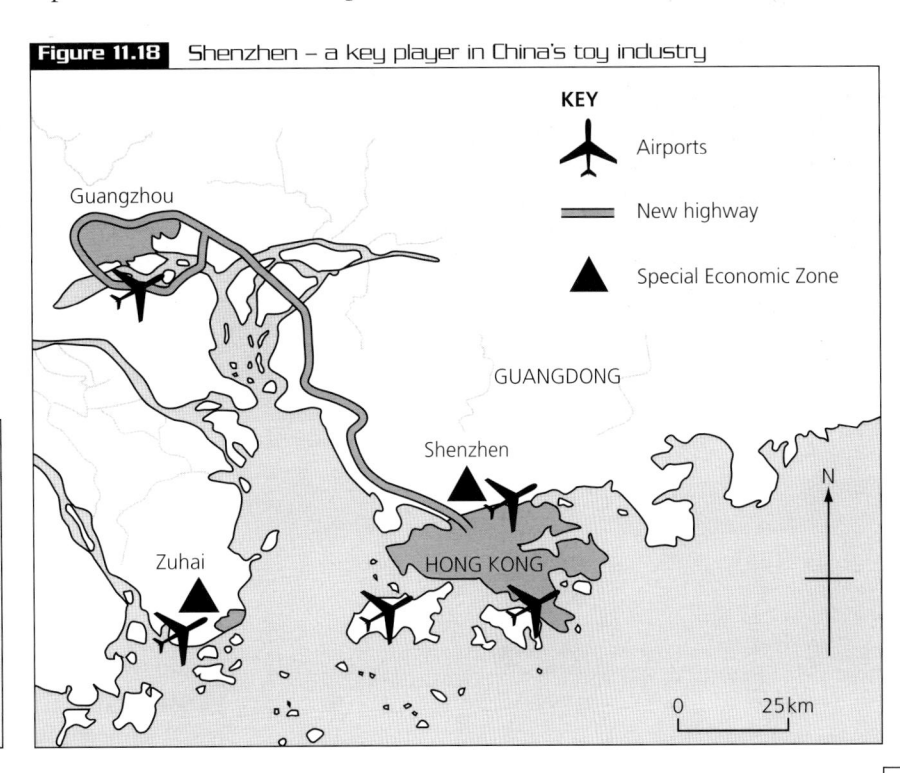

11

Air pollution in Beijing

Beijing, the capital of China, is sited between two rivers on the north-western border of the Greater North China Plain **(Figure 11.19)**. Its population is about 11 million people and its population density over 25,000 people per square kilometre in the central area. Winters in Beijing are very cold whereas summers are hot and humid. These temperature extremes, combined with the city's dependence on coal for heat and power, produce a large difference between Beijing's winter and summer air pollution levels – particularly levels of sulphur dioxide (SO_2) and suspended particulate matter (SPM) **(Figure 11.20)**.

Beijing is a city full of potential sources of pollution. Over 5700 industrial enterprises operate in Beijing, including 24 power plants, over 50 metal smelters, 194 chemical plants, and 483 metal products factories! Coal accounts for 70% of all energy used in Beijing. The city government has attempted to control industrial pollution by relocating industries away from the central area, and new enterprises are actively discouraged from entering the city.

Industrial sources account for 87% of SO_2 emissions. Of these, more than half come from just 24 power plants and 18 coking facilities. Household stoves account for 73 000 tonnes of SO_2 (13% of the total), but their relative contribution is much higher in the cold winters.

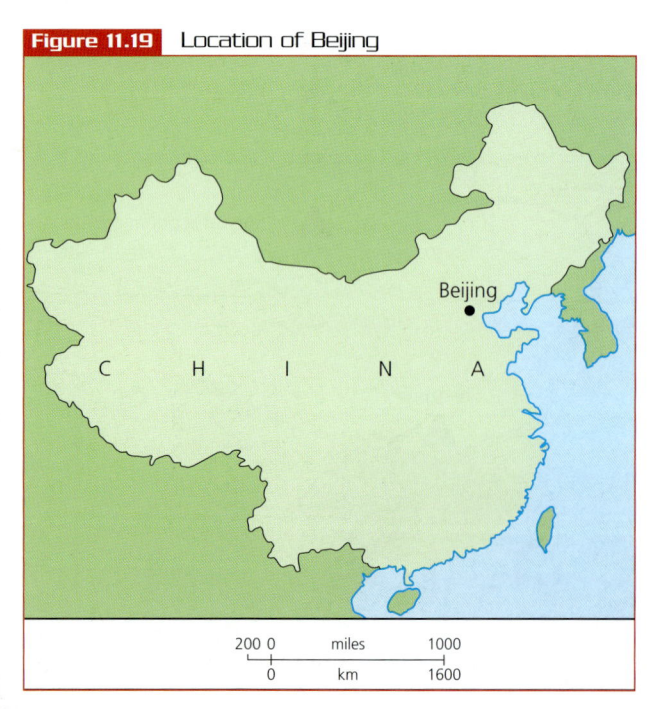

Figure 11.19 Location of Beijing

Many Beijing residents are exposed daily to high concentrations of SO_2, SPM and CO during the long, cold winters. A specific pollution problem results from the many small domestic combustion sources. Although the total amount of emissions from these small sources is relatively small, the sources contribute a high proportion of the SO_2, SPM and CO in the air because household stacks are low and pollutant dispersion is limited.

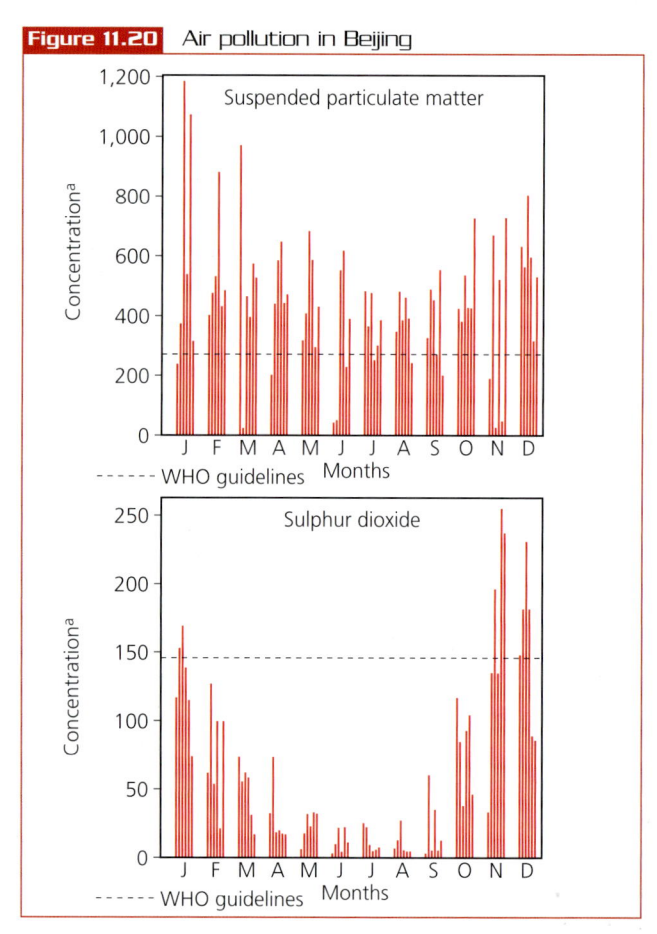

Figure 11.20 Air pollution in Beijing

Questions

33 Using an atlas, draw a climograph to show the contrast in Beijing's winter and summer temperatures.
   a When are the highest levels of SO_2 pollution in Beijing? Suggest reasons to explain this pattern.
   b Briefly explain the daily pattern of pollution levels in a Beijing household.
   c How and why does pollution in Beijing differ from that of a UK city?